NOTHING IS IMPOSSIBLE

To Ryan
all the best,
♡ Sarah Schiffer-Duffy

NOTHING IS IMPOSSIBLE

STORIES FROM THE LIFE OF A CATHOLIC WORKER

SCOTT SCHAEFFER-DUFFY

Haley's
Athol, Massachusetts

Haley's
488 South Main Street
Athol, MA 01331
haley.antique@verizon.net
800.215.8805

Cover photo by Tanya Connor.

Other photos from the author's collection unless otherwise credited.

Copy edited by Elsie Uffelmann Boucher. Proof read by Mary-Ann DeVita Palmieri.

The author gratefully acknowledges Worcester Art Museum, *Inside Worcester, The Catholic Free Press, Worcester Magazine,* and *Worcester Telegram&Gazette* for permission to use their photos in this book.

Library of Congress Control Number: 2016933638

Cataloguing in Publishing data:
Schaeffer-Duffy, Scott.
   Nothing is impossible : stories from the life of a Catholic Worker / Scott Schaeffer-Duffy.

Athol, MA : Haley's, 2016.

244 pages 25.4 cm

ISBN: 978-0-9916102-5-9

1. Schaeffer-Duffy, Scott. 2. Catholics--United States--Biography. 3. Catholic Worker Movement. 4. St. Francis and St. Thérèse Catholic Worker (Worcester, Mass.) 5. Civil disobedience--United States. 6. Pacifists--United States. 7. Human rights workers--United States. I. Title.

BX4705.S334 A32 2016

for my best favorite
Claire
and our children,
Justin, Grace, Patrick, and Aiden

People say nothing is impossible,
but I do nothing every day.

—Winnie the Pooh

Contents

Illustrations

Anything Is Possible

a preface by Scott Schaeffer-Duffy

My dad, Charlie Duffy, was an Irish Swedish Catholic. My mom, Barbara, was an English Scottish Protestant. His motto was "Buy now, pay later." Hers was "Neither a lender nor a borrower be." He got up before dawn. She was a night owl. He was shy. She was outgoing. He drank. She did not. The one thing they had in common was a sense of humor. As a member of a social club called The Gabbers, my mother donned a wild costume as a semi-bald cowboy to pose for a photo that appeared in *The Woonsocket Call*, a Rhode Island newspaper. When my father refused to hire professionals to wallpaper our living room, my mother and her friend Jackie Thibeault papered the walls with the Sunday comics. When we moved to Pelham, New Hampshire, a town whose colonial homes advertise their ages on plaques, my father put a sign on our fifty-year-old house that read, "Circa 1675." He later dragged an old toilet into our front yard, filled the bowl and tank with dirt, and planted marigolds in it.

Barbara and Charlie Duffy

photo by Christine Zerillo

Like anyone, I am a product of my parents' genes and contradictory example but also defined by my experience and will. Although geometry teaches us that the shortest distance between two points is a straight line, how many of us reach life destinations that way? Most biographies are replete with false turns, diversions, and regressions before the protagonists become the figures we know and admire. Even Jesus had to grow into his vocation. Who knows what Jesus was up to until he was thirty? He may have tried his hand at many things. Most of us do. The entirety of our experience, even what we consider irrelevant or injurious, goes into the blender, for better or worse, to produce our mature selves.

The following stories concern a summer in a haunted house, a year in a Franciscan friary, expeditions to war zones, time in jail, adventures in mountain climbing, a love affair, an unorthodox running of the Boston Marathon, and more. My experience has been so varied that I've often felt that I was on a kind of incoherent funhouse ride peppered with surprises and thrills. But unlike the Spanish surrealist filmmaker Luis Buñuel, who held that life is episodic without coherent theme, I believe everything has a definite purpose.

In 1977, a friend took me to an Irish pub where I saw people crying their eyes out at an anti-war ballad, laughing at a sea chanty, and then crying again at a song of lost love. I couldn't understand the wild mood swings, but I have come to realize that the deepest human emotions exist in close proximity to each other, giving them greater value. This book runs the gamut of emotions. The stories in this book are as true as my notes, media reports, court records, and my memory allow. They are not chronological. They can be read in practically any order.

In my fifty-seven years, I realize that all of us have invitations in life to take risks, invitations that we usually refuse. Most of us don't climb Mount Everest, not only because it's very difficult, but also because we are afraid of what people will say if we undertake such an expedition. And like JRR Tolkien's hobbit, Bilbo Baggins, we don't want adventures. We are lured by conventionality into the misconception that the most predictable lives are the happiest. We also routinely sell ourselves short. "I could never do that," we exclaim, when confronted with myriad opportunities that do not, in fact, require extraordinary skill.

These pages include my own and many others' decisions to take a walk on the wild side. I can assure you that my associates and I are neither lunatics nor heroes but ordinary people who, like Henry David Thoreau, did not want to come to the end of life only to "discover that we had not lived."

I hope that this book will inspire readers to say yes to their personal invitations to make themselves and the world better. If any of these stories help someone do that, I am well satisfied.

On an unseasonably hot May evening in 2015, a Haitian block party took place at the end of my street. As I strolled past the deejay and bouncy house full of leaping children, I saw a two-year-old black boy wearing a T-shirt with a picture of a ship in a bottle and the motto, "Anything is possible." When I saw him, I couldn't help but think of the white comedian Steve Martin's outrageous opening line from the movie, *The Jerk*, when he says, "I was born a poor black child."

Anything is possible, indeed.

Catholic Workers Scott and Claire Schaeffer-Duffy, right middle wearing hats, with their Saints Francis & Thérèse Catholic Worker sign during a Human Rights Day protest at Worcester, Massachusetts, City Hall

Saint Benedict's Catholic Worker

logo by Ade Bethume

the logo of the Catholic Worker Movement

My chair wobbled. Either a leg was busted, the floor wasn't level, or both. Not surprising, given that everything else was mismatched—the furniture, curtains, and even the people. The crowd packed around me was of many colors, ages, incomes, and states of psychiatric wellness and sobriety. Some were clean-shaven, well-dressed folks from the suburbs while others sported scraggly beards and thrift store attire. Most had their eyes on Father Jim Connolly who was celebrating Mass on a makeshift altar, but a few were distracted, and at least one person was asleep. The Mass at Worcester's Mustard Seed Catholic Worker was unlike any I'd attended. The "chapel" had only minutes earlier been a dining room and would minutes later be a TV room. To call the place a firetrap would be an understatement. Indeed, like many Catholic Worker houses, it did eventually go up in flames.

And then, as if the scene weren't surreal enough, a drunken man started banging on an outside window yelling, "Let me in, you bastards!" His mantra escalated to a line I would hear many a time later on: "You call yourselves fucking Christians!" Finally, he threw a rock that shattered the glass and skittered across the floor, landing near the altar.

No one seemed surprised or distraught.

Catholic Worker Rich Kuzlowski said calmly to the Mustard Seed's co-founder, Mike Boover, "I'll go talk with him" and slipped quietly outside. The Mass went on.

I was sure of only one thing—volunteering in such a madhouse was not something I could ever do.

The Mustard Seed Catholic Worker is part of the Catholic Worker Movement founded in 1933 by Dorothy Day and Peter Maurin. The Catholic Worker Movement aspires to "build a new society in the shell of the old," to "create a world where it's easier to be good." In 150 inner-city houses of hospitality and a dozen farms, the Catholic Worker mystifies scholars. Unstructured and unfunded by the church and the state, run by volunteers with no special skills or training, and serving the most needy and volatile while trying to promote peace and justice, the Catholic Worker is either a crazy house built on sand or a testament to God's miraculous power on earth. Maybe it's both.

Before I became a Catholic Worker, I took my religious studies degree from The College of the Holy Cross in Worcester, Massachusetts, in a more conventional direction by joining the Capuchin-Franciscans. That experience was at once wonderful and disappointing. The kind of voluntary poverty and peacemaking I aspired to was not the focus of most friars. As I prepared to leave the friars, my novice master advised me, "Don't just take up where you left off prior to coming here. Challenge yourself by trying something you have never done before."

So I spent a year working at a nursing home, nursery school, and group home for the mentally challenged and disabled. Afterwards, I figured I'd give the Catholic Worker a go. So I wrote to several houses asking if they needed help.

On July 8, 1982, Michael Kirwan at Saint Benedict's Catholic Worker in Washington, DC, answered:

> . . .I was so thrilled to get your very touching letter with an offer of HELP that I felt compelled to get one off before you made other arrangements . . . . There is so much I could write about the houses, but I think the best thing is to come and visit and experience them for yourself . . . .
>
> I never intended to start a house of any kind. I have never not been associated with the Worker. My parents knew Dorothy (Day) back in the forties . . . . I worked at the Worker in New York for a couple of years, but then came back to Washington to go to George Washington University to work on a master's in sociology. Anyway, in 1978, I was out walking one night around the State Department, which is near the dorms, and I met a guy on the heating vents that line the government buildings here in Washington—men and women use them in winter to stay warm from the exhaust. He asked me for some food, and I went to the dorm, fixed him a meal, and brought it to him. I've been doing it every night since at the same vents for approximately fifteen people that congregate there year round.
>
> Those same people and others asked for a place to clean up and live after I had been going down there for a while. That winter, I had fifteen people in my dorm room—it was like that for one and a half years until, after two deaths in the dorm room, the university took me to court to have me evicted. I then found the little house we are in—Saint Benedict's—and last year I bought a house two doors away—Mary Harris House—for women. The houses are only four rooms each (not four bedrooms but four rooms). Last winter, we had about thirty-five men in the men's house and twenty women at times in the women's house. I have, ever since the days of the dorm, had an open door policy. The houses are small, crowded, in

much need of repair; noisy—incredibly hot in the summer—but still, I love it. I thank the Lord for stumbling on that guy on the grate that day—it was all so accidental—so unplanned—so spontaneous—it still is. It just happened as Dorothy said in her autobiography, *The Long Loneliness.*

Scott, because the house was so unplanned and because in the dorm and now in the houses I never had any privacy—it was always so crowded and uncomfortable—the few people who came to volunteer wouldn't stay. There are no volunteers as I said. The people that come in off the street "run" the houses or don't "run" them for that matter. I work full time at the George Washington University Hospital as an office clerk for the department of anesthesiology. I would have loved to have worked as an orderly, but I can't do work like that because I would have to be on call, and I can't do that with the houses and taking food down to the grates at night. So I have kept an office job that gives me tremendous free time if I have to go home during the day for an emergency.

But because of that time away from the houses—with no one responsible there—the houses are often chaotic. I come home after work oftentimes to find everyone gone—the houses empty and wide open. Oftentimes there have been fights and vandalism . . . . It's not a good way to manage two houses—yet, by the grace of God, it is almost four years, and we are still here. Lots of good things have happened . . . yet so much more could be done . . . . The need is so great. I very much feel the need for a real community of Workers with all that entails. I especially miss the prayer life we had in New York with Morning Prayer, Vespers, liturgies, etc . . . .

One point I have to clarify, Scott. I now have a room set aside for volunteers if any come. I realized after those couple of bad experiences with no room for volunteers that all of us need our quiet, our privacy, our respite. Even going to one's room is often not enough—the sounds of the house and its commotion follow everywhere—but it is a beginning. I have set aside a room in the women's house and a room in the men's house. I alternate now between the two to keep an eye on both. Anyway you can look at it when you come. It is not a life for everyone, Scott. I don't ask that or deny that in anyone. I know, myself, over the past years, it has often gotten to me. But so much of that has been the frustration of going it alone so often. I am in love with the Worker ideal and Ideal it is—we never quite make it, but we keep plugging along. Please come if you can—with no obligations or commitments.

Yowser! Here was a challenge. I wrote back to Michael immediately and went down to Washington two weeks later. The Greyhound bus was air-conditioned to the point that I had to wrap myself in a sweatshirt to keep from freezing, but, when I stepped outside, it was so hot that my feet actually sunk into the asphalt. I walked up to Fourth Street past brick row houses with black people sitting on the stoops. I was the only person walking around. The humidity was eighty percent or more. There wasn't a speck of breeze. I later learned that a large part of DC was built over the Foggy Bottom Swamp. No surprise there.

I did not think a human being could be more uncomfortable until, twenty minutes later, I entered Saint Benedict's Catholic Worker house. The walls of the tiny row house were crawling with cockroaches, and the air was hotter than a blow dryer's. Michael was making soup in a huge pot that he stirred with a wooden plank. How he could cook soup in such an inferno, not to mention how anyone could want to eat hot soup under such conditions, was beyond me.

Michael introduced me to some of the men and then asked for my help ladling the soup into mason jars, which were then put in boxes for transport to the men sleeping on the grates. Why those men would still want to sleep over the warm exhausts in summer was another mystery that I would not solve. We loaded three or four boxes full of jars into an old car and drove off. We left the jars and three loaves of white bread with an assortment of men who asked Michael for this and that favor. A fellow said he needed a pair of shoes, so without hesitation, Michael took off his Nikes and gave them to the guy. I never saw anything like it. He assured me it was no big deal and that he'd have new shoes before the day was out. And, thanks to a generous donor who noticed Michael's stocking feet, he did.

And then Michael, in stocking feet, and I gathered up empty jars and, to my surprise, drove out to Alexandria to spend the night at Michael's mother's house. Even there, in a clean, spacious bungalow with ceiling fans, I slept in a pool of my own sweat. New England had never prepared me for what I thought was the Deep South.

I left the next day, promising to return four weeks later on the same day that a woman volunteer, Sue Burke, was expected. When I arrived late in the afternoon of August 15, I saw a white woman who turned out to be Sue sitting on the stoop of Mary Harris House surrounded by suitcases, reading a book by psychology's chief apostle of behaviorism, B. F. Skinner.

I said to her, "I don't know much about the Catholic Worker, but I'm pretty sure you can throw that book away."

When I asked why she was sitting outside, Sue explained that the women guests had thrown her out of the house and locked the door. I coaxed them to open it again only to find the inside hotter than Hades. A guest named Dorothy, who wore her winter coat year-round, had cranked the oven with its door open to "take off the chill." All of the windows were closed, some with plastic insulation covering the outside. I turned off the oven, opened the windows, removed the plastic, and encouraged the women not to reject Sue again. She thanked me and then jumped at the sharp sounds of what could have been fireworks, a car backfiring, or something worse.

Sue asked anxiously, "What was that?"

"They're shooting the white people," I deadpanned.

I probably should not have teased her. When I went into Saint Benedict's, I was not met by Michael Kirwan's friendly face but by a belligerent alcoholic named Burton who rode me like a Shetland pony.

"You know, this isn't Georgetown," he needled. "Look around. You be lost. A white boy like you isn't going to last long here . . . . I won't even bother to learn your name. You're a twenty-four-hour man. I'll wake up in the morning, and you be gone."

In a way, I'm grateful for Burton. His trash talk only served to stiffen my prideful determination to prove him wrong. I found myself a place to sleep in a small upstairs bedroom with three other men (apparently Michael's resolve to save me a private room had evaporated). I got up the next day and made myself as useful as I could doing things like washing dishes and sweeping the floor.

When I started killing cockroaches, a guest named Roger White told me, "It says in the Bible, 'Thou shalt not kill those damned things.'"

A prim and proper older gentleman named Arthur said, "For every one you kill, there'll be fifty at his funeral."

As the day went by, I really started wondering where Michael was. The mystery was solved when he appeared that night. He saw Sue and me on the sidewalk and said with astonishment, "You actually came!"

He went on to explain that Sue and I were the only prospective volunteers who had ever returned after having seen the houses.

The next morning, I walked over to Saint Francis Catholic Worker on Sixth Street, another community I had inquired about. Theirs was a more substantial row house, wider than Saint Benedict's and three-stories tall, but I was immediately put off by bars on the windows, a common sight in DC. When I went inside, I met Catholic Workers Paul Magno and Marcia Timmel, who told me that they had a young woman named Claire Schaeffer, recently graduated from the University of Virginia, staying with them for the summer.

"She had a difficult encounter on the street with a black man a few days ago," said Paul.

"We don't expect her to last long in the Catholic Worker," confided Marcia.

So much for prognostication.

As fate would have it, Michael Kirwan turned over complete responsibility for Saint Benedict's and Mary Harris Houses of Fourth Street to me, while he continued to feed the men on the grates and worked to start a Catholic Worker Farm in West Virginia. After five weeks "running" the houses by myself, Claire decided to join me. On the night she left the relative comfort of Saint Francis house for the mayhem on Fourth Street, I confessed to a guest named Billy that I was a little worried about how things would work out. Billy told me, "God in his infinite wisdom has made yet another good mistake."

Claire and I were religious idealists who saw the Catholic Worker as the perfect canvas on which to paint a Gospel masterpiece. We had both spent much of our college years discussing the writings of Tolstoy, Dostoevsky, Gandhi, Thoreau, Martin Luther King Jr, and Dorothy Day. We saw living in the little row houses on Fourth Street as a fantastic opportunity to try to take Christ literally—to welcome the stranger, to give to those who beg from us, to love the enemy, to take nothing for the journey, to pray unceasingly, and to rejoice in the Lord always.

Not everyone thought as we did. Sue Burke left swiftly. A former Carmelite nun named Sharon left after three weeks but not before saying, "I can handle the dirt, the roaches, and the physical work. What I can't handle is the people. They are so ungrateful. I've come to realize that I just can't stand poor people!"

I almost fell off the same cliff. On a night when our house was especially crowded and I was sleeping on the floor in the narrow front hall, I was awakened at midnight by a man named Earl asking for a place to stay. I told him that every bed and all the floor space was in use. He asked if he could bed down next to me in the hall. I recalled how a Catholic Worker old timer named Stanley Vishnewski used to say, "There's always room for one more if you aren't superstitious and don't mind sleeping thirteen to a bed" and then told Earl, "Okay."

There wasn't room for us both to lie down on our backs, so we each turned on our sides. Before too long Earl began murmuring amorously in his sleep, "Shirley" and then wrapped his arms around me.

"I'm not Shirley," I reminded him as I pushed him away.

Then he started snoring, which a few jostles seemed to cure, but finally Earl began to fart so pungently that I feared I would pass out.

So much for thirteen in a bed. I got up and searched high and low for another spot to lie down, finally settling for the top of our kitchen table, which had two men snoozing underneath. I lay down, pulled the greasy vinyl tablecloth over me, and fell immediately to sleep.

Not ten seconds later or so it seemed, the kitchen light was blazing above me, the sun was up, and a guest named Willie Fayson was asking, "Mr. Scott, can I get car fare to Fairfax?"

Thoroughly spent, I went outside to the curb where Claire and I usually met for Morning Prayer and complained to her, "You give and give to these people and their only response is to ask for more."

Completely unruffled, Claire said, "And isn't that exactly how we are with God?"

It was not the sympathy I wanted, but it was a reminder that a Catholic Worker's job is not to accumulate appreciation but rather to witness to the gratuitous and unshakable love of God.

Thankfully, a number of other volunteers came forward to help us, the most extraordinary of whom was Carl Siciliano, a deeply spiritual person who loved to sing Janis Joplin's "Mercedes Benz" and the Beatles' "Yellow Submarine." Despite being only eighteen, Carl showed remarkable maturity, courage, and good humor. He persevered through many trying days.

On one of those tough days, when a guest named Uncle John fell down drunk and cut himself badly enough to warrant an ambulance, one of the neighborhood kids ran up to Carl and me saying, "Pooh Pooh is stealing a roll-away bed from your house." We rushed inside and out the open back door into the alley where I saw the very poorly nicknamed hoodlum pushing a bed.

"What's going on?" I asked.

"One of the men sold me this bed for ten dollars," he answered—not a completely unbelievable story given the number of alcoholics in our house.

"If this were my bed," I told him, "you could have it, but it's Calvin's bed, and we have rats so he can't sleep on the floor. So let's go back to the house, you can show me who sold you the bed, and I'll get your money back." (I slept on the floor at that time and woke up one night with a rat sitting on my chest.)

"No," he said, "you go back and I'll wait for you here."

Now, being a Christian does not mean being a chump, so I said, "No, I'm taking the bed back."

His fist disagreed with me, knocking me to the ground. I got up slowly and repeated, "It's still Calvin's bed, and I'm still taking it back."

Pooh Pooh looked confused. In his world, people either fought back or ran away. My middle way was a mystery. In his hesitation, I thought, "Aha, here is the victory of nonviolence."

And then he punched me again with similar effect on my face and keister.

I rose much more slowly and stood in silence. After a few seconds, I looked down on the trash-strewn ground only to see an old piece of wood with a rusty nail sticking out of it. When I looked up, I saw that, by miserable Irish luck, Pooh Pooh had spied it too.

This day seemed certain to go down the proverbial toilet, when a police car pulled up to the other end of the alley, fifty yards or so away.

"You gonna put the police on me?" he asked.

"We don't need the police to resolve this," I said, turned, and began pushing the bed back to our house. I half expected to feel that rusty nail rake down my back, but, thankfully, I did not.

The experience had shaken me, though. Previously, I had imagined martyrdom as an uplifting affair over some weighty issue, with a stenographer on hand to record my last words. I never pictured dying alone in the garbage over a roll-away bed.

Interestingly, a week later, Carl and I were sentenced to three days in DC's massive jail for a protest against the MX missile. While waiting to be processed by the jail nurse, Carl pointed to another inmate and said, "Look who's here." Pooh Pooh, of course. Although Pooh Pooh, Carl, and I were not assigned to the same cell, we did share a day room from morning until night. This strange coincidence made me especially grateful that I had not used force in that alley. If I had left Pooh Pooh with a grudge, that three-day sentence might well have been my last days on earth. Maybe nonviolence was wise after all.

At Saint Benedict's we kept our front door open, and we gave away virtually everything we had when we had it. We might as well have done so, since people would just steal everything if we didn't. We lived off donations, and when those failed, we went door to door in the Catholic University neighborhood to beg for food to make dinner for our guests. We broke up fights and smashed bottles of booze against a cement block outside our front door. Claire, Carl, and I once had a rat sit among us during Evening Prayer. We buried three of our guests, one of them quite literally when we took her body out to the Catholic Worker farm in West Virginia. We hosted men like Adolphus Minor, who walked out of the house once with a bottle of vodka in one pocket and a hammer in the other. We set off bug-bomb spray cans at regular intervals to kill the roaches and then swept them up into two or three thirty-gallon trash bags. We fed as many as forty people a day, most from the Deep South but some from exotic locations, including a Swede named Sowli Limpa who did not speak a word of English and an Ethiopian refugee, Johannes. Roger yelled at him, "Who died and made you king, yo' highness?"

We even had a guy named Andrew Hython who, for a time, thought he was Jesus. When anyone sneezed, he'd say, "I bless you," and when anyone said, "What a nice day," he would add, "You're welcome." A guest named Everett Foy said at Vespers, "I'd like to pray for that great evangelist, Neil Armstrong."

Our women guests were as colorful and wild as the men. Ruth had an intense loathing, bordering on phobia, of chicken. A fundamentalist named Mary fasted, prayed, and spoke in tongues for Claire, Carl, and me to be saved from Catholicism. Our neighbor, a squat woman called Ladybug, loved to talk to everyone, especially Claire, but no one ever understood a word she said. Chrysilia threw water from the toilet on me. An incredibly short woman from Central America gave Claire and me odd gifts when we went to Saint Patrick's church for morning Mass.

So much happened. We hosted a block party that blew every fuse in both houses and was featured in a *National Geographic* profile of DC. Two young men knocked me down in broad daylight and stole a backpack full of my dirty laundry. Our van was stolen, and we could not call the police because no one knew the license plate number. The CIA dropped off a delivery of toys and asked us to send a thank you to: "Santa Claus c/o the Central Intelligence Agency." When Saint Stephen's Church gave us several cases of Guinness Stout, Carl and I drank a bunch of bottles in Lafayette Park and spent the better part of a night yelling at Ronald Reagan to come out and explain to us why there was so much poverty in DC. We held a party after a mean dog named Satan, who had bitten Claire twice, died. Claire and Carl took a bunch of neighborhood kids to the CW farm in West Virginia and, when they stopped on the way at a McDonald's, lily white Carl peeked in and said in dismay, "We're the only black people in here."

There did come a time when we owed hundreds of dollars and had run out of people to ask for help. Carl and I walked to the post office to see if a donation had arrived in the mail. Everyone in our neighborhood had a post office box because regular mail got stolen. We reached the post office a bit early, so Carl suggested that we pray a litany to the saints appealing for a donation. I agreed but hesitated when he actually knelt down on the post office's lobby floor. He insisted that we'd only get results if we did the prayer by the book so to speak. So we did:

"Saint Joseph," Carl began.

"Pray for us," I responded.

"Saint Mary."

"Pray for us."

"Saints Peter and Paul."

"Pray for us."

You get the idea.

This went on as a bored postal worker could be seen sliding mail into the various slots getting ever closer to ours. Carl and I had used up all the saints we could remember and were starting to ask for the intercession of people like Dr. Martin Luther King Jr., Flannery O'Connor, and Thomas Merton when our mail finally arrived. We opened the box and stared in disbelief at three more bills.

We moped home to Saint Benedict's only to discover an envelope sticking out of our mailbox, the only letter I ever saw delivered in eighteen months. We opened it to discover a thousand-dollar donation. At least one of those saints must have heard us.

Thirty-three years later, Carl wrote to Claire and me:

> . . . I wanted to tell you how grateful I am for the time we lived together in the service of God's poor. I have so many joyful memories. Mostly of the remarkable sense of closeness and friendship I had with both of you. I remember with so much happiness waking up early in the mornings and walking to the Little Sisters of Jesus convent for Mass. (And getting to eat a real breakfast and contemplative prayer afterwards!) . . . . I remember (our guest) Tyra's funeral service in the kitchen of Mary Harris House, us singing "Swing Low, Sweet Chariot," and my having to throw myself on her casket to prevent it from flipping over when Truman drunkenly fell on it. Driving to the Catholic Worker farm in West Virginia and digging the grave through the night. . . . Claire coming to my rescue when Robert was repeatedly bashing my head into the pay phone in the hall when I wouldn't let him rape a drunken woman on Uncle John's bed. Scott calling me Mr. Potato Head!! All those double features we would watch for a dollar in the afternoons, as much to be in cool air as for the films. I think my most cherished memory is of the nights we sat in that little bedroom, drinking hot chocolate and reading from Andre Schwarz Bart's *The Last of the Just.*

I don't think I've ever had such a sense of family and community and closeness (outside of being in love with [his current and former partners] Raymond and Gary) . . . .

The battered charm of Saint Benedict's and Mary Harris Catholic Worker was hard to capture, but in November of 1982, we tried to do so in a two-page newsletter, which a fellow named Walter Marx printed for us in the same way it was done during Ben Franklin's day, with individually set type and a hand-cranked press. In our tract, Claire wrote:

The floors of Mary Harris House are terribly uneven. The coarse plywood that covers the holes trips everyone who walks across it. To an outsider it would seem as if we had no balance here. We permit so much. The other evening Ulysses told me we cannot run a house the way we do. "You can't do it this way, man. This place is supposed to be a mercy shelter, a f— mercy shelter!" But isn't that what we are? That very same evening, someone from outside threw ammonia into Ulysses eyes. One of our woman cared for him. Frances washed out his eyes. She washed out his sweater and found a shirt and vest for him. Her giving was all the more powerful when I considered that she had been a victim of violence many times over . . . . We sleep with violence here and hope to sow love."

Claire always had her eyes open to the ugliness *and* the beauty. This gift would serve her well after an incident with lasting repercussions.

On a night in late 1983, when Claire was the only woman volunteer at Mary Harris house, a conflict arose at midnight after a guest named Pat started cooking. Other guests asked Claire to get Pat to turn off the lights and go to bed. Pat, a former student of Harvard University, was furious with Claire, whom she chided as a wealthy white woman doing just enough time in the ghetto to write a book before returning to the easy life. She said Claire had no idea what it was like to be involuntarily poor and black, to carry poverty with you in life. Somehow, her tirade escalated into physical violence. When I arrived at 6:30 in the morning to see if Claire wanted to go to Mass, Pat stormed out. I found the guests crying and Claire a little bruised. Everyone was shaken up.

While sitting on the stoop and thinking what to do, I made a rosary out of string and some sticks lying on the ground. It then occurred to me that Holy Cross Trappist Abbey in Berryville, Virginia, had a standing offer for us to take a retreat. So, we did.

When we returned the next afternoon, the women at Mary Harris house told us that Pat had stormed in the previous night wielding a long knife shouting, "Where is that bitch?"

The next morning, we received a call from Saint Elizabeth's mental hospital telling us that Pat was there and that she had a history of violent outbursts when she was not on meds. A few days later, the hospital called again to say that Pat was released on a day pass and did not return. For a while, we had extra volunteers around in case she came by to kill Claire, but Pat never did, and we gradually forgot the incident.

Two years later, after Claire and I married and moved to Worcester, an eight-months pregnant Claire and I were walking down Main Street and whom did we see coming our way but Pat?

Yikes!!

"Maybe she won't recognize us," I hoped, but she did.

"Claire, Scott, how are you?" Pat asked cheerfully.

"Good," we replied.

"Where are you living?" she inquired.

"Around," I said.

She seemed fine, but it was jarring to see her nonetheless. More shaken than I, Claire had nightmares about Pat punching her in the abdomen and killing our baby.

A few days later, Claire went to the library and, when she turned into a row of books, Pat was at the other end of the aisle. Part of Claire wanted to flee, but another part of her was nagging about how we should love the enemy and forgive. Pat approached Claire, and they started a conversation that became more relaxed as it progressed. Ultimately, Pat asked how the pregnancy was going and Claire told her about some swelling in her ankles that had just appeared. Pat warned her that this might be a sign of preeclampsia, a serious condition whose only symptoms are swelling and high blood pressure, which you cannot feel. Pat urged Claire to call the doctor, which she later did. The physician was not concerned since Claire had already had a prenatal checkup only a week or so earlier, but we went into Saint Vincent Hospital prenatal clinic anyway and discovered that Claire's blood pressure was through the roof. They had her lie on her side to try to bring her pressure down and, failing that, induced labor. Our son Justin was born without complication. Later on, the doctor told us that, if we had not come in when we did, Claire and Justin may have died.

Loving the enemy saved their lives. Thank God for Pat. Thank God for the Catholic Worker.

The Haunted Hallway

The summer of 1978 began innocently enough in Worcester, Massachusetts. My friend and college classmate Joe and I had found third-shift cooking jobs at a Howard Johnson's restaurant while another friend Mark discovered an apartment we could sublet. It had four bedrooms. We planned to share it with two other Holy Cross students, Laura and Sue. The rent was $105 a month, only $26.25 per person, a remarkable deal. Even at minimum wage, Joe and I could save money for school and still have plenty left over to have lots of fun. Little did I know (an expression Dustin Hoffman claims to have taught an entire college class on in the film *Stranger Than Fiction*) what that summer held in store for me.

Since the previous tenants were Holy Cross seniors who wouldn't vacate the place until graduation on May 22, Joe, Mark, and I remained in on-campus housing till then. Coincidentally, May 22 was the date of my very first demonstration for peace, a rally for nuclear disarmament outside the United Nations in New York City. Joe and I planned to join Clark University students on a bus leaving at eight in the morning. We left work at seven and walked over to the new apartment to leave our bags and grab a quick shower before departing.

Mark had made all the arrangements for the rental, so this was Joe and my first time at the place. We reached the apartment by climbing the open-to-the-air, back-porch stairs to the third floor. We didn't have a key, so we had to wake a soon-to-be-graduated-and-gone senior to get in. A very hungover student eventually opened the door, grunted, let us in, and went back to sleep. There were hundreds of beer cans and bottles everywhere. *Animal House* came to mind.

Joe took the bathroom first while I explored. Even amidst the debris, I spied an ornate fireplace, polished wooden sliding doors, a brass chandelier, high ceilings, and a cozy alcove well-lit by three windows—all of which spoke of a much fancier abode than I had expected for the dirt cheap rent we were paying. I noticed three doors oddly situated side by side along a wall to my left. I opened the farthest to the right and saw that it led to a front hallway with a small enclosed porch to the right and stairwell straight ahead. I took a step onto the landing when Joe burst out of the bathroom saying, "Where are you going? We gotta hurry up."

This innocuous first visit to our apartment sticks in my memory because these many years later, I would *never* enter that building, never go to the third floor apartment, and most especially, never enter that hallway again! I won't even give you the street name, lest one of you foolishly seeks the place out.

As much as it amazes me that within seconds of entering the apartment I was about to penetrate its ebony heart, I'll try not to bore you again with echoes or hindsight. The truth is, my early days in that apartment were wonderful. Joe and I came home from our night shift around 7:15 a.m., slept until two or three in the afternoon, went to a matinée movie for a dollar, had pizza or pasta for dinner, drank cold beer, and felt like kings. Our only worry—that a third floor apartment would be incredibly hot—proved unwarranted as the place was remarkably cool. Less than a week after we moved in, our roommate Sue eloped with the manager of Hojo's, which freed up her room for guests. Joe, Mark, and I quickly began to refer to our last remaining female roommate, Laura, as our mother, an endearment she could have done without. A second job I picked up at Catholic Charities gave me access to wicked cool hats, uniforms, and other outfits, which I loved to sport. Joe learned how to bake bread. Mark worked at Saint Vincent Hospital. Joe, Mark, and I had dates. Laura had a steady boyfriend. The weather was fine. Life was good.

Although all of us hailed from working class backgrounds, Mark yearned to live above his station. When some of his siblings came for a visit, Mark refused to bring them up the open back stairs because the sight of laundry on the clotheslines spoke to him of poverty. Mark made a point of bringing guests in the more formal front hallway. Joe and I razzed him to no end about his pretension.

A couple of days after the visit from Mark's sisters, when we decided to go see a movie, Joe said in an aristocratic tone of voice, "Let us exit through the front door, my good man."

"Yes," I replied. "We mustn't let our attire be sullied by the common riff and raff in the rear."

Like Walt Disney's Chip and Dale, we linked arms, put our noses in the air, and paraded into the front hallway. We had not gone far between the second and first floor when the darkness became so complete that we had to slow our pace considerably.

As we felt our way to the front door, Joe said, "There ought to be a window on this landing."

And then we turned to the first floor where light spilled in from a window in the front door. We opened it and sped off to Showcase Cinema.

On our return, we entered the front hall again. This time, the adjustment to the darkness was more difficult since we had just come inside from bright sunshine. In order to get our bearings, we actually had to stop on the landing between the first and second floors. While doing so, I brushed against the outer wall and discovered the heavy molding and a sill for a window that had apparently been covered.

"Hey Joe," I said. "There was a window here. I wonder why they covered it."

"Who cares?" Joe replied distractedly, as his focus was already on the prospect of dinner.

Taking a page out of my literary high school playbook, I sat down and transcribed the day's events. You see, while growing up, I was, among other things, a fan of horror novels and films. I read Poe, Lovecraft, Hitchcock, and early Stephen King. I saw all the classic horror movies and was a subscriber to Forrest J. Ackerman's magazine *Famous Monsters of Filmland*. I fantasized about writing top-notch, truly terrifying short stories. To advance that end, whenever I found myself in even the least unusual circumstance, like discovering an object in an unlikely place or walking through a cemetery at night, I documented the event. I saved the nuggets as plausible foundations for future fiction. I figured that the most credible horror was rooted in personal experience.

The peculiarity of the covered window prompted me to write down an account of its discovery and to promise myself to check it out more thoroughly. So, later that evening, I went downstairs with a flashlight and confirmed that an ornate frame did exist on the landing between the second and first floors. The opening, covered with cheap paneling, admitted no light at its edges and gave a little to the touch as if there were insulation underneath. Apparently, this weatherizing must have kept heat out as well as in, because it was quite cool, almost cold, in that dark space. The frame seemed rather large, so I brought down a chair and climbed up to measure the dimensions, which turned out to be three feet wide by six feet tall. I wondered if there had been a decorative stained glass window in the space. I knew of a Victorian mansion on Oberlin Street where Longfellow's tragic character Evangeline is immortalized in glass. I had also seen stained glass windows in the front hallway of other Worcester triple deckers, but in those blue-collar dwellings, the windows were much smaller and less ornate. Indeed, the Oberlin Street house showcased its stained glass at the head of a sweeping, open staircase. Evangeline is gloriously visible to those inside by day and outside by night. In contrast, our hall window frame was on the far side of the house with an alley between it and another similarly aged building. It wouldn't have made sense to put a large and expensive piece of art in such a narrow and out-of-the-way location.

When I returned to the third floor, I asked Laura a series of don't-you-think-it's-strange questions, which irritated her sufficiently for me to teasingly offer to escort her into our "haunted hallway." She refused, making it clear at dinner that she didn't appreciate my attempts to frighten her. Joe and Mark thought my curiosity was peculiar, if not ridiculous.

Two days later as I bounded up the back stairs clad in a white sailor suit, a stern voice coming from the second-floor screen door stopped me: "Your bathroom is soaking mine!"

"Excuse me," I offered.

"Water is leaking from your bathroom," the voice continued.

"I'm sorry," I said. "Maybe my housemate Joe took a shower with the curtain outside the tub. I'll check and make sure it doesn't happen again."

A quick trip upstairs proved my theory, and a few towels mopped up the excess moisture. I learned from Mark that the man (call him Mr. B.) was a long-term tenant.

The next day, clad this time in a Second World War Eisenhower jacket, I bumped into Mr. B. on his porch. I could see that he was about sixty years old, moderately heavy, and a bit stooped in the shoulders. I asked him if the leak had disappeared. He said yes and thanked me for attending to it.

On a whim, I also ventured, "I noticed that there's a frame for a window in the front hallway. Do you happen to know why the window was removed?"

Mr. B. straightened up slightly, grinned, and said, "Now that's a strange story!"

Are you kidding me? In every B-horror movie I had ever seen, there is a creepy character using that exact line as a prelude to reveal a legend of diabolical evil and unspeakable danger.

"You see," he went on, "there used to be a stained glass window there."

I knew it!

"The window had a gorgeous, intricate design. My wife and I loved it. She put curtains around it and flowers on the sill. But then, three years ago, in the late spring, I went away for a month, and the original owner died without an heir. The bank sold the building to a stranger who in turn sold the window and had the opening covered with mahogany. When I got home, I told off the new owner but good, and he moved out soon afterwards."

Bummer. The mystery was just a case of an opportunist selling off an antique fixture for a quick buck.

But, as I turned to leave, a question came to mind: "You said the opening was covered with mahogany, but it looks more like paneling over fiberglass."

"That's because the bastard covered it so poorly," he answered, "that there was a cold breeze coming through the window into my apartment, so I insulated and covered it as you see it now."

Clear enough. I thanked him for his time and went upstairs, a bit disappointed that my summer mystery was so banal. But then I began to think about what Mr. B. had said. I grabbed a flashlight, chair, and plastic straw and went back down into the front hallway. I discovered holes in the upper corners of the window molding, holes consistent with braces for curtains—but the considerable width and depth of the holes, which I checked with the straw, led me to believe that the braces had been meant to support heavy drapes rather than lacy curtains.

As I climbed down from the chair, I wondered, "Who the heck puts drapes on a stained glass window?" and "Who puts flowers in front of colored glass?" And then I asked myself, "Why would a greedy new owner cover the opening with such a heavy and expensive wood as mahogany?" And finally, I asked, "What kind of cold breeze could be so strong in early summer as to disturb somebody in an apartment half a floor higher than the window frame? Cold air does not rise."

Suddenly, the hall didn't feel merely cool but uncomfortably cold.

Once upstairs, I wrote down the day's events. Perhaps a real mystery did exist, but other matters took precedence. Baseball, romance, cooking at Hojo's, and the genuine pleasure of living away from home in my first apartment pushed the mystery aside—that is until one of the former tenants came by to pick up a weight-lifting bench he had left behind. I asked him if he'd had any problems with our apartment. He said no at first, but, when I pressed him, he said, "We did have one problem, but it won't affect you guys."

"How is that?" I asked.

"Well," he replied, "the apartment is hard as hell to heat. It has a parlor heater in the living room, which we didn't expect to distribute the heat very well, but this thing worked so badly that we had the gas company out twice to look at it. The second time they came, the guy told me, 'I don't know what's going on here. There's nothing wrong with your heater. With the amount of gas it's burning, it should be able to heat an outdoor tennis court to seventy-five degrees. It's not a problem of insulation because there's a ton of snow on your roof.' Pretty weird, eh?"

After he left, I took a thermometer off the outside back porch and placed it on the windowsill down in the front hallway. Twenty minutes later, I retrieved it and saw that the temperature was forty-six. Pages of the *Worcester Telegram & Gazette*, scattered on the living room floor where Joe usually discarded the paper, informed me that the day's temperature was expected to be in the upper eighties. Suddenly, our "comfortable" apartment felt much less inviting.

Time went by. Normal events transpired. The mystery, such as it was, slipped out of my mind. We saw some terrific movies, like *The Deer Hunter.* We also saw some pretty bad films. We didn't discriminate. This was the pre-video, pre-Netflix, pre-internet era after all in an apartment without even a rabbit-eared, black-and-white television. Movies in Worcester were so cheap, we basically saw every one of them, the good ones multiple times.

And so, it comes as no surprise that, in early July, Joe and I saw Gregory Peck in *The Omen*, a decent horror movie about a diplomat whose son is secretly murdered and replaced with the Antichrist. As Joe said, "Hey, shit happens." On the morning after seeing the film, I returned from Hojo's, said hi to Laura, who was eating a bowl of Cocoa Krispies in the kitchen, and plopped myself down in our one comfy chair in the living room alcove. Warm sunbeams, made visible by the dust we never vacuumed, streamed by me to the center of the living room floor, where they intersected with a much duller beam of light that extended from the keyhole in the door leading to the third-floor landing in the front hall. That light originated from a small westward-facing window.

As a religious studies major at Holy Cross, I was curious about the biblical quotes in *The Omen* and resolved to check them out. I suspected that Hollywood jazzed up the Bible to enhance the movie's script. In particular, I wanted to find the quote about the number of the beast being 666. I knew it was somewhere in the Book of Revelation. Unfortunately, the only Bible we had on hand was one Joe stole (or "borrowed," as he claimed) from the classics department. It was in Greek on the left-hand side with Latin on the facing pages. I had endured two semesters of Latin and hoped that I could ferret out the 666 text. I opened to Revelation and read the first line I found. My Latin is now quite nonexistent, save grammatically incorrect quips like "Semper ubi sub ubi" (Always where under where) and wasn't that much better then. I read Revelation 13:5, "Quis similis bestiae? Et quis poterit pugnare cum ea?" Although the words meant nothing to me, I felt a very sudden chill down my spine, looked to my right, and saw the keyhole to the hallway door go completely black.

I cried, "Laura, come quick! There's someone in the hall!"

She raced in, and we opened the door but found the hallway empty. No one answered at either Mr. B.'s or the first-floor apartment. And the front door to the street was closed and locked.

Despite these facts, I knew someone (no, that's not accurate), I knew some *thing*, something malevolent, had been behind that door, something that consumed all the light, heat, and joy out of that space as surely as one of Harry Potter's Dementors did.

At first, Laura chided me for trying once again to scare her, but, seeing how shaken I was, she hesitated and eventually let the matter go. I could not move on so easily. To this point in my life, I had always assumed that terror grew by degrees from reasonable beginnings to irrational heights under the influence of mental exaggeration. Poe's murderer in "The Tell-Tale Heart," for example, is gradually driven by guilt and fear into the supernatural delusion that he can still hear his victim's beating heart from under the floorboards of the room where he had interred her corpse. Terror, I always believed, was contextual. If I heard noises in the middle of a stormy night while reading *Dracula*, my mind might well trick me into imagining that I was being stalked by the undead. But on that sunny morning, many hours after seeing *The Omen*, could the suggestion still be strong enough to scare me so viscerally? Many of Poe's characters went mad. Was I entering a world of visual hallucinations?

I had no desire to embrace lunacy, so I resolved to renounce supernatural ruminations and plunge myself into shallow joys more typical of a college sophomore. As Bluto Blutarsky says to Flounder in *Animal House*, "My advice to you is to begin drinking heavily." I organized a pizza party for that night, bought an abundance of beer, and surrounded myself with friends. The atmosphere was so festive that I asked if anyone wanted to see our haunted hallway. Several people, including a couple of waitresses from Hojo's, Roxanne and Sally, were game, so I grabbed the old-fashioned key to unlock the hall door. To my frustration, I found that I couldn't make the key work. After several attempts by others and me, we gave up. I turned the knob a few times and gave the door a pull without effect before turning back to my guests. A few minutes later, though, Roxanne noticed that the door was ajar. I reinserted the key in the lock and found that it opened quite easily. Weird.

Roxanne, Sally, and I went down to the landing where we examined the covered window by the tiny flame of a Bic lighter. I could have used a brighter flashlight but opted instead for a spookier effect. Nothing untoward transpired, and we returned upstairs. The party lasted a couple of hours more without incident.

The next day, I told Joe about my problem with the key, and he wondered if the front hall key would fit any other doors. For the next ten minutes, we tried it in various closet and room doors without success, and then, Joe remembered there was a door on our outside back porch, a door we had presumed led to an attic. We tried the key there with no more luck than elsewhere.

At eleven that night, I arrived for my shift at the restaurant. I was a line cook, as was Joe. We prided ourselves on our efficiency and good humor at work. The waitresses and dishwashers were more friends of ours than coworkers. We had lots of laughs. My routine didn't vary. My first task was to go into a small changing room adjacent to the staff bathroom to put on the bright orange jumpsuit cooks were obligated to wear. The changing room was painted aqua blue and Day-Glo orange, HoJo's trademark color scheme. When we went inside the changing room and closed the door, a bright fluorescent light came on automatically, accompanied by a small fan and the sound of Muzak piped in from the dining room.

On that particular night, I was in a fantastic mood and looked forward to my shift. I trotted inside to get vested, but the instant the door closed behind me, I felt an identical chill to the one I'd experienced when the keyhole in our apartment turned black. I was overwhelmed with an indescribable fear and fell back into the kitchen where my concerned coworkers told me that all the color had drained out of my face. Terribly embarrassed, I collected myself and re-resolved to stop letting my mind play tricks on me. I kept the tenor of the rest of my shift purposely light, even going so far as to spray whipped cream on Joe's hat and to inhale helium to distort my voice.

When morning broke, I walked home freshly determined to put the supernatural behind me. As I neared our building, I decided to waltz confidently upstairs right past the covered window, giving it no mind whatsoever, but the second I opened the front porch door, a blast of cold air struck me as forcefully as it did when I opened the walk-in freezer at work. I stopped dead in my tracks and, without closing the door, walked backwards until I came to rest sitting on the front lawn. I could no more enter that hallway alone than I could fly to the moon. I slunk dejectedly up the back stairs.

When I reached our apartment, it occurred to me that I had never translated that line from Revelation, so I looked it up and painstakingly learned that it meant: "Who is like the beast? And who can make war upon him?" The text went on to say, "The beast was allowed to boast its boasts and blasphemies and to do whatever it wanted; and it mouthed its blasphemies against God, against his name, his heavenly tent and all those who are sheltered there. It was allowed to make war against the saints and conquer them."

These struck me as significantly more frightening lines than the reference to the number of the beast being a triple six. Although Revelation is an almost incomprehensible book of the Bible, with huge divergence in its interpretation by scholars and religious sects, I did remember that the general idea of the Antichrist is that God will give this dude some slack for a period of human trial and tribulation before everything will be set right once and for all. Good people will take some pretty hard knocks during God's hiatus. Like all prophecies, there's nothing anyone can do to prevent their fulfillment. In fact, those who try to prevent them, like Saint Peter who rails against the idea of Jesus's crucifixion, are denounced: "Get behind me Satan! Because the way you think is not God's way, but man's" (Mark 8:33).

Was I screwing around with something diabolical or . . . ? Father Karras in *The Exorcist* presumes that the child played by Linda Blair must be mentally ill because she claims to be possessed not by some minor demon but by the Devil himself. The priest, who is also a psychiatrist, says such pretension is characteristic of a deluded mind, like people who think they are Napoleon.

When one starts believing he or she might be threatened by the Devil, aliens, or secret agents of a shadow government, it's a good time to seek rational advice. My housemates already concluded that I was a whack job, so I called a skeptical religious studies professor at her home in an adjacent town. The phone rang a few times and then made a jarring sound I had never heard before, a cross between a busy signal and that high-pitched beep used for the Emergency Broadcast System. I called the operator, who told me that there was trouble on the line. Undeterred, I called a Jesuit priest who taught philosophy at Holy Cross. He answered on the first ring and seemed pleased to hear from me, but, before I could explain why I called, he excused himself to take another call. When he returned, he apologized saying he had an emergency and had to leave town right away. Disappointed but not ready to admit defeat, I tried a classmate of mine in upstate New York. Her phone also made the trouble-on-the-line clanging.

Before I could slip from frustration to paranoia, I changed tactics and wrote a letter describing recent events to a friend named Joe C. in Philadelphia. Joe C. planned to enter the Jesuit seminary in September. He introduced me to Malachi Martin's book *Hostage to the Devil* on the history of exorcism. Joe C. was too superstitious to be objective by a long stretch, but he was no intellectual slouch. After I sealed and addressed my letter, I gave it to my roommate Joe to post on his way to pick up a pizza.

Later on, I asked Joe if he had remembered to mail my letter, and he said, "I had it in my pocket, but when I got to the mailbox it wasn't there. I figured it must have fallen out, but I didn't see it on my way home. Sorry."

I grabbed him by the shirt and shouted, "What do you mean, it wasn't in your pocket?!"

He pushed me away saying, "Hey, don't get your knickers in a twist. Just write it again. Jeez, Louise!"

I did write another letter, only this time I merely invited Joe C. for a visit. I said nothing about the hallway or my concerns. I mailed the envelope myself and, four days later, I received a cheerful reply from Joe C. promising to visit that very weekend.

On one of the intervening nights, Laura's parents came for dinner. Apparently, Laura had never informed them that Sue had moved out. She feared that her parents would be upset she was the only woman in an apartment with three men, so she put a few feminine items in our guest room and pleaded with Joe, Mark, and me to pretend that Sue still lived with us. At dinner, Laura pointedly referred to Sue so often that Joe and I couldn't resist having some fun.

"So, Laura," Joe asked, "what time will Sue be in tonight? Shouldn't your parents meet her?"

Despite furtive dirty looks from Laura, I beamed to her mother and father, "You'd love Sue. She's such an easy-going roommate, it's almost as if she didn't live with us at all."

Afterwards, Laura called us jerks, as if that would insult us. How little some women understand the adolescent male psyche.

The next morning, I went downstairs to the first floor to return a colander Mark had borrowed to strain spaghetti. The woman who answered the door thanked me and said, "Do you mind if I ask you a personal question?"

"Not at all," I replied.

"How much are you paying for rent?"

"$105 a month."

"Unbelievable. We pay more than twice as much."

"What was this about?" I wondered to myself, but said aloud, "What did the tenants before the college students pay for our place?"

"There were none," she answered, "The third floor apartment was left vacant for two years until the students came and got it for a pittance."

"That's weird. Have you ever asked the landlord about this?"

"My husband and I wrote him a letter to complain about the rent and about heating problems we were having. He gave us no explanation about the rent but said that, as far as repairs to the heating system were concerned, we could hire someone to look into it but that under no circumstances would he ever return personally to the building."

She paused and went on, "I can tell you that something is not right here. We're moving out next week. I'd advise you all to do the same."

As I climbed back upstairs, it occurred to me that the third floor apartment was left empty about the same time Mr. B. said the new owner sold the window and moved out. Why would this owner not rent the third floor for two years and then rent it well below the going rate? Why did he refuse to come back to our house? What the flip was going on?

These questions were set aside as we prepared for Joe C.'s visit. Mark, Joe, and I, all friends of Joe C., decided to give him a creative welcome. We set up a long table in our kitchen with chairs on only one side, covered it with a white sheet, and placed a wooden chalice in the center. We made a big banner that read in Latin, "This is your last supper, Turkey." We dressed like daVinci's apostles and put Joe C. in the center spot, teasing him that his entry into the seminary was like Jesus's ill-fated entry into Jerusalem. He got into it, blessing the bread and wine before quoting the Gospel of John, "So you do indeed feel grief now, but I am going to see you again. Then your hearts will be full of joy, and no one will take your joy away."

After supper, Mark went off for a twelve-hour shift as a tech assistant at Saint Vincent Hospital, and Joe left to spend the night with his girlfriend.

"I'm sorry," I apologized to Joe C., but I have to work from eleven till seven at Hojo's. I'm off tomorrow, so I can spend more time with you then. Make yourself at home. Feel free to play the stereo and eat anything you like in the fridge."

Joe C.'s face darkened.

"What's wrong?" I asked.

"This may sound weird to you," he began, "but I have always felt a strong sense of what God wants me to do, and I have an uncanny feeling right now that the last thing God wants me to do is to spend a night alone in this apartment."

He made this pronouncement with no knowledge of my suspicions.

Despite my pleading, he refused to stay by himself, preferring instead to join me at Howard Johnson's where he spent the night napping in a secluded booth. The next morning, I told him every peculiar thing that had happened that summer. He advised me to leave well enough alone and move out immediately. Then Joe C. cut short his visit, returning to Philadelphia by the first available bus.

I decided to get away too, but only for a short visit to my parents' house in New Hampshire. On the bus ride, I had the creepy feeling that the other passengers were Satanists like the denizens of the brownstone in *Rosemary's Baby*. No matter how innocuous they seemed, I was wary lest they try to thwart my flight from Worcester.

Once I got home, I tried to tell my mother, a conservative Methodist, whose only nonconformist belief was in UFOs, about my experience. She gave me the kind of look that made me change the subject before I had gone very far into it. She'd accept ET long before she'd even consider ESP or anything paranormal.

I had better luck with my friend Briand. He not only heard me out but insisted on calling a parapsychologist he knew at the University of New Hampshire. This fellow was so excited by a thumbnail sketch of my experience that he drove down from Durham, picked Briand and me up, and took us to Worcester so he could investigate the site himself. I called to let Joe, Mark, and Laura know that I was returning with a ghostbuster, an occurrence they found more than a little humorous.

When we arrived at the apartment, the professor came into the house with a big case that he didn't even open before saying, "Oh yes, I definitely sense bad vibrations here."

Several times, he closed his eyes, splayed his fingers, and moved his outstretched arms slowly, as if he were gathering a huge swath of cotton candy. Then he exclaimed, "The aura is strong" or something equally weird. Mark thought he was hysterical. Even I found his manner over-the-top.

After spending an hour upstairs, the investigator insisted that we go outside to examine the exterior of the covered window. Interestingly, since it is on the side of the building away from the main street, I had never actually seen it before. Briand, Dr. Demento, and I looked up at the blank gray wall for a minute before realizing that the regular house shingles were made of wood while those covering the former window opening were of a lighter shade, probably made from a cheap material not unlike stiff cardboard.

The professor put his case down on the ground beside the house and climbed on top of it to get a closer look. He reached up and tapped on the surface once or twice looking perplexed. Without a word, he gestured for each of us in turn to climb up and try the same experiment. By the time I did it, he spoke out loud what we all already knew was under the cheap covering: "Glass!"

The stained glass window had not been removed. It was merely covered over. But why would the owner protect the inside with mahogany, wood so heavy it does not even float, and the outside with cardboard? And why would he lie to Mr. B. that he had removed the window? What the flying flip was going on in this place?

The parapsychologist couldn't have been more excited. He promised to return with more sophisticated equipment, interns, and even a few colleagues.

"This might be one of the most significant paranormal finds of our time," he declared before shaking my hand vigorously, saying he'd call the next day and then leaving with Briand.

"Finally," I thought, "there's someone, even if it's someone semi-rational, who's going to look into the mystery for me. I can give it up and enjoy my summer."

Unfortunately, things didn't work out that way. I never heard from Dr. Strange. After two days went by, I called Briand, only to learn that the professor had been sick in bed with the flu since his visit to Worcester. I called the professor and left many messages which all went unanswered. I finally received a letter from him saying: "Despite my initial suspicions that paranormal activities are occurring in your house, I have decided to close this investigation. I strongly advise you to do the same. Please DO NOT contact me again on this matter." End of story. What's a sophomore to do?

And then, just when I thought it couldn't get weirder, it did. Father Ted, the vocations director for the Capuchin-Franciscans, came to visit me. He sat on a couch to the left of the hallway door. While we talked, Joe unlocked the hall door and went out. When he returned, he locked it again and sat down to talk with the affable Father Ted. A minute later, I heard the distinct sound of the doorknob to the hall being turned from right to left several times as if someone were outside trying to get in. I excused myself, got up, and unlocked the door figuring Mark was out there, but the hall was eerily empty.

When Father Ted left, I asked Joe if he had heard this clicking sound from the knob. He insisted he hadn't, which I found hard to believe since he had been sitting with his back less than three feet from the knob. He suggested that the noise I heard was an "after-click" from when he locked it.

"Maybe the tumblers were slow falling back into place," he offered.

"No way, Joe," I argued. "What we both heard was the knob turning not once but several times." Not until ten years after the fact did Joe admit to me that he had heard the knob turning but that he didn't want to admit it because he felt it would throw fuel on the fire of my sleuthing.

The conversation about the knob and key reminded me how the door wouldn't open at first during my pizza party but opened easily minutes later. I recalled this to Joe and asked him if he would like to try the key once again in any of the apartment's locks. He agreed, and we found that this time the fickle key opened and closed every one of them. Neither of us could fathom what was going on, save the possibility that humidity had previously caused the doors to stick.

We sat in silence on the couch a bit, and then Joe's face lit up.

He exclaimed, "The porch door!"

We rushed out, easily opened the lock, and bounded up a short flight of stairs to an unfinished attic. The dusty space was chock-full of boxes filled with books on obstetrics, gynecology, and veterinary medicine. We also discovered several cases of prescription medicine, including codeine and other narcotics. Joe turned up a number of letters and business cards with the name Faisal D. from New Jersey as well as a couple of letters and cards from a Worcester lawyer named Barton. We took his business card, a cool sign that said "The doctor is in," and a neat stool. Then we went downstairs.

Joe reached a quick conclusion that the incongruous collection of human and animal medical paraphernalia indicated that this Dr. Faisal had been a veterinarian up front and an illegal abortionist on the side.

"After all," Joe argued, "abortion has only been legal in the US for five years. Someone performed them before that time."

I was skeptical of Joe's theory but was sure that I wanted to know more, so I suggested that we call the Worcester lawyer and make up some cock-and-bull story about accidentally finding this stuff and wanting to know if we could help locate its owner. Joe agreed, and I made the call.

The lawyer himself answered. From the outset, he was suspicious and stern: Who were we? What exactly did we see? Did we open anything? Didn't we know that the lease signed with the original Holy Cross students prohibited subletting?

Only with great difficulty did I get off the phone. Joe and I were sure that we'd be evicted, get sent to jail, or be shot by gangsters.

Worries are as ephemeral as cobwebs, though, when you are twenty years old. Mark came home all excited to point out that there was an ad in the *Worcester Telegram* placed by a man named Mohammed Merri from Qatar who was looking for a typical American family to live with for a month. Since Laura was our surrogate mom, we boys felt certain that we could legitimately rent Sue's empty room to this man from a country none of us had ever heard of. Mark dialed Merri's number while Joe and I pressed our ears up to either side of the receiver. Mohammed Merri had a wonderful singsong accent not unlike the Indians from the nearby Annapurna Restaurant. He promised to be back in touch and closed his conversation with, "Thank you very, very much, maybe please." The prospect of hosting him put us all in a festive mood. We retrieved a few more medical accoutrements from the attic to spruce up the living room and ordered three large pizzas.

The next morning, Joe was in the shower while I ate breakfast and a dark-skinned fellow peered in through the window of the porch door. I opened it and asked, "Mohammed Merri?"

"No," he replied coldly. "Faisal D."

A split second later, a towel-clad Joe emerged from the bathroom and asked, "Who's the swami?"

With an even frostier tone, Mr. D. said, "Your landlord."

Yikes!

We put on our best manners and offered tea, coffee, and Cheerios all while trying to stand in such a way as to obscure the various items we had already pilfered from the attic. Joe spread his towel over the stool. I leaned against the mantle stretching my arms to block the doctor-is-in sign. We were terrified and braced ourselves for dire consequences, but Mr. D. went downstairs without a word. His two sons returned and began removing everything in the attic. Joe and I were so scared we volunteered to help. The four of us carried all the boxes down to a U-Haul trailer parked out front. In my multiple trips up and down, I never saw Mr. D. until I peered around the right side of our building to find him staring up at the space where the window had been covered over.

In less than two hours, everything was packed up. To our surprise, instead of having us arrested, Mr. D. gave each of us ten dollars. And then, without explanation, he and his sons got into their car and left for good. Joe and I didn't know what to make of the affair but did manage to buy wicked cool sandals with our windfall. As far as my mystery was concerned, I was more confused than ever.

Again time passed. Our first-floor neighbors moved out, leaving us alone in the building with the creepy Mr. B. And then, on a warm August night, I left Laura and her boyfriend Ed in our living room while I went out to get a pizza. All the outside back porch landing lights were on as were the lights in the empty first floor apartment. I walked to the corner of the main street and glanced back at our building. Through the uncurtained trio of windows in our living room, I thought I saw a huge, dark hand reach up and douse the chandelier light.

"This must be a tropical delusion," I chortled, unwilling to accept any more bizarre occurrences.

When I returned though, the entire building was in darkness. No other houses on our street were without lights, so I knew it wasn't a power failure. As I climbed the back stairs by skimpy moonlight, I tried the pull chain on each porch light without success. Were it not for the soothing aroma of pizza, I'd have turned back. At the top landing, not only did the light fail to come on but the outside door was closed as was the inner door to the kitchen. This meant I had to enter through a pitch-black hallway. I did so quickly, shouting, "Laura! Ed!"

Ed poked his head out of the fully-lit living room and asked, "What's up?"

I explained that the power was out in the rest of the building, but, when we went outside on the porch, we discovered that all the lights were on including those inside the first-floor apartment. Laura and Ed insisted that the living room chandelier had never been extinguished.

The following evening just about sunset, I was alone in the apartment talking on the phone with a waitress from Hojo's about the previous night's incident when I heard the doorknob of the front hall door turn behind me. I told her about it and begged her to stay on the line while I ran into the front room to get a bow tie for work. If I successfully completed this mission, I'd pick up the phone, say goodbye, and skedaddle to Hojo's several hours early for work but all the safer. She agreed with my plan.

I set the receiver down on the mantle, looked at the silent hall door, ran past it into the front room, and fumbled in my drawer for a tie. While doing so, I not only heard the out-of-sight knob turning but also furious pounding on the door. I sprinted back to the phone, passed the once-again silent door, picked up the receiver, and heard my coworker exclaim, "Am I glad to hear your voice!"

"What do you mean?" I asked.

"Well," she answered, "if this were a movie, there'd be a close-up of a huge, dark hand hanging up the receiver, I'd hear the dial tone, and never see you again."

"I'm sure glad you aren't directing my life," I replied before escaping out the back door.

After this incident, I took time to reflect. It was coming close to the time when we'd all return to Holy Cross. I was of two minds. The rational part of me assumed I had allowed my imagination to run away with itself. The murkier side wondered if I were being warned off by supernatural forces, or worse still, being threatened by them. The dark option was just too kooky to contemplate, so I didn't. For the final two weeks of summer, I made no more inquiries and was pleased to see how uneventful those days and nights were. And, you'd better believe that was fine with me.

On the last day in the apartment, as Laura and I finished loading our stuff into Ed's car, I remembered that I had forgotten to take down the crucifix my grandparents had given me. It featured a white plaster figure on a black wooden cross affixed to the wall by two eye hooks, one at the top and the other at the bottom. When we moved in, the first thing I did was put that crucifix up on the wall in the front room where Joe and I ended up sleeping. After telling Laura to wait for me, I went up the back stairs, passed through the kitchen, living room, and sliding doorway. When I turned to my left to retrieve the cross, I found it hanging upside down. A familiar chill came over me as I screamed until Laura came up to see what was wrong. She insisted that the nail from the upper eye hook must have fallen out, but neither of us could find it anywhere on the floor despite a lengthy search.

Three months later, my friends and I went to a Halloween showing of the 1968 classic film, *The Night of the Living Dead*. Afterwards, we hung out in the campus pub where people began exchanging spooky stories over pizza and beer (perfectly legal for nineteen-year-olds in that enlightened age).

All of their tales struck me as rather tame, so I said, "I have a story to tell. It happened to me last summer, and it's true."

Catching their attention, I plunged right in. Before I had gotten very far, though, I absently touched the top of my ear and discovered blood on my finger. I didn't feel any pain, so I was more curious than concerned. I grabbed a stack of napkins from the table, pressed them gently to the side of my head, and resumed my tale, but, when I pulled them away a minute later, I was shocked to see the formerly pristine rectangles soaked in blood. An icy hand stroked my spine, prompting me to stop talking and head to the infirmary. The nurse on duty told me I had an inch-long cut on my ear that appeared to have come from a razor or something equally sharp. She refused to believe that it could have just started bleeding spontaneously.

Two years later, when I was a Capuchin-Franciscan novice, I figured that I was in about as safe a place as there could be to get my story on paper. During the few spare hours of free time we had each evening, I typed in the second floor classroom of Saint Francis Friary in Garrison, New York. A couple of days after I began writing, I left my room on the third floor to go to Night Prayer in the first-floor chapel. To promote an atmosphere of reverence, the halls were lit only by night lights. I entered the stairwell and felt a wave of cold. In my peripheral vision, I could see a body hanging from the solarium railing on the floor above. The upper portion of the corpse was shrouded in darkness, but a chalk-white hand came only inches from my face as the body swayed slightly. The cadaver was so close that the hand would have brushed against my nose if I turned for a direct look. Well, I can assure you, there was no danger of that happening. I ran headlong down the stairs, tripped on the knotted cord about my waist, and landed unceremoniously at the feet of my disapproving novice master who chided me, as he always did with, "Brother! Jesus calls us to be child-like, not childish."

To make matters worse, that night's reading was from 1 Peter: "Your opponent the Devil is prowling like a roaring lion, looking for someone to devour."

Creepy? Yes, but not enough to dissuade me from my appointed task. The following day between Evening and Night Prayer found me typing away in a classroom. Since it was sultry, I left the windows open on both sides of the room. They afforded me a clear view of the other well lit wings of the friary. Within an hour, I had a neat stack of say a dozen completed pages.

And then, without warning, the lights went out.

Suspecting that my mischievous brother novices pulled a fuse to scare me, I said, "All right, guys. Very funny. Turn the lights back on."

No one replied or snickered in the dark hall beyond. I wondered if it was a power failure but noticed that lights were still on in other windows.

I resolved to get up and investigate, but before I could push my chair back, I was overwhelmed by a sense of mortal peril. The temperature plunged ominously (in the movie version, this will be captured by striking the lowest chord on a piano). Just as suddenly, a fierce wind rushed through the window behind me and scattered my papers. I was out of the room faster than Cornwallis left Yorktown. The next morning, I gathered the pages and tore them up.

I tried yet again to write this story in 1983, when I lived for a brief time with my friend Tom Lewis in his brownstone in Worcester, Massachusetts. As I banged away on his manual Smith Corona, the wind howled outside and rustled the plastic insulation on Tom's windows. I jumped when his rotary phone rang, but was relieved to hear the voice of my friend Mary Donnelly.

"Whew! Am I glad to hear your voice, " I said.

"Why is that?" she asked.

"Because I've just started writing about something that frightened me years ago, and I spooked myself."

"That's funny," she answered. Then she continued:

A friend of mine just shared a strange experience of his with me. You see, he was trying to buy some property up here in Maine, only the elderly husband-and-wife Realtors seemed skittish about selling it and evasive when he asked them why. It was a large, undeveloped, mostly wooded parcel that seemed innocuous enough, but, after my friend walked through it on an overgrown dirt road, he discovered the burned-out ruins of a house. Later on, when he asked the Realtors about it, they hesitated, until the wife reluctantly told him that a superstitious man used to own it. He collected occult artifacts and hosted parties with macabre themes. When he acquired a medieval book that purported to have a spell that could invoke the Devil, he gathered his people for a midnight trial run.

"So, what happened?" my friend asked.

The wife swallowed hard and whispered, "He came."

The husband put his arm around her and concluded, "The guests fled. The owner, whose hair turned white overnight, burned his own house to the ground and abandoned the property. That's why it's going for so little."

My friend says it was then that he noticed how the Realty office was festooned with crucifixes and religious statues. He told me that he left without buying the land.

The fact that Mary, an ordinarily sensible person, had chosen to share this preposterous story with me at the precise moment I was trying to write about something equally far-fetched, disquieted me. After I hung up the phone, I took the sheet of paper out of the typewriter and left it crumpled in a wastebasket.

I stopped writing my story not because I'm normally a squeamish person nor because I routinely see dead people like that Olmert kid in *The Sixth Sense* but because I do not enjoy being frightened. In fiction, a character hears sinister noises behind a door and invariably opens it to his or her doom. In reality, people play it safe and hightail it in the opposite direction. Rational people do not enter cursed Egyptian tombs nor split up to search for homicidal maniacs. A nice, boring, and safe life is fine and dandy, thank you very much. Nothing ventured, nothing lost.

But I am a slow learner, so I sat down once again in 2012 to write this tale. Only this time, as you can see, I carefully avoided any identification of the location of the house. Maybe that had nothing to do with it, but I have had no more scares.

What I've told you is as true as memory allows. I've tried to be clear about when I was speculating, and maybe that's the only thing I can leave with you.

Remember how Mr. B. said the window was of an intricate design that his wife honored with drapes and flowers? Could that design have been occult? Could they have been treating it as some kind of altar? When Mr. B. was away, the new owner, Faisal D., moved in and had the window covered on the inside with the heaviest wood on earth and on the outside with cardboard. Was he trying to keep something from coming in? When Mr. B. returned, Faisal lied to him about selling the window, was chastised by Mr. B., and, shortly thereafter, moved out so suddenly that he left behind expensive, if not incriminating, items that he failed to retrieve for three years. What frightened him so much that he fled and told the first-floor tenant that "under no circumstances" would he return? Why did Faisal refuse to lease the third floor for two years until he rented it to a group of hard-partying students? Did he hope that rowdies would not go poking around like some foolish religious studies major, whom he never intended to rent to, eventually did? Could it be that, when Faisal bought the building, he recognized the sinister design of the window, approached it, took out a quarter, scratched the surface, and put an eye up to the cold glass? Could it be that what he saw was not the side yard, but a grotesque place of unmitigated evil?

Upon reflection, I realize that there are only two possibilities: The first is that my roommates were correct that I am a victim of my imagination. The second is that there really was something diabolical going on in that house. If I went back and uncovered the window, I would either find nothing remarkable or a horrific Lovecraftian reality. I could be mildly disappointed or insanely terrified.

If Milton was right in *Paradise Lost*, though, and Lucifer parted company with God in a jealous rage over God's love for humanity, the Devil's purpose is not to lurk around gratuitously frightening people. The Devil's goal is to break our bond of trust with God and discourage us from becoming the saints we are called to be. In a homily I heard, the priest said, "The opposite of faith is not doubt but fear," and Saint Mark tells us, "Fear is useless." The nice, boring, and safe life that fear dictates is not without cost. It crushes our potential.

And so, maybe not today or tomorrow, but, despite my earlier insistence that I would never go back to that house, I like to think I eventually will. And when I do, should I come face to face with the Prince of Darkness, I hope I can stiffen my spine and reply brazenly, like the French defenders of a besieged castle in *Monty Python and the Holy Grail*, with "I fart in your general direction."

In the Sandals of Saint Francis

My earliest childhood memories of Catholicism revolve around the dying days of the Latin Mass offered by an ancient French Canadian pastor named Father Lucier. He was the absolute monarch of Saint Theresa's Parish in Blackstone, Massachusetts, where he thundered against the "sacrilege" of wearing sneakers or shorts to church. Father Lucier's accent was so pronounced that I had nightmares for a week after he preached, "I t'ink it is important t'at you should fear the rat' of God." To tell the truth, the clerically conjured image of a giant rodent bearing down on me out of heaven was no stranger than my neighbor's shouting, "T'row me down the stairs my shoes." In a French Canadian neighborhood, there were a few certainties: Everything had gender ("The car, she don't go"), and everyone was Catholic. Mass was a life-or-death obligation reinforced by *The Baltimore Catechism*, which had all the answers:

"Who made me?"

"God made me."

"Why did God make me?"

"To know Him, love Him, and serve Him in this world, and to be happy with Him for all eternity in the next."

Who could argue with truths so confidently delivered by nuns in midnight black habits? The Catholic Church seemed like an immovable rock.

With seven children, my parents could not afford to send us to Catholic school, which meant we attended public school and had to go to catechism classes for our religious education. Luckily, my first teacher was Sister Rose, who was not improperly named. Her gentleness and conviction persuaded me that the almost impossibly dry Communion wafers were not only miraculously transformed into the Body of Christ but that their reception was a personal encounter with God, second-to-none. I had a similarly positive introduction to the Sacrament of Confession. Paradise was set before me while Hell was hardly ever mentioned. I'm happy to say that I never saw a nun smack anyone with a ruler nor a clergyman abuse anyone. Catholicism got off to a good start in my life.

As with many situations, though, the honeymoon was not to last. The Second Vatican Council introduced sweeping changes by the time it concluded in 1965. Nuns as we knew them in black habits vanished, our church was stripped of statuary, and the Mass was dramatically changed. Our new pastor, a military chaplain named Father Rattay (we called him Father Ratty behind his back) "celebrated" a kind of staccato English liturgy not unlike rap music without the rhyming. In place of Latin chant, we had silly "music" with lyrics like "Allelu, allelu, everybody sing allelu, for the Lord is risen, it is true." At Mass, we were expected to turn to strangers in the pews and shake their hands. Sometimes we were asked to hold hands with them during the Lord's Prayer. For a second-generation Irish-American like my father, this "touchy-feely stuff" was intolerable. He resolved to spend his Sunday mornings in a lounge chair reading novels instead of going to church.

This should have finished things for me and Holy Mother Church, but my actual mother saw to it that it did not. Although she was a lifelong Methodist, she honored a promise she made when she married my father to raise all her children as Catholics. Even though my dad stopped going to church altogether, my mom insisted that my brothers, sisters, and I go to Mass and religious education. Her integrity was such that all seven of us were eventually confirmed as Catholics. After Confirmation, though, she figured we were free to spend our Sundays as we pleased.

Unfortunately, from 1966 until 1975, I was subjected to a collection of Catholic preachers so incredibly dull that it was a real chore to remember a shred of their sermons a minute after they mercifully concluded. One priest was so boring and long-winded that parishioners began boycotting his liturgies. This prompted him to make a promise not to preach longer than six minutes. His pledge was to be enforced by a timer set up on the pulpit, but all it evoked, when it rang, was an impatient "Damn!" from the priest, who went on and on anyway. If I had to characterize the clergy of those years with a color, it would be gray. Had any of them opened a homily with the words "Blah, blah, blaah," I don't think a single member of the congregation would have been surprised.

There was an exception. One priest took to the 1960s with sparkle. His name was Father Dorrais. He made an association with Catholicism that I seldom heard from anyone else. He connected it with a person named Jesus. This priest was able to communicate that Christ was a truly likable human being and a fine example of what divinity should act like when God comes to earth.

Father Dorrais's example prodded me to consider the priesthood. The experience I had in various school plays convinced me that I was already a better public speaker than the boring, gray priests. Maybe I could be a Sister Rose or Father Dorrais for someone else. It inspired me to think so. On the other hand, my Methodist mom and post-Catholic dad would hardly jump for joy at having a son announce that he wanted to be a priest, so I stashed the idea in the back of my mind behind what I imagined might be a more acceptable career as a lawyer, geologist, archaeologist (the biggest word I knew until I was sixteen), chef, actor, or comedian. When you're a kid, the possibilities are endless.

In 1972 when I was fourteen, my family moved to Pelham, New Hampshire, where, by the time I was a high school senior wallowing in self-pity over my latest breakup, priesthood was far from my mind. Even though I had a perfectly miserable track record with girls, miracles like the 1969 World-Series-winning Mets continued to fuel my hope that a self-perceived Charlie Brown could succeed in romance. I wrote yards of adolescent poetry singing sentimental praises of love. I was a mushy-hearted sap who fell in unrequited "love" embarrassingly often. Although my social skills had the power to condemn me to celibacy, I was not about to embrace it voluntarily.

Until then in my life, I had always assumed that friendship and love could be secured only by putting one's best foot forward. Since I was not a jock, and academic prowess makes a poor high school come-on, I relied on my sense of humor, eventually capturing the ultimate prize of class clown. The strategy worked well for me as a rule but obviously not during my romantic post-partums. During those dreary periods, I did my best to punish the offending female by dragging my normally cheerful countenance in the dust. I subscribed to the notion: "If you can't get love and respect, go for pity." The fact that the tactic never brought a former girlfriend back into my arms did not dissuade me.

Everything changed, though, when I was busy sending woe-is-me vibes to an ex named Valerie, whom I particularly missed. One of the most popular girls in my class, Kyle Chapman, asked how I was doing and actually listened to my monologue. I was in a most decidedly unfunny state of mind, but she warmed to me nonetheless. Before I knew it, we were fast friends, so close that it seemed perfectly natural for us to go together to the senior prom. There was nothing physical between us, but in every other imaginable way, it was a romance.

This relationship not only pulled me out of my funk but was something of a religious revelation as well. Although I had heard quite a bit about God loving me at church, I had previously assumed that God's love depended on my good behavior and that God's love itself, devoid of sexual intimacy, could never be emotionally fulfilling. My relationship with Kyle at once reminded me of God's love for his oftentimes less-than-adorable chosen people and convinced me that I could embrace celibacy without giving up emotional intimacy.

In August of 1976, the year I graduated from high school in New Hampshire, I went off to the College of the Holy Cross in Worcester, Massachusetts, while Kyle attended Western New England College outside Springfield. In November, she came to spend a weekend with me. After meeting her at the bus station, we walked past Worcester's iconic Coney Island Hot Dogs diner. My focus was to share all the "wisdom" I had gained in my first two months as a religious studies major, and I did so in a high-speed monologue. My pontificating was interrupted when we bumped into a homeless man begging for food. Hunched over with a scraggly beard and gloves missing a few fingertips, he reminded me of Jethro Tull's Aqualung or Fagin in *Oliver Twist*. I had a five-dollar bill and a one in my pocket, but, when I reached for the one, I pulled out the five. I had elaborate plans for Kyle's stay, plans that had a claim on the bigger bill, so I reached into my pocket a second time and still came up with the five. After trying a third time and failing yet again to get George Washington, I put Lincoln in my back pocket, drew out the one, and placed it in the beggar's hand. I never so much as looked in his eyes. I was preoccupied with keeping my train of thought and resumed talking at once.

We hadn't gone five steps, though, before I noticed that tears were streaming down Kyle's face for what was probably the first homeless person she'd ever seen. I felt ashamed that I hadn't responded more personally to the man, but when I turned around, the sidewalk was empty. Now, it was possible that he had hustled into the bar farther down the block, but at this point in my religious development, I thought, "Yikes! It was Jesus . . . . And all I gave him was a buck."

Ironically, my plans for the weekend proved disastrous. We arrived late to an expensive Holy Cross versus Boston College basketball game in Boston after a Green Line train got stuck for an hour in a tunnel. BC upset Holy Cross. We missed the last bus back to Worcester by five minutes and managed to catch it only by running six blocks in traffic. When she prepared to leave on Sunday, Kyle told me, "You didn't have to spend all that money. I would have been just as happy to hang out with you."

It was then that I realized that the encounter with the homeless man, which struck me at the time as an inconvenience threatening to ruin my weekend, was actually an invitation to take a leap of faith that would have saved it. I not only could have given the man all six of my dollars but also could have scalped the basketball tickets and put the guy up in Worcester's best hotel. I had seen the presence of the homeless man as a roadblock on my way to happiness when actually he was a kind of angel. Ironically, I would have impressed Kyle much more than with all the blabbering I did about faith. I resolved never again to be so callous toward someone who begged from me.

I also found that living on a wealthy campus in a blue-collar city with plenty of poverty helped remove another of my reservations about the priesthood. Growing up not too far above the poverty line, I bitterly resented not having all the things money could buy. For a time, if someone asked me what I wanted to be, I would have said, "Rich." But at Holy Cross I was turned off by snobbish rich kids who came back from spring break parading their tans. Students who worked with me in the campus dining hall, as well as Worcesterites I met while employed by Catholic Charities in the summer, helped me discover working class pride. Like the Grinch, I gradually learned that Christmas does not come from a store. I began to appreciate the joys of simple living that saints, Thoreau, and Gandhi wrote about. Ultimately, I identified with the man in the parable who finds a buried treasure in a field and sells everything he has to buy it. Like Saint Francis of Assisi, I felt spiritually richer in voluntary poverty.

Providentially, the weekend after Kyle's visit found me in my home parish where Father Jack Rathschmidt, a visiting Capuchin-Franciscan, served as guest preacher. To my mind, Capuchins were cool priests who, in their brown robes and untrimmed beards, looked like Saint Francis. I approached Father Jack after Mass and secured an appointment with the vocation director. It wasn't too long after that I applied to become a postulant, someone who thinks seriously about formally entering religious life.

As a Capuchin postulant continuing at Holy Cross, I enjoyed occasional weekend retreats at friaries, spiritual direction with a friar named John McHugh, and spare time spent reading biographies of Saint Francis, all of which fed my enthusiasm.

As a do-it-yourself Catholic with a Protestant mother and lapsed Catholic dad, I found the world of religious orders a mystery. I had no idea that Saint Francis's followers had split themselves into three branches: The Conventionals, the Franciscans, and the Capuchins. When I met the Capuchin vocation director, a jolly cookie-jar friar named Ted Corley, I asked him about the difference between the three orders. "The Capuchins," he told me, "have a stricter interpretation of voluntary poverty." Considering my father's prejudice against parish priests as lazy bums who worked only one day a week and drove around in Cadillacs as well as my own admiration for Francis's austerity, I replied, "Great!"

Later on, I learned that the concept of voluntary poverty so divided Franciscans that rival factions of friars once set up cannons facing each other in Assisi. At other times, groups of friars tried to have their rivals excommunicated. Saint Bonaventure ordered all other biographies burned after he wrote his version of Francis's life. Some of this turmoil arose because Francis wrote three separate rules or documents of conduct for his friars: the first conveniently lost by those who deemed it too demanding, the second rejected by the pope for the same reason, and the third which got the official stamp of approval. A bumpy start like that is bound to encourage idealists like me to reform.

The Conventionals are the oldest branch of Franciscans, deriving their name from their residential convents, including the one beside the church in Assisi where the saint is buried. The Franciscans were an early reform community, while the Capuchins are a much later reform effort. The origin of the name Capuchins seems to have come from their long hoods, known as capuches in Italian. Capuchin detractors like to say they got their title from their resemblance to an African monkey of the same name. Whatever.

With a mischievous sparkle in his eye, Ted Corley told me, "Capuchins have the spirit of Saint Francis, Conventionals have his body, and Franciscans have his name."

I took to the ideal of voluntary poverty as if it were a spiritual life raft. Each Friday, I gathered up all my possessions and divided them into three piles: those I absolutely needed, those I wanted, and those I could give away. I marveled at the way objects migrated, over time, from the first pile to the second and then to the third. I thought I had simplified my life pretty well when my spiritual director came for a visit to my college dorm room. With a sweeping gesture, I proudly described my remaining possessions as gifts from different people "reminding me that everything is a gift from God."

"Which we must take in turn and give to others," he retorted, successfully trashing my main excuse for holding onto many objects.

Eventually, I adopted what I called "the beer-box principle." Whatever I couldn't fit into an empty case of Moosehead beer had to go. Christ's admonition "Take nothing for the journey" morphed into "Take only what you can carry in one trip from the liquor store." I got around the compromise by telling myself that simpler living would embroil me in the sin of pride, something I was too familiar with already.

To my delight, Ted Corley introduced me to another Holy Cross student who was also a postulant with the Capuchins, a math major named Tim McCaffrey. Unlike my unchurched background, his family was clerical city with an older brother and an uncle who were Capuchin priests. In spite of his kin being a bit of a priest factory, Tim wasn't a dowdy church mouse. With a terrific sense of humor, brains, good looks, and athletic physique, he defied the stereotype that religious life is a refuge for those who can't make it elsewhere.

We became fast friends and applied for acceptance to the Capuchin novitiate after our graduation.

Before the Second Vatican Council, the Catholic Church scooped up clerical hopefuls early on and sent them to high school seminaries where they were to be kept safely away from sins of the flesh, but bad experience with homosexuality, child abuse, and clerical desertion in those seminaries taught the Church to try a different approach by the time I became a postulant. Before you could become a Capuchin friar, the order strongly encouraged you to complete at least a bachelor's degree, preferably at a coed school. This policy assured more mature applicants and, as a bonus, saved the order a bundle on what it previously had to shell out to educate friars.

In those days, a prospective friar entered the order as a postulant with limited commitments. After graduation, he applied to become a novice, a process that involved psychological tests, a long application, and several interviews. If accepted, he spent the next year—a contemplative year—as a novice. After that, he could be invited to take simple vows of poverty, chastity, and obedience. The vows are called simple not because they are easy, but because they last only twelve months. A novice spent that year as a brother in a foreign mission or an inner-city parish. If all went well, he renewed simple vows annually during studies and pastoral training for ordination to the diaconate, followed by the priesthood. At that point, he took final vows meant to last a lifetime.

Tim and I both had exciting goals we hoped to accomplish as friars but felt united around the idea that the novitiate was a kind of boot camp one suffered through in order to reach those goals. As extroverts, we didn't look forward to a year of prayer, manual labor, and isolation.

In the three months between graduation and entrance to the novitiate, Tim asked, whenever he opened a bottle of beer, "Hear that sound?" and then said, "We're going to miss that sound."

Nonetheless, we took the plunge.

In mid-August 1980, Tim and I arrived at Saint Francis Friary in Garrison, New York. The three-story brick building sat just off scenic route 9D on the east bank of the Hudson River. From our backyard, we could see the US Army's military academy at West Point, several miles upstream from us. We could see a ridge of low mountains lining the river valley on both sides, and one mountain called Sugarloaf right across the street from us. A castle built in the 1920s by a lovesick millionaire as a gift for his sweetheart tops another tree-covered peak.

This is Washington Irving's Sleepy Hollow country: idyllic, beautiful, and still peppered with Dutch names like Peekskill, Fishkill, and Van Ness. For some incomprehensible reason, the heavily wooded area had become the abode of numerous religious communities, oftentimes alongside homes of the very rich. To the left of our property, for example, beyond a small stand of trees, sat a gorgeous mansion used only as a summer home. A half mile to our right lay Saint Conrad's, a much bigger Capuchin friary for those studying theology. Beyond that was a lavish golf course. None of us could escape the irony of coming to the second richest county in America in order to emulate the little poor man of Assisi.

In my class were eighteen novices ranging from nineteen to fifty-eight years old. The elder of our group was Lou Massinet, a talented artist who had been a Capuchin novice many years earlier, left the order, and was giving it another shot. There was also a diocesan priest named Ray Frias who was making the switch over to communal life with the Capuchins. The youngest novice was a short Italian American named Carmine with a pencil-thin mustache. Our class included a curly-haired, heavyset, charismatic Catholic named Jerry Rocco and a tall fellow named Bob Lombardo who had the distinction of always wearing wing-tipped shoes with his habit. Another tall novice, Paul Norman, was a laconic chain-smoker who rolled his eyes and said, "Puh-leeze!" at anything sentimental. He was offset by the most earnest person I've ever met, Ken Osborn. Jim Keating represented a kind of skeptical idealist. Another heavy smoker was the short, cheerful, dandruff-plagued Dave Cronin.

A nice guy named Kevin Burke had a disconcertingly goofy laugh. A pious and austere bass player named Stanley Fortuna assured us that we'd never be lacking in musical accompaniment at Mass. Tim McSweeney was a tight-lipped New Yorker who snickered like the cartoon character Dick Dastardly's dog, Muttley. A streetwise New Yorker named George Dash had extensive carpentry and automotive skills. Another Gerry was a shy second-time novice like Lou. To make things even more interesting, we had three novices from the Capuchin mission on Guam, Isidro Ogomoro, whom we called Sid; a young man named Paul; and a heavyset, quiet fellow named Joe. We were all fish out of water, but these guys from Micronesia had the especially hard job of adjusting to a different climate. Sid never tired of complaining how cold it was.

The staff of the novitiate included four priests and two brothers. In command was Father Paul Minchak, a novice master whose reputation as a conservative and strict disciplinarian was legendary. A credible rumor circulated that once upon a time, Father Paul punched a high school seminarian for swearing. Very much beneath the novice master was Father Matthais Wisnowski, a long-suffering friar who never directly challenged Father Paul, but, when alone with us, played the jaded idealist in an attempt to shore up our values. Another priest in the house was Father Darius (pronounced duh-RYE-us). He was a good-humored handyman, mechanic, and cobbler. An ancient retiree, Father Roy, also lived in the novitiate. He was included in the regular rotation of celebrants at Mass but mostly shuffled around the house from meal to meal. He clearly enjoyed food more than anything else. Our cook was an older brother named Jerome, a broad-smiling sadist who ran his kitchen like an Afghan warlord. This guy delighted in telling me that we were going to have something I enjoyed like pasta for lunch only to serve something evil laced with sauerkraut. The last member of the team was Joe Nolan, a thirty-year-old brother, who ran the house laundry and tailor shop. Joe was congenial, lanky, and quiet. We occasionally had guest speakers, but, for the most part, those four priests and two brothers were our models of Capuchin reality.

Upon arrival at the novitiate, each of us was assigned a dormitory-style, single bedroom on the third floor. With cinder block walls, a desk, bed, and curtained closet, these rooms were austere but made more cheerful by a beautiful view of the Appalachian Mountains or Hudson River, depending on which side of the building you had. By order of the novice master, the third-floor hall where we lived remained in perpetual darkness,

.. only by sporadic floor-level nightlights. This haunted-house effect was supposed to engender a spirit of quiet prayerfulness in an area of the novitiate where casual conversation was forbidden. Ear-splitting shouts of "SILENCE on the third floor!" from Father Paul were employed to remind anyone who forgot the sanctity of this rule. Among some novices, such a controlling arrangement may have fostered the desired solemnity or a bitter resentment, but in our group it only engendered mischief.

I remember one afternoon when we all thought the novice master was out for his daily run. From my room, I could hear at least a dozen voices echoing from the bathroom at the hall's end when a friar from the house of theology came up the stairs and knocked on Father Paul's door. To my surprise, the novice master himself peered out wiping sleep from his eyes. Apparently, he had not been feeling well and decided to forgo his usual exercise. His visitor started telling Father Paul that he was needed at Saint Conrad's, but bulging veins in the novice master's forehead made it clear that the only thing he could hear right then was full-bodied laughter coming from the bathroom. Our angry superior pushed his way to the open door and bellowed his mantra: "Silence on the third floor!!" Three guys shaving at the sinks instantly froze, but Tim McCaffrey was in the shower and went on singing something ludicrous like "Beautiful Dreamer."

Seeing the novice master's obvious fury, the visiting friar tried to save Tim by pleading, "We need to go, Father." Caught between two responsibilities, Father Paul made a mental note to deal with the third-floor-noise issue later and barked one last "SILENCE!" to which Tim, who assumed the command originated from a pranking novice replied, "I CAN'T HEAR YOU." I can assure you, only the urgency of the novice master's required presence elsewhere saved Tim's life.

But I'm getting ahead of myself. We called the novitiate Retrea' because the sign above the entrance to the novitiate was missing its last letter and read "St. Francis Retrea'." The order devoted our first week to a special retreat led by Tim's uncle, Warren Smithbower. Father Warren was widely respected in the order for years of faithful service, but, like many friars I would meet, he had his peculiarities. Father Warren's eyesight had deteriorated with age until he was left completely blind. Nevertheless, he wanted to maintain his independence by fooling people into thinking that he could still see. With a Boy Scout's "be-prepared" attitude, he devoted his days of dwindling sight to memorizing the distance between all the stationary objects and landmarks at Saint Conrad and Saint Francis friaries. Long after he went blind, the years of practice enabled Father Warren not only to get around without assistance but even to boldly point out statues to his companions.

Both Tim and Father Paul warned us that the previous class of novices had sorely offended the senior priest by laughing at his retreat-closing song. None of us had actually heard the song but were under strict orders to sing it with all due respect. Written by Father Warren himself, the tune had already been designated as part of the priest's legacy. Shortly after its performance during a brief ceremony, each of us would be "vested" with a novice's habit. From that point on, the formal novitiate year would begin.

the Saint Francis Retreat building in Garrison, New York, which
the Capuchin-Franciscan novices called "The Retrea'" because
the sign over the main door had a missing "t"

Father Warren's retreat consisted of prayer, confession, Mass, and daily talks, which he gave himself. The talks were fairly inspiring and marred only by his tendency to get a bit turned around. Usually the consequence amounted to nothing worse than his facing a few degrees to the left or right, detours he corrected after hearing our voices answer a question from the chapel pews before him, but once he moved so dramatically as to stand before us at a complete right angle. He punctuated his perpendicular talk with a gesture towards a religious painting that would have been in the direction of his extended arm if he had faced forward. Nonetheless, not a single novice gave a hint of his error. We were not going to be insensitive like those immature novices of yesteryear. This blind man had wisdom to share with us. We would not be sidetracked by a quirk.

At least that was our intention until we actually heard the song, "Mary. My Mother." Even pious Lou rolled his eyes at the lyric "Jesus told us that you were a queen." Half the novices were from Manhattan, a couple from Greenwich Village, for crying out loud, where "queens" were plentiful but hardly virgins. With red faces and stifled titters but, thanks be to God, no outright guffaws, we finally performed it. The incident reminds me how language changes over time. *Everybody's Saint Francis*, a biography published in 1912, for example, constantly calls Francis's followers "gay" men whom others considered "queer."

From that Sunday on, the fact that each of us now wore a religious habit most of the time drove home the seriousness of what we had undertaken. The dark brown, one-

novices at Saint Francis, including the author second from right in the second row,
on the day they successfully sang "Mary, My Mother"

piece robe had a long hood and two side pockets sewn into it along with a larger pouch over the midriff. The sleeves fit almost tightly, but the waist was enormous. I would have felt extremely insecure wearing it except for the stout cord that we each tied around our middles. We were taught to include three knots in this white clothesline to represent our prospective vows of poverty, chastity, and obedience. Some guys kidded about how they'd tie slip knots for the vows they weren't too enthusiastic about. On top of the whole ensemble, we wore a flap of identical cloth called a caperone. The small addition marked us as novices rather than full-fledged friars.

I thought the habit was really cool to wear, although it did take some getting used to. At a meeting we attended with a group of nuns, I sat with my legs wide apart unable to understand why the novice master kept glaring at me from across the room. I had a thing or two to learn about the advantages and drawbacks of wearing a dress. Apparently, it was not good religious decorum to show my underwear to nuns.

Along with two habits, each of us received a pair of blue jeans, a blue denim shirt, and a jean jacket. We used this prison-like attire during non-religious chores. Every article of clothing, all the way down to our socks and underwear, was fitted with a name tag to facilitate sorting house laundry. Ordinary BVDs bore distinguished labels, "Brother Scott Duffy," "Brother Paul Norman," and so on.

On the day our clothes returned from the tailor shop, Tim stood ashen-faced in his doorway staring at the name tag on his underwear.

"What's wrong?" I asked.

Pointing to the label, Tim replied, "It's kind of like reading your own obituary."

Tim's trepidation notwithstanding, we began our real life as novices. Each day was marked by six formal prayers: Morning Prayer at 6:30 a.m. followed by a twenty-minute meditation and then Mass; the Angelus at noon and Midday Prayer; Office of Readings at 5; Evening Prayer at 7; and examination of conscience followed by Night Prayer at 9. All told, we

Brothers Scott, the author, left, and Tim

spent about three hours a day in the chapel where we sat according to seniority with the youngest friars in the front row and the oldest in the back.

We had to learn how to use the Breviary for prayers. A ninth-century collection of psalms and other scripture, the Breviary was Saint Benedict's monastic answer to Saint Paul's admonition that Christians pray unceasingly. With monks, friars, diocesan priests, sisters, and brothers reciting such prayers all over the world, someone is indeed always in prayer. It's a great idea, and the Second Vatican Council encouraged lay Catholics as well as clergy to take advantage of the practice. The Catholic practice of consecrating different hours of the day to prayer would one day become a point of commonality for me with a devout Muslim in the Gaza Strip. He rolled out his prayer rug by my side so he could perform a similar ritual. Praying the psalms of the Breviary would also see me through many a difficult stretch of jail time when I was allowed only religious books.

Some of the novices wanted to learn to chant psalms like the Trappists at the Abbey of Gethsemani in Kentucky, but the novice master was quick to point out to us that we were friars, not monks.

"A monk," he told us, "is a contemplative religious with a commitment to stability, but a friar is an active religious, a mendicant living out in the world."

Prayer would constitute a central part of our lives but not its totality. Father Paul did allow us to chant Saturday and Sunday Night Prayer, though, and I fondly recall the beautiful melodies.

Each of us received a four-volume set of breviaries called *The Liturgy of the Hours*. The hefty books correspond to different parts of the Church year, and each includes an array of colored ribbons to mark a day's readings. One needs several markers, because the prayers are not always contained in a single section. If the day comprises a "solemnity" or "memorial" or any one of a dozen other special categories, one might need to get psalms from here, readings from there, and petition prayers from elsewhere—not to mention our opening and closing hymns.

You had to be a rocket scientist to understand all the rubrics. It could take five or ten minutes to set up a Breviary each morning. If designated as the first or second acolyte (novices who read the antiphons and serve at daily Mass), you had to be on top of things. If you read from the wrong page, Father Paul wouldn't just tell you the correct one. Oh, no. That would be too easy. He was loath to have any conversation in church so, instead, he rapped his knuckles sharply on his pew. He did it again and again in a trial and error fashion until you got it right. We hated it.

Beyond prayer, our life included two hours of classes each morning and an equal amount of time in manual labor on weekday afternoons. An hour or two of recreation time was wedged in before and after dinner with quiet hours owning the rest of the day. Each of us went once a week on a social apostolate of some kind. Jerry Rocco and I taught religious education at a nearby parish. We also went en mass once a week to the Franklin Delano Roosevelt Veterans Hospital in Montrose.

During our first visit to this enormous complex of depressing psychiatric wards packed with shell-shocked vets from the Vietnam, Korean, and even Second World wars, I had my first experience of how it felt to be a clergy person. While standing against a wall in a smoke-filled, institutional rec room crowded with vets, a man approached me and asked, "Father, would you hear my confession?"

Taken aback by the question, I told him, "I'm not a priest. I'm just a novice."

Undeterred, the guy bowed his head and began saying, "Bless me Father, for I have sinned . . . ."

Unable to think of anything else to do, I snagged Dave Cronin as he walked by and said to him, "Dave, stand here please," while I scurried away to the other side of the room where I tried to look less clerical.

Each Thursday afternoon, Jerry Rocco and I drove one of the community's mid-sized cars to teach seventh-grade religion classes. The students, from well-off families, were very polite to us in our costumes, a complete switch from when I tried to teach religious education in high school. Back then, I commanded no respect. When I asked third graders to make Christmas cards, a boy named Ricky Bruckner produced a sheet of paper colored pitch black. He said it was "Bethlehem at night." But our students seemed to like us, and so did their parents. Religious garb lent us credibility.

As Christmas approached, one of the parents gave Jerry and me a bottle of Frangelico. In a nifty bottle shaped like a monk with a cord around his waist, the liqueur presented a problem for us. We were not forbidden to drink alcohol. The rec room cooler at the friary was stocked monthly with two cases of Piels Light, the worst beer on earth, bar none, believe me. I still shudder at its mention. We were allowed to enjoy a brew or two on Friday and Saturday nights, but everyone realized that eyes were on us to determine whether or not any of us had "a problem with alcohol." Trust me, such scrutiny puts a damper on any party. Jerry and I didn't look forward to seeing the Frangelico wasted in such an uncomfortable setting. Plus, the bottle wasn't that big. If we turned it over to the novice master, as we were expected to do with any gifts, he would share its contents equally with all twenty-five members of the community. Talk about a buzzkill. It wouldn't do.

So, Jerry and I concocted a personal interpretation of the vow of obedience, a corollary if you will, completely compatible in its spirit with the letter of the law.

"God certainly does want good friars to hold their possessions in common," we agreed, "but our Lord and Savior also made plenty of wine at the wedding in Cana for his first miracle."

And so, we concluded, "Such a generous party host would not want spirits doled out with an eye dropper."

Armed with rationalization, we smuggled our precious cargo into the Retrea' and selected three other novices as representatives of the entire community to join us after hours in the attic. At the risk of certain death from Father Paul, we stole away at ten that night, gathered some chairs around a lantern, and toasted the holidays. Tim enhanced the celebration by dragging over large statues of the Three Kings hidden in a corner. Before we snuck back to our beds, we felt good enough to sing a few carols arm in arm with Caspar, Melchior, and Balthazar, the Three Kings.

Our escapade went undiscovered but not without consequence. The journey into the attic alerted Dave to the fact that we had Christmas decorations on hand. Since it was already mid-December, he carried down a box and festooned our otherwise dreary rec room. Unfortunately, Father Paul took note of the tinsel and spoke of it at the opening of the next day's classes.

"I noticed that someone has put up Christmas decorations," he began ominously.

"What liturgical season are we in?" he asked.

After a pregnant pause—Where was he going? This could not end well, we answered nervously, "Advent?"

"Correct." He plowed on in a voice deeper than James Earl Jones's rendition of Darth Vader. "And what kind of season is Advent?"

He didn't wait for us to reply.

"A penitential season," he reminded us.

We could see the storm clouds on the horizon.

"Christmas decorations," he declared, "will be taken down and not replaced until Christmas season actually begins on the eve of December 25."

As Father Paul turned to the blackboard, Tim whispered in homage to Charles Dickens's *A Christmas Carol*, "Are there no prisons? Are there no workhouses?"

Tim often pushed the envelope with the novice master. Given Father Paul's short temper, Tim played a dangerous game. When we went to the refectory for meals, Tim often positioned himself a few feet behind Father Paul and mimicked his manner of walking. The pose was subtle, but the shit-eating grin on Tim's face was not. During class time, Tim also reveled in trying to catch sunlight on the face of his wristwatch in just such a way that when Father Paul turned around from writing on the blackboard, he would be temporarily blinded by the light. Joe went even farther by sometimes writing swears on notepaper and holding the sheet up until the very last second before Father Paul faced us. On other occasions, someone tied Jerry Rocco's cord to the kneeler in church and placed a pinecone on his pew so that when Jerry sat back, he sat on the pinecone. In the atmosphere of strict discipline Father Paul insisted upon, pranks let off a lot of steam.

On the other hand, genuine prayerfulness seemed to grow on us almost in spite of ourselves. When three novices and I worked outside laying concrete for a garage under construction, we could not go into the chapel for Midday Prayer lest the cement set improperly. Nonetheless, when the chapel bell rang for a midday litany called the Angelus, all four of us reflexively knelt to pray, "The angel of the Lord declared unto Mary, and she conceived by the Holy Spirit . . . . " Prayer was becoming an integral part of our lives, not just rituals we performed in the chapel. The spectacle of our kneeling outside in blue jeans reminded me of Jean-François Millet's 1859 painting of farmers in a field stopping their labor to pray the Angelus.

To his credit, Father Paul employed many methods to deepen our prayer life. Besides all the liturgical prayer, he took us to a meditation session led by an Indian Jesuit, he taught us scriptural prayer techniques, and he instilled in us the importance of opening and closing anything we did, from a class to a meal to an outing, with prayer. Years later, I would find similar devotion in a peace activist friend, Tom Lewis, who never missed a chance to initiate and punctuate a protest or court case with prayer.

In Lent, Father Paul divided us into small groups and asked us to prepare a special service once a week before Night Prayer. Stanley, Dave, Tim, and I made elaborate preparations to ensure ours would be the best. Our plan was to open with the chapel in complete darkness. From the back corner, Stanley would play "The Cry of the Poor" on the string bass. Sitting next to him, Dave used a penlight to read the scriptural passage, "Jesus Christ, though he was in the form of God, did not regard equality with God something to be grasped. Rather, he emptied himself, taking the form of a slave, coming in human likeness." Simultaneously while kneeling in darkness, Tim would turn a flashlight on a statue of the Virgin Mary holding the Christ Child. When the reading finished, he would switch off the light and direct it towards a statue of a grown-up Jesus while Dave read, "My commandment is that you love one another as I have loved you." Then again, Tim would extinguish the light, and Dave would say, "Jesus humbled himself, becoming obedient to death, even death on a cross." Then Stanley would turn a switch in the back of the chapel to activate an outdoor spotlight that would illumine a stained glass scene of the Crucifixion. Lastly, Dave would read, "O death, where is your victory? O death where is your sting?" Stanley would flick the switch for the light above the tabernacle, and then I would complete the tableau by ringing the bell in the closet off to the side of the altar. We felt proud to compose such a short but moving tribute to the life, death, and resurrection of Jesus with sufficient Catholic overtones sure to impress Father Paul.

Unfortunately, we had over-practiced the meditation to the point that, when the moment of truth came, Dave read the first scripture and Tim turned on a dying flashlight. Dave had his back to Tim, so he had no idea what was going on. The congregation caught a faint glimpse of the first statue before it plunged back into darkness. When Dave read the second text, Tim faced the statue of Christ and smacked the flashlight hoping to restore it to life. When it failed, he muttered audibly, "Damn!" The stained glass window lit on cue as did the tabernacle, but I was so eager that the bell should ring loudly that I leapt up onto the rope to pull it down with all my strength. The infernal cord lifted me up, I struck the door, and everyone in the chapel had a view up my habit as I swung into and out of sight near the altar.

We were lucky not to be excommunicated.

From what I had heard of previous novices, though, our failings were more or less typical. So the novitiate year went on.

In order to help us deepen our faith lives, we each had to choose a spiritual director. Fathers Darius and Matthais were popular choices, but I was possessed with a sudden urge to stretch myself. I figured that I would learn more from someone as unlike myself as possible, so without guile or irony, I chose Father Paul Minchak. One refers in retrospect to such inclinations as temporary insanity. Father Paul and I met weekly but never really became the kind of chums who have heart-to-heart chats.

He did challenge me, though. On one occasion, shortly after the rapes and murders of four American missionaries in El Salvador, I heard that a special prayer for peace would be offered at Saint Patrick's Cathedral in Manhattan. We went into the city once in a while for talks at Fordham University, so I asked Father Paul for permission "to sit before the Blessed Sacrament at Saint Patrick's to pray for peace." He asked me if I really thought prayer would help, and I enthusiastically said, "Oh, yes, Father, I do."

"All right then," he replied. "You have my permission to pray for peace at that time in our own chapel."

Father Paul wasn't merely theologically conservative. I suspected he supported Ronald Reagan. No way would Father Paul allow me to have an activist moment under his watch.

Providentially, we did go into the city on a different day that allowed me the chance to visit Mary House, The Catholic Worker in Manhattan's Lower East Side. Jim joined Tim and me for the expedition. En route on the subway, I shared tales of Gospel poverty and radical pacifism I was certain we would encounter at the motherhouse of The Catholic Worker Movement. I was extremely excited when we entered the front door of Mary House only to have an elderly woman perched on the top of the inside stairway point directly at me and shout, "You good for nothing pimp! How dare you come here! Damn you to hell!!"

Before I could react, she leapt onto me and began pounding furiously on my chest. My religious companions stood wide-eyed, but Frank Donovan, a longtime community member at Mary House, poked his head around the corner, smiled, and said, "Welcome to the Catholic Worker."

No explanation was ever offered as to why this woman, whom I later learned was named Lena, displayed such hostility to me. I heard years later that when Mother Theresa visited Mary House, Lena asked the saintly nun for a cigarette. I would also learn that tolerance for characters like Lena forms the bread and butter of the Catholic Worker.

Coincidentally, our visit to Mary House turned out to be only three days after the Catholic Worker's co-founder, Dorothy Day, died. Her funeral took place the day before at her parish church on the lower East Side, but that evening, Terence Cardinal Cooke held a memorial Mass for Dorothy at Saint Patrick's Cathedral on swanky Fifth Avenue. This time I didn't need permission to go to the massive edifice. The Cardinal was in an awkward position, since he never agreed with Dorothy's opposition to the Vietnam War. But he could not ignore popular consensus about her saintliness. In his homily, he focused on her work with the poor and skirted her pacifism.

Returning to the Retrea' after a day in Manhattan felt like descending to the bottom of the ocean in a submarine. Isolated not only physically but culturally, we walked around in twelfth-century garb that underscored the countercultural character of our future locked morally into place by vows.

For some, it was too much.

Carmine was the first to drop out. Soon after he left, Carmine called us from a disco in the Village where he delighted in saying, "I'm wearing alligator boots!" Ken and Jim moved on after Christmas, although their objections concerned something more lofty than limitations on our apparel. The departures of Ken and Jim were difficult to bear because, for better or worse, we each had a growing awareness that we were becoming a kind of family. Lou said that in the old days there was so much shame and trauma involved in leaving religious life that novices sometimes slipped away in the middle of the night. He recalled being told by his novice master to check on a friar who failed to come to Mass only to discover an empty room save the remains of the now former novice's beard in the trash barrel. Although we were not under that much pressure, we didn't consider leaving lightly.

That's not to say we didn't have fun. The Three Kings incident hardly constituted our only lark. One evening just before Night Prayer, I heard furtive laughter coming from the unlit bathroom at the end of the corridor. Upon investigation, I discovered Bob crouched down by an open window with a mischievous smile on his face.

"You want to see something funny?" he whispered. "Take a peek out the window."

I peered out from the T-shaped Retrea' and could see Jerry Rocco alone in the classroom one floor below. Bob nudged me aside and called softly, "Jerry. Jerry!"

A light wind gave Bob's voice a mysterious enough quality for our charismatic brother to reply hopefully, "Yes, Lord."

Bob fell on his knees in hysterics, which he curtailed long enough to intone, "Rebuild my church!" (the words Saint Francis heard during prayer at San Damiano Church.)

Although I thought Bob's prank particularly evil, Jerry looked so much like a Botticelli angel that I never had the heart to disabuse him of his "revelation."

Another time when a jazzy, red convertible crashed into a tree across the street from the friary, a number of us rushed out to see if we could help. The dazed but otherwise unhurt driver looked up at us in our brown robes and pleaded without irony, "I'll change. Please give me another chance!"

Even friction inevitably turned to good humor. During a period when I had been particularly argumentative about what I saw as the laxity of our voluntary poverty, Paul Norman began stopping me to point out an object in my possession and ask, "Could a poor person afford that?"

Not to be outdone, I responded by getting rid of the offending material object. The back and forth progressed until I had discarded my desk lamp, mattress, and blankets. Undeterred, Paul sauntered into my virtually empty room and gestured towards the polished crucifix on the wall. I promptly took it down, stowed it in the attic, went outside, picked branches from a thorn bush, and fashioned them into a cross. When he saw what I had done, Paul laughed and laughed. That night, when I went to bed, I found seven mattresses piled on my bed frame. My good-humored brothers had even slipped a pea underneath them all.

We experienced aggravations, though, like one I had with the cook. Brother Jerome took each Sunday off and scheduled a novice to take his place. As a person who spent five years working in various restaurants, I very much looked forward to my turn but was disappointed to discover that Jerome was such a control freak that he left strict instructions about exactly what to serve in his absence. I had had enough sauerkraut. The larder overflowed with ample supplies for me to make a sumptuous baked macaroni and cheese and wonderful peach cobbler. So I went ahead and cooked them, and everyone loved them, even Father Paul. But I foolishly stored leftovers in the walk-in fridge.

When Brother Jerome returned that night and discovered my transgression, he went directly to the novice master. I was called out of bed near midnight and given a lecture about religious obedience and courtesy toward a man whose life revolved around the kitchen. Under orders to apologize for making macaroni and cheese, I stood fuming outside Jerome's door for ten minutes before I could bring myself to knock. As a deprived pasta lover, I swore to myself, "If I ever get out of here, I'll have macaroni and cheese every day for a year!"

As ridiculous as this sounds now, such petty things loomed large then. Only much later did I learn that Saint Thérèse of Lisieux had similar fits of anger over peculiar noises that a certain sister made with her teeth during chapel. With prayer, Thérèse overcame her aggravation, but how many others left religious life or marriage over such little things? For all we know, Jesus may have had a speech impediment that drove Judas crazy. Whole empires may have fallen for the lack of macaroni and cheese.

Ultimately, the time in the novitiate focused seriously on whether or not God wanted us to be Capuchin-Franciscan friars for the rest of our lives. Different individuals had different struggles with that salient choice. Many agonized over chastity. Some chafed at obedience. Several feared that the novice master or someone else on the staff would ask him to go home after one of the three "scrutinies" (religious vocation evaluations) that had to be overcome in order to be invited to take vows.

I was a queer duck (there's that word again). My anxieties centered on concerns that the Capuchin view of voluntary poverty was not austere enough and that, as a friar, I would not be able to continue working for peace. I shared these concerns with Father Paul Steffan, the religious superior of our province, during a visit he made to Garrison.

He told me, "You know, I've never had to chastise a friar for living too simply."

"Of course," I answered. "I understand that I could choose to fast, to wear only my habit, and to take on other aspects of simple living, but I would still be assigned to live in a comfortable house, on valuable property, and never have to worry for any material thing for the rest of my life. This seems to me to be asceticism, not poverty. The truly poor person is not someone who merely chooses to walk instead of using his or her car but someone who actually doesn't have access to a car at all."

I went on to ask Father Steffan if I could attend peace demonstrations after my ordination. He replied, "Our order is moving towards greater involvement in peace work and would welcome your activism, but you have to realize that there are much older friars who would resent an inexperienced priest going off in a new direction. You would probably have to do traditional parish work for some time before you could do peace work."

"Fair enough," I said, "but how long do you think I would have to wait?"

When he replied, "Ten years," I admitted, "I don't know if I'd be the same person after that long."

I was torn. For real Church renewal to occur in matters dear to me, I had to have a long view and lots of patience, and a decade-long wait for something with a strong foundation made sense. I just wasn't sure of myself. Would I grow complacent in a comfortable rectory? Would I lose the desire to own nothing and depend completely on God? Would I become a cookie jar friar? I just didn't know.

As the end of the novitiate year approached with my recommendation for vows, my indecision grew. I tried all kinds of methods to clarify my thoughts. I used a decision-making technique of Saint Ignatius of Loyola that entailed making lists of pros and cons until one side outweighed the other. Unfortunately, every time I compiled a list, the advantages and disadvantages of the Capuchins came out exactly equal. Time was running out. So much of my personal identity wrapped up in Saint Francis's vision of Christian life that the idea of leaving loomed momentous to say the least.

Tim and I talked about what we planned to do. He had plenty of complaints and uncertainties but felt that by being a friar he could do something good with his life.

"Isn't that worthwhile?" he asked.

Tim's rationale tempted me. After several novices and I had dinner at my Uncle Bob and Aunt Claire's house in Millville, Massachusetts, he told me that we novices had "an aura of goodness which the world sorely needs." Could I hope to accomplish anything remotely similar outside of religious life, and if so where? How? I had no answer.

In the end, I didn't decide my vocation at all. I let it be decided for me. This came about when we all went to Milton, Massachusetts, for a fund-raiser called a penny sale in a church hall packed with old ladies. We novices were used as props to encourage donations via carnival-type games. The Bingo atmosphere depressed me. I felt uncomfortable, demeaned. I just couldn't see Francis of Assisi as a carnie even if he was huckstering for a good cause, so I slipped away to hide in the bathroom. After sitting on the throne in a very dark stall for so long my butt lost feeling, I spied the outline of a penny on the cement floor. It seemed significant to me to see such a humble coin at an event where, despite its name, we were intent on raising much bigger sums.

"What the heck," I thought, "My indecision has gone on too long."

"God," I prayed, "if that penny is heads, I will see it as your will that I leave the Capuchins, but if it is tails, I will remain for the rest of my life."

When I picked the coin up and saw Lincoln's bearded profile, I knew my decision was made. The following day, I told the novice master that I was leaving.

"I'm sorry to hear that," he replied, "I think you have a vocation to religious life." (Now he tells me.)

"No, Father," I answered calmly. "God has revealed to me that I should go."

Not the best decision-making method I'll vouchsafe, but one that worked for me. Although I am deeply grateful for many things I learned as a friar, I have never had a serious moment's doubt that the penny on the floor was a signpost from God telling me not to become a priest.

Can a Loser Ever Win?

In 1970, the Bee Gees of later disco fame recorded a sappy, vibrato-laden song asking, "How can a loser ever win?"

In romantic terms, for much of my life, I'd have to answer, "I cannot." If I didn't screw things up myself, it seemed like outside forces conspired to keep me alone. To say that I identified with Charlie Brown would be to understate my romantic insecurity. On one of my rare self-confident days, I unintentionally biked into a telephone pole and knocked myself out. On another occasion, after feeling particularly close to God at Mass, a member of the congregation told me that my pants were split from top to bottom. When I said to a former girlfriend, "Everything I touch turns to mud," she agreed.

Although it would soon go sour, my romantic career had a promising start. In 1967 while visiting my friend Henry, I managed to amuse his cousin Michelle enough that she consented to be my first girlfriend. Since we were both fourth graders living a town apart, our courtship was pretty much confined to letters, but oh, how my pen did woo her and hers did me. You'd have to go back to the days of Shelley and Byron to find such prose. I thank God that my sister Christine never found one of those embarrassing epistles. She'd be holding it over my head still.

Perhaps because later breakups would be so very much more traumatic, I hardly recall what ended my postal love affair with Michelle. Maybe it was my dislike of the Beatles' song of the same name. Maybe it was her reluctance to part with a nickel for each first class stamp. Maybe we just drifted apart. I saw Michelle many years later at Henry's father's funeral and felt just like Harry Chapin in his taxi. Whatever we had once was gone.

Being without a girlfriend had no social consequences until seventh grade when it seemed to my loser comrades and me that all the cool guys had girlfriends. By eighth grade, we were convinced that we had missed the last romantic boat. We lacked the confidence to ask anyone to dance and would have panicked if a girl had invited us onto the dance floor. None of us had a clue how to dance. The Twist was the beginning and end of my repertoire. It was an awkward time.

But then I saw her. She had the face of an angel, the eyes of a tiger, and the hair of a young Elizabeth Taylor. She was an Irish Catholic named Sue. Like a knight of the Round Table, I loved her chastely from afar, not wanting to sully her aura with my unworthy presence, but friends detected my ardor and contrived a meeting. To my everlasting astonishment, this celestial beauty suggested a date. I was so elated that I nearly departed without confirming the details of our prospective encounter, but she, being wiser as well as more comely than I, asked where we should go.

"Let's take a bike ride to the fire tower," I suggested. And she agreed. The time was set for our ride to the pinnacle of our town, and she glided away.

Her assent to go out with me made her, at least in my mind, my girlfriend. This knowledge made the three days before our rendezvous heavenly. We didn't hold hands, pass notes in school, or dabble in any other such trivialities to cheapen our romance. We carried on in the tradition of secure lovers eschewing crass public displays of affection. Like the fiat of the Virgin Mary to the Angel Gabriel, Sue's "yes" to our bike ride was a complete act of pure love.

The momentous Saturday was upon me all too quickly. I arrived at her house twenty minutes early. After a brief hello to her mildly curious mother, Sue and I set off but had hardly pedaled more than two blocks when she suggested that we set down our bikes and take a walk in the woods. Why, this goddess could have asked that we watch dandelions grow, and I would have said, "Splendid idea!" As we started down the deserted path, Sue took my hand. My heart leapt. This was my first actual physical contact with a girl outside of fights with my sisters, and Sue had initiated it. I nearly fainted with delight.

After strolling a short while in silence, Sue steered me to the side of the path, where we sat down together on some dry leaves at the base of a hill. She reclined, trapping my left arm in back of her neck and forcing me to lie down also. Then she moved her head onto my chest where my heart was beating so fast I thought it would explode. For the next twenty minutes, I lay as still as a fossil caught in amber, convinced that no romantic moment could be more complete. It never occurred to me that I should hug her with my free arm or, God forbid, kiss her. Lying as we were simply could not be improved upon.

Unfortunately, even perfection has its limits. My arm eventually fell asleep, and round about that time, Sue sighed and sat up. She brushed the leaves from her hair and said that she should probably go home. I saw nothing alarming in her suggestion. After all, we had communed in a way that would be written about for generations.

Imagine my dismay when Sue telephoned me that very next morning to say that she was breaking up with me. After her call, I threw myself on my bed and begged God to bring her back, but our inscrutable Lord and Savior left me without comfort on the rocky shores of Jiltdom, a desolate place I would come to know so very well.

Three years later, I fell for another Irish Catholic classmate named Valerie. This romance was equally chaste, brief, and tragic. I bumbled it quickly and patched it together with an uncharacteristically sensitive and mature phone call, only to bumble it again shortly thereafter. My postpartum grief nearly cost me my only accolade in high school, a yearbook designation as class clown. Were it not for the friendship of my friend Kyle, I'd probably still be moping over the loss of Val.

Since Kyle was fresh from a breakup of her own, she agreed to go with me, as a friend, to the senior prom. I asked my father if I could use the family car, and he said yes.

I told him, "I might be back late."

"That's okay," he replied without concern.

"I might be back real late," I emphasized.

"Not a problem," he answered without looking up from the newspaper he had started to read.

Somewhat miffed at his attitude toward a night when many of my peers would be driving drunk and doing their best to "go all the way," I tried one last time to get a rise out of him by saying, "I could be out all night."

Still, with a no-big-deal tone of voice, he said, "Fine."

"Aren't you afraid I might get into some kind of trouble?" I asked in exasperation.

Genuinely mystified, he asked, "Like what?"

"Thanks a lot," I replied.

It's one thing to be considered a nerd by your classmates but quite another to be given no credit for possible mischief by your own father. When my friend Richard Bates called my house, he mistook my father's voice for mine and asked, "Is Stupid home?"

My father answered, "No, he's out registering the car."

As Rodney Dangerfield loved to say, "I don't get any respect."

From my senior year in high school to my freshman year in college, I'd like to say that I acquired romantic experience, but that would be a lie. I made identical mistakes with Lumpy Everhard, her sister Julie, and Kathy Henderson, who reminded me so much of the original Lumpy that I called her by the same name. Women love those quirky endearments, do they not? I had moments of romantic brilliance, like the time I gave the elder Lumpy my high school ring, the time I wore a white tuxedo to the Holy Cross College spring ball with the younger Lumpy, and the time I secured the role of the Scarecrow opposite Julie as Dorothy in *The Wizard of Oz*.

The play's director was a wicked witch if there ever was one. During a dress rehearsal, she threw some folding chairs, pointed at the stage, and screamed, "What's that?" Answering her own question, she snarled, "A bra strap! A bra strap on a Munchkin! From now on, I don't want to see any Munchkins with bras." To which the Wizard of Oz trumpeted from behind a piece of scenery, "All right!" Yet, this director loved the sincere way my eyes moistened at the climax of every performance when I faced Dorothy and said, "The best thing about brains is that they let you think about those you love." If I'd had half a real brain, I might have noticed the daggers in Dorothy's eyes.

About that time, I began seriously to consider becoming a Catholic priest, but the vocation director stressed that amorous incompetence was not the same as a vocation to celibacy. Prior to entering the seminary, I was encouraged to attend a coed college and remain open to the prospect of romance.

But while *National Lampoon's Animal House* depicted college as an alcohol-driven, sexual free-for-all, I was told by an upperclassman, "Holy Cross is the only place you can go to regain your virginity." Casual dating was very rare. Those students who slept together were usually couples planning to get married on the day after graduation. Female companionship was so hard to come by that my good friend, Joe, referred to our first two years at Holy Cross as "the drought."

And yet, toward the end of that arid period, I had my first kiss. I'd like to say that it came as the poetic culmination of a long and chaste courtship, but it didn't. It was more like making out with a virtual stranger in the mental confusion of an all-night study session. Since there was no relationship whatsoever, the experience was unencumbered, cheesy, and briefer than a college basketball time-out.

The summer of 1978 changed everything. Joe and I found jobs at a Howard Johnson's restaurant where all the attractive young waitresses were eager to date us. We couldn't believe our good fortune. When even a blue-eyed, drop-dead gorgeous beauty named Eva agreed to go to the movies with Joe, he proclaimed, "The drought is over. Prepare for the flood."

Despite her external charms, a few minutes of conversation with Eva convinced me that she was not very bright or interesting. I warned Joe, "You can't judge a book by its cover."

To which he replied sagely, "But you can judge a cover by its cover."

One waitress did stand out, quite literally, among the others. She was six feet tall, college educated, and a little shy. Call her Sally. She was a Polish/Irish Catholic whom Joe included in his dating mix. I considered asking her out also but wanted to be sure that he wasn't serious about her first, so I asked Joe if he minded. He good-naturedly wished me well.

Sally and I had dinner on the outdoor patio of a nice restaurant called Pickwick's adjacent to the Showcase Cinema. We talked late into the night enjoying each other's company, but, when I woke the next day, I found Joe moping around the apartment like I'd killed his dog. He was so depressed that he took all the money he had saved thus far for the next semester and bought an expensive amplifier for a stereo system. It was a pointless purchase, since Joe did not own a turntable, speakers, or any record albums. For years afterwards, whenever Joe encountered romantic disappointment, we'd ask him to work it out at a hi-fi store.

Despite Joe's melodrama, Sally and I went on a couple more dates but could not escape the feeling that we were dancing on Joe's grave. After a week (the outer limit of all my previous romantic interludes), Sally and I arrived at a moment when it seemed appropriate to say good night with a hug. To both of our surprise, the embrace was awkward rather than sensual or romantic, kind of like hugging an aunt or uncle. With my arms still wrapped around Sally, I never felt more convinced that I was called to be a friar. Happily, she shared my unease, and we agreed to be just friends.

As a side note, an older friend once told me, "There will come a day when you'll receive a telephone call from a girlfriend who'll say, 'I like you as a friend, but . . . . ' As soon as you hear those words, hang up, because your self-respect is about to go down the toilet."

The next morning, I woke Joe with the news that Sally and I had broken up. He looked up at me from the couch and said earnestly, "Thanks a lot."

His gratitude came across as the sexist presumption that Sally was a commodity I could dispense to him, so I replied, "Go fuck yourself." Those were the last words we exchanged on the matter.

Later that day, Joe resumed dating Sally, monogamously this time, while I stopped dating altogether, seeing as I was contemplating the priesthood and battling supernatural forces in our haunted apartment described earlier. By the way, nothing cools passion better than fear. If a man is scared enough, his penis will actually retract into his body to cower in private. That's a fact. I read it in a magazine. But I digress.

Oddly, although Sally and I had no romantic interest in each other, our brief platonic relationship made Joe so uneasy that he virtually never entertained her in my or any other guy's presence. She became something of a ghost. Joe would disappear for a period of time, and all his friends assumed he was "Sallying," as we came to call his absences. On rare occasions when I did see Joe and Sally together, he always kept a proprietary arm around her as a physical reminder of their bond. There could be little doubt that he considered her the woman he would marry.

The summer after my junior year, I met another waitress at HoJo's. Call her Pam. Since I was only a postulant, a thinking-about-it friar, I was encouraged to date. So Pam and I went out. On our second date, we saw Dudley Moore and Liza Minelli in the romantic comedy *Arthur*, a film set in Manhattan. Afterwards, Pam bemoaned the fact that she'd never been to New York City, so I suggested that we go.

"When?" she asked.

"Why not right now?" I replied, "It's only nine o'clock. We can be there by midnight."

Since neither of us had to work until eleven the next night and Pam had her own car, she agreed to go. In no time, we were looking at the Statue of Liberty across the harbor and then strolling through a mostly deserted Chinatown. We watched the sun rise over Central Park and had breakfast in Times Square. Pam, who proclaimed it the most romantic night of her life, slept while I drove back. Given how little I actually knew about New York City at that time, I was as surprised that we weren't mugged as I was by her compliment.

Once, I took my younger brothers Chipper and Tom to a restaurant with Pam. When a waitress came to take our order, Chipper looked up from his menu and said to me, "I know it's my day, Dad, but let Tom eat today." The waitress looked at me like I was a monster. Word to the wise: never take your siblings on a date.

I wish I could say that the remainder of Pam and my courtship was equally sweet, but it was not. Under the influence of too much alcohol, I lost my virginity. My grandmother always said, "When the booze goes in, the brains go out." Then, while she remained flush with romance, I began confusing lust with love. Friends and family encouraged me to break off the affair, which I finally did after two months, but Pam did not go easily. She pursued me, sometimes with tears and other times with anger. I had always assumed that it was painless for the one initiating the breakup, but I learned otherwise. I felt miserably guilty for hurting her. When she called, I heard her out at great length, which would inevitably give her false hope that we'd get back together. The idea that couples could sleep together without emotional baggage exploded in my face as a sexist myth. I felt like a dirtbag because I was one.

Armed with newfound humility, I steered clear of women for the waning days of my senior year and went into the Capuchin-Franciscans as a novice. Leaving the friary in 1981 was difficult and not related to celibacy. Voluntary poverty and peace activism constituted my sticking points. Regardless of my reasoning, the day I left Saint Francis Friary disoriented me. I had a degree in religious studies. I had spent years contemplating a religious vocation and left it behind without a ready alternative.

I returned to Worcester where my friend Mark put me up for one night. With half an eye toward the plight of the homeless, I slept on a porch the following night and in a tree the next while I spent the days looking for a job. Before my departure, my novice master suggested I find work I'd never done before. He also said that, if I changed my mind and wanted to return to the friary, I could come back in two years. I told him that I'd never worked with the elderly or with children, and he suggested I do so. Burning with unfocused energy as I was, I applied at a nursing home, a hospital, a nursery school, and at a group home for mentally challenged adults.

Near the conclusion of my interview for a job as an orderly at Saint Vincent Hospital, I was asked, "Would you have any problem with catheterization?"

Having absolutely no idea what that was and wanting to impress, I said, "Absolutely not."

The surprised interviewer asked, "So you have no problem handling other people's genitals?"

I nearly fainted and did not get the job.

But, thanks be to God and persistence, Saint Agnes Day Care took me on as a volunteer, and Bancroft House Nursing Home hired me as an orderly, a job that involved plenty of contact with naked patients, excrement, and urine but no catheterization, thank you very much. I was also hired part time at the group home with a promise of a full-time, live-in position come September. With so much income and no bills, I was able to rent the three-bedroom apartment (not the haunted one) my friends and I shared during the summer before I entered the friary. I didn't need more than one bedroom but welcomed the familiarity and fond memories I had of my previous stay. The spacious apartment had the added advantage of being located only a block from the group home and almost as close to the nursing home.

During my first visit to the group home, I ran into Sally, who chatted with me about her engagement to Joe. While we talked, Joe, who also worked at the group home, entered the room, and I reflexively took a step away from Sally. Noticing, Joe put an arm around her shoulders, smiled, and said, "That's not necessary now that she's mine."

It creeped me out a bit, but I was glad to see him finally over his jealousy, especially since the nursing home that hired me also employed Sally.

My responsibilities at Bancroft House were challenging: cleaning incontinent patients three times a night and changing soiled johnnies and linens. I had to turn elders who had lost the ability to roll over, something essential to avoid terrible bed sores. Since I worked eleven at night until seven the next morning, I had plenty of interaction with patients, quite a few of whom were insomniacs.

It took me a long time to get over the idea that, at twenty-two, it was actually possible for me to handle naked grandmothers and grandfathers. My heart broke for their

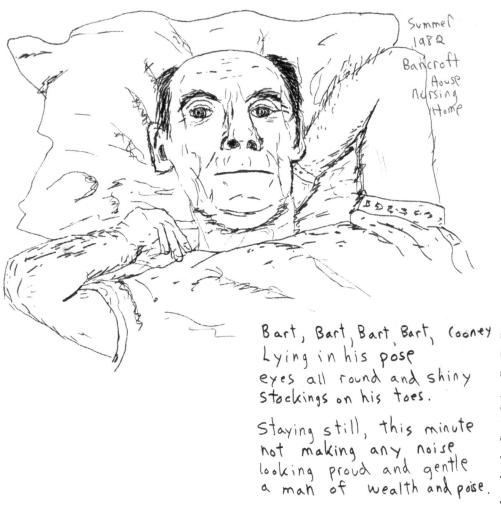

Summer
1982
Bancroft
House
Nursing
Home

Bart, Bart, Bart, Bart, Cooney
Lying in his pose
eyes all round and shiny
stockings on his toes.

Staying still, this minute
not making any noise
looking proud and gentle
a man of wealth and poise.

drawing by Scott Schaeffer-Duffy

Bart Cooney

humiliation. I wanted so badly to return to them any dignity I could. Some patients made it easy. Just listening to them did the trick. Many of these folks turned out to be charming, giving more to me than I ever gave to them. Other patients slept through my ministrations, were too disoriented to complain, or were openly hostile. A Polish woman named Sophie would throw her colostomy bag at us when we entered her room. Bart Cooney rocked back and forth, repeating the same word with increasing rapidity until we left him alone. Amanda Mason suffered horribly from bone cancer, which made any physical contact a torment. Another woman startled me by speaking through her tracheostomy. I had no doubt in my mind that my work was going to be a challenge and an education.

And yet, in that institutional atmosphere with pitifully few mementos left to each patient, some elders retained the very best of themselves. Mary Agnes Gallagher never complained about her circumstance, preferring to inquire about the well-being of others.

She had marvelous blue eyes that sparkled as she bestowed her kindhearted smile on anyone who came into her room. Like screen legend Helen Hayes of *Arsenic and Old Lace* fame, Mary Agnes epitomized aging gracefully.

I viewed the patients as treasure chests stowed away in a seldom-visited attic. I began asking the insomniacs questions between my rounds: "What was the most beautiful place you ever visited? What was the most romantic thing anyone ever did for you? What advice would you give a young person? What did you think of FDR? Of Senator McCarthy? Of Greta Garbo?" Perhaps they could not recall what they had for dinner that evening, but they could describe events from decades past with brilliance.

Another thing surprised me. To most of us, old age is a calamity to hold off by all means. Wispy gray hair, wrinkles, sagging flesh, and protruding bones suggest inevitable death more than lasting beauty, and yet, I often saw something quite attractive in the elderly. The lines on their faces told of years of laughter and generosity. The dimming eyes still shone with mystery and wisdom. Even some of their bodies were more alluring than decrepit. I began to count myself lucky to have that job.

On the other end of the age spectrum, my work at the nursery school was also an eye-opener. Four- and five-year-olds are easy to fall for, and their fresh insights were wonderful. They loved it when I read aloud and even more when I made up stories on the spot. Watching them play dress-up with such seriousness and seeing them cooking in the mock kitchen as if they were master chefs was a hoot. They could imagine anything. Sometimes they'd put an ordinary object, like a wooden block, in my hands and tell me to guard it from an evil dragon who wanted it because it was magical. I especially enjoyed the youngest of the four-year-olds because some of them still had a touch of the high voice of really small children. It made me feel like I was working with Munchkins in the merry old Land of Oz.

The job at the group home provided an altogether different side of the human condition. Six of the eight residents were mentally challenged, including someone diagnosed with schizophrenia, and one was deaf with cerebral palsy. The latter two ended up in the custody of the Massachusetts Department of Mental Retardation because of misdiagnosis and bureaucratic unwillingness to correct it. Alice C., the deaf woman, was institutionalized in the 1950s on the mistaken assumption that her physical disabilities implied cognitive damage. Actually, she was as bright as can be. All of the residents had spent years in brutal state "hospitals" where they were neglected and often physically and sexually abused. What cognitive and emotional progress they might have made in life had been seriously stunted in those cruel and impersonal environments.

Thankfully, after a number of exposés, the people at our group home had been de-institutionalized. In Worcester, they lived in a stately Victorian home with a gorgeous Japanese maple tree by the front porch. With three full-time, live-in staff and me as a live-out parttimer, the residents enjoyed a fair amount of personal attention. We not only taught them more independence, but we also socialized with them and brought them on vacations with us. The program director, Marilyn Bulger, and I took two residents, Roger and Bob, to the Bahamas for five days in April. Roger had the time of his life while Bob told us we were all nuts for going in the ocean because "Everyone knows it's too cold to swim in April."

Another resident, Kevin, took me to all the Arnold Schwarzenegger movies and a fair number of World Wrestling Federation competitions. Kevin was a body builder who bought a waterbed, which he surrounded in his room with posters of Pat Benatar. Time with Kevin and the other residents often struck me more like hanging out with interesting people than working. Were it not for the rigmarole the state made us go through and the paperwork it required us to file, I would have done the job for free.

Three weeks after I left the friary and soon after I began working, Joe said to me, "Sally is renting a room kind of far away with restrictions on visitors. I know you have that big apartment all by yourself right here. Would it be possible for her to share it with you until September, when you are going to move into the group home?"

Wow! I guess he had come a long way, but, then again, I did have three empty bedrooms. I slept on a shelf in the butler's pantry. It's a long story for another day. Joe was my best friend. How could I refuse?

Sally and I shared many shifts at Bancroft House. After she moved into my apartment, we started walking home together at seven in the morning to eat breakfast before going to sleep. In the sunny kitchen, we talked about the patients. The conversations acted as a kind of decompression after the difficulties of caring for lonely people facing disempowerment and death. Sally's compassion impressed me. We so enjoyed those morning reflections that we began stretching them out a bit and widening the topics of discussion. I shared why I left the friary, and she told me, without bitterness, how she had to drop out of college, go home, and help support her family when her father lost his job. Her selflessness amazed me.

And then, one morning, we had a champagne breakfast, a perk of having too much income and too few bills. After talking about a patient who was very near death, we turned again to our families. I told her about my break with my father and how he had boycotted my college graduation as well as my brother Michael's wedding rather than see me. Somehow she ended up embracing me. I can still vividly recall the warmth of her arms around me and the feel of her hair on my face when I realized, "Hey! Idiot! She is your best friend's fiancée!" It was an excellent juncture to step back, clear my throat, and make an apology, but I was so taken with the contrast between this embrace and the awkward hug from three years earlier that I hesitated. The Capuchins had drilled into me that the novice was not unlike a person engaged to be married, the job of both individuals being to discern God's will and not simply march on without question toward a vow. My tired, lonely, confused, and slightly-intoxicated self argued, "If this feels so natural, maybe it's not God's will that Sally should marry Joe. Maybe this embrace is part of the divine plan." Yeah, maybe I was the King of Minnesota or, more likely, full of crap. I couldn't just "sin boldly" as Martin Luther advised. No, I had to recast betrayal as a holy act. The chutzpah!

Having loosened my moral restraints, I let myself go, and we didn't stop until there was nowhere left to go. Suspecting that I was falling in love but not wanting the budding relationship to be underhanded, I said, "We have to talk to Joe right away."

Sally disagreed, arguing instead that we give it some time. I foolishly acquiesced. And so we carried on a clandestine romance for a week, during which I felt terrible whenever I saw Joe but helpless and happy when I was with Sally. I was adrift. Thankfully, Sally was not. Saying that her relationship with Joe was too precious to lose, she ended the affair on the seventh day.

By mutual consent, we laid off the wine and reduced our contact considerably. A couple of weeks later, Joe, Sally, and I went to the Tipperary Pub, (a sad-to-say long lost Worcester treasure). Although Joe was one hundred percent Polish, he and I had spent so much time together at Irish-American sing-a-longs that I gave him the nickname Itchy Monahan. On this particular night at the Tip, the three of us were soon singing, clapping, and swaying to the band's renditions of "The Wild Colonial Boy," "Whiskey in the Jar," "The Black Velvet Band," "Step It Up Mary," "The Wild Rover," and of course, "Finnegan's Wake." As is the practice in any decent Irish pub, rowdy songs balanced tear-jerkers about the famine, the troubles, or the First World War. When the band struck up "The Four Green Fields," Sally and I sang the rebel ballad aloud, but Joe stared wistfully in our direction. I suspected that he felt a trifle left out because he wasn't really Irish. So, when Joe went to the bathroom, I impulsively followed to try and reassure him.

In a fit of insanity, I leaned against a urinal and said, "Joe, you looked sad tonight, perhaps with a touch of the old jealousy about Sally and me. Well, I want you to know that I fell in love with her this summer. I thought she might love me, but she did not. She loves you, not me. If she stayed with me, she'd regret it. Maybe not today. Maybe not tomorrow, but soon and for the rest of her life, because she's a part of you, and you belong together."

He paused for a tense moment and then gave me a bear hug saying, "That was beautiful."

"I know," I said, quoting Woody Allen, "It's from *Casablanca*. I've been waiting my whole life to say it."

Before we left the bathroom, I gave Joe the keys to my apartment and told him that I'd sleep on the group home couch so he and Sally could have romantic privacy. He thanked me again, and I felt pretty darn noble.

The next morning at eleven, I went home and was shocked to see furniture overturned and Sally red-eyed from crying. Joe appeared out of nowhere, grabbed me by the throat, and shouted, "Tell me why I shouldn't kill you right now!"

Apparently, on his way home from the pub, Joe began wondering how amorous my romance with Sally had been. When Sally reluctantly admitted we had slept together, Joe went ballistic.

Seeing his anger and hurt, I felt completely deflated, so I answered him, "Go ahead and kill me. I guess I deserve it."

But Joe did not strike me. Instead he let me down slowly saying, "This is how it's going to be: You and Sally will continue living here as planned until September but will not speak a single word to each other. You will both move into the group home as planned. You will come to the wedding when it is held. I will not be cuckolded!" This was the only time I've heard that word used outside of *Othello*. It somehow added weird gravitas.

I meekly agreed to all of Joe's demands and slunk away. How far had I fallen from the "aura of holiness" my uncle had ascribed to my fellow novices and me. What a bitter disappointment I had become to my seraphic father, Saint Francis of Assisi.

I blamed myself entirely and scrupulously followed Joe's instructions. In public, Sally and I were cordial while in private, we did not so much as glance at or speak to one another. I went to Mass every day for a week but sat in the back without going to Communion because of my betrayal. Finally, I went to confession before Monsignor Sullivan at Saint Peter's Church. He was a high-church, no-nonsense pastor who wore a long black cassock with red piping and a biretta with a red pompom to stress his ecclesiastical rank. Parishioners in his parish still knelt for Communion twenty years after Vatican II encouraged standing. I expected the Monsignor to give me a tongue-lashing and severe penance. The Irish Catholic in me was never more certain that I was going to Hell. But the formidable cleric took me by surprise. Apparently, he'd heard worse sins than mine. After absolving me, he said I needed to truly believe that I was forgiven and that God still wanted me to have a holy and happy life. This was spiritual water in the desert, a great grace.

Perhaps that grace is what sustained me over the next six months when I lived at the group home in the room next door to Joe and Sally. I prayed the Morning and Evening Prayer, went to Mass, volunteered at the nursery school, and worked at the nursing home and group home all without a shred of familial or social support. At Christmas, in a spiteful moment, Joe gave me my only present, a book on sexual dysfunction by Sigmund Freud. When I returned to my room that night, I found a neat pile of everything I had given him since we met in 1976. Books, records, cards, letters, and a bust of the Polish composer Chopin lay there like trash waiting for the garbage collector. Joe had erased me from his life.

I coped poorly. I bought two rabbits and built a complex hutch for them in my bedroom. The bunnies were a big hit at the nursery school and cheered me up as they silently hopped around wiggling their noses. After my "boys" delivered four babies (the pet shop sales person lied to me), I put a poster on my door depicting a quantity of rabbits and Oscar Wilde's words, "Nothing succeeds like excess."

And you know what? While many things adults say about nature are nonsense, like the business about storks delivering babies and elephants never forgetting, the stereotype of rabbits as prolific breeders is spot on. Before I knew it, I felt like Captain Kirk in "The Trouble with Tribbles" episode of the original *Star Trek*. I could barely see over all the fluffy tails and had to give every one of my pets away.

Interestingly, no one in the group home paid me much mind. Because my room was on the third floor, they let me be. I was no more peculiar, after all, than Caroline, the laconic epileptic in the room below me, or Roger, the compulsive eater and Fats Domino fan, or Alice M., the sweet old lady who typed shocking letters to her archenemy, "that fucking Irene Nalto." Living in a group home relativizes normality.

Time may not heal all wounds, but it can cauterize them. Joe gradually softened, and, by February 1982, he seemed more like his old self around me. Sally even started saying hello in passing. Plans were under way for their spring wedding. Joe took classes in computer technology to beef up his hardly marketable religious studies degree. He bought a Triumph Spitfire, a wicked cool, bright red, sport car. He loved it so much that he took the top down whenever the sky was clear, even if the temperature was only forty degrees. My life was still an empty wasteland of loneliness, but I began feeling vicarious happiness for my old friend's future life.

And then, on a weekday in late February, Sally surprised me by inviting me to lunch to discuss the wedding. She suggested a restaurant called Chopsticks that had a very good buffet, plenty of vegetarian items, and wasn't too pricey. How could I resist? My social calendar was open forever.

We walked from the group home and had a nice lunch. She spoke mainly about details for the Mass and reception. Joe and I had attended several weddings together and agreed about what was fun and classy as opposed to bogus and tacky. At one wedding Mass after the priest invited the congregation to offer their own prayers, Joe and I whispered simultaneously, "For an open bar," and God did not disappoint us. Good music, good food, good company, free beer, and lots of dancing were much more important to us than a ritzy hall, flowers, a limo, or tuxedos and gowns.

Sally, who had often spoken about her desire eventually to finish a degree in early childhood development, asked me about my volunteer job at the nursery school. After I told her briefly about storytelling with the children, she wanted to know if she could accompany me on the following day. I didn't see why not. All in all, the first conversation I had with her since August seemed remarkably easygoing.

On our walk home from lunch, Sally asked me if we could stop at a bar for a drink to take the chill off. Once inside, she confided to me that she was nervous about the wedding.

"I imagine that's perfectly natural," I replied.

We continued on our snowy way up Main Street, and Sally asked if we could stop at Moynihan's Pub near the group home, for another drink. Half way through her wine, she confessed, "Sometimes, I'm not attracted to Joe."

I stressed to her that, from what I've heard, that too was nothing to worry about. Physical attraction probably waxes and wanes throughout married life. Again, perfectly natural. Actually, from day one of my marriage to this very moment more than thirty years later, I have been consistently and passionately attracted to my wife. Perhaps, I'm an exception.

Instead of going home, Sally then asked if I'd keep walking and talking with her for a while. One drink later, in a bar on Chandler Street, she complained, "Sometimes, Joe disgusts me."

With a bit less confidence, I repeated don't-worry-be-happy platitudes.

Eight o'clock found us in Leitrim's Pub on Park Avenue. We had moved in a very wide circle around the group home. In a high-backed wooden booth under the influence of wine beyond counting, Sally looked me straight in the eyes and said, "Actually, I don't love Joe. I love you."

Whammy! I choked on my beer and couldn't have jumped back quicker had a tarantula just fallen on the table. My first instinct was to see if there was a lawyer in the place who would notarize an affidavit testifying that I had never touched her nor made the slightest romantic advance. I had suffered too much emotional grief trying to recapture a shred of my friendship with Joe to see it all go down the toilet again.

But, on the other hand, I was incredibly lonely. But, on the other other hand (just how many hands does a person get?), her remark could still be nothing more than pre-wedding nerves exaggerated by drink. I had to escort her home straight away and delete all her comments from my memory. Neither task was easy. I still remember vividly what she said that night, and walking her home was almost impossible. She swayed and slipped on the ice, pulling me down into snowdrifts several times. She sang, laughed, and, most frightening of all, pleaded with me to spend the night with her. Meanwhile, like the protagonist in Jack London's "To Build a Fire," I mostly wanted to escape freezing to death.

With great difficulty, we managed to reach the group home around nine. I escorted her to an empty room on the third floor, where I intended to leave her, but she clung to me and continued to offer herself. Joe was due home at ten. The rational part of me suspected that Sally wanted us to be discovered together to force a breakup with Joe. Not only did this mean I was being used, but it also meant that Joe would probably kill me. While you might think these factors would squelch passion, one must never underestimate the dominance of sex over reason in men.

I had half my clothes off, right on the verge of saying, "What the hell?" when my coworker, Dawn, opened the door, gasped, apologized, and closed it again. Thoroughly embarrassed, I broke away and fled to the first floor where I tried to act natural watching TV until Joe walked by shortly thereafter. A close call indeed.

The following morning as I prepared to go to the nursery school, Sally waylaid me. She said she still wanted to accompany me. I told her that I would chalk up everything she had said and done the previous day to premarital stress.

"Do nothing of the kind," she admonished. "I stand by every word I said. Can I go with you to Saint Agnes Day Care?"

It was daylight. The school was a public place. I didn't know what to make of her comment but saw no harm in her coming with me.

The children were especially charming, right at the tail end of their helium-voices, but before the dawning of impertinence. I read *Frog and Toad Are Friends* aloud and made up stories featuring each of the children as a character. We also made soapy bubbles and built castles out of wooden blocks. How different one day can be from another.

On our way back to the group home, Sally told me, "I've thought about what I said last night and have decided to talk to Joe this afternoon and break our engagement."

There was no alcohol in her, and yet, she still professed a preference for me over her fiancée. After a few moments of shock, I said that I would not even consider dating her unless she and Joe broke cleanly followed by a decent period of mourning. She agreed.

Back at the group home, she invited Joe up to the third floor for the momentous conversation while I cooled my heels in the living room at the bottom of the stairs. Three hours passed. Finally, Joe bounded downstairs, smiled at me, and went out the front door.

What in the world had transpired?

I crept upstairs only to find Sally seated at Joe's computer playing Space Invaders. I asked what had happened and, without even turning to face me, she said, "You lose."

While I stood dumbfounded in the hall, she both literally and figuratively closed the door on me.

Only much later did I learn that Sally had indeed broken her engagement only to find Joe so willing to support her free choice that he became much more attractive to her. In the light of her hesitation, Joe suggested that, despite his imperfections, he and Sally were deeply bonded in a spiritual way. Apparently, he was correct. My wife Claire and I saw them years later, and they seemed like a very happily married couple.

If I could pick any two days in my life as the most confusing and miserable, that day and its predecessor would be front runners. In less than thirty-six hours, I had been taken on a harrowing emotional roller coaster. I felt like a battered yo-yo.

In my despair, I went outside into the cold and walked to a nearby school playground where I sat on the monkey bars, pledging to remain there until a compassionate someone came to collect me. I perched on those icy bars for nearly three hours. It was well past dark, long after my shift at the group home should have begun when I realized bitterly that no one would come looking for me, not even Sam, the house dog.

I often say, "If you can't get love and respect, go for pity," but what do you do when you can't even get pity?

You soldier on. That's what you do. As trite as it sounds, it's still the best policy. Wallowing is tempting but not therapeutic. Working for others is. So, I walked back to the group home and did my best to help those I'd been hired to serve.

Joe and Sally married two months later. I attended the wedding and wished them all the best.

A few days afterwards, I lay on my bed thinking about Gene Wilder in Mel Brooks's comic masterpiece, *Young Frankenstein*. In imitation of one of Wilder's scenes, I began turning from side to side, repeating, "Destiny, destiny, no escaping, that's for me." On my third turn, my foot knocked the old screen out the window and I nearly fell three floors to the ground below. It occurred to me that had I fallen and been killed, my friends would have assumed that I had committed suicide. No one would ever guess the silly truth.

61

"That's it," I cried. "I've gotta' make a change. Moping is not a vocation."

I grabbed a copy of *The Catholic Worker* newspaper, found letters from a couple of communities appealing for volunteers, and wrote to both houses offering my services.

Not four days later, Michael Kirwan invited me to Saint Benedict's Catholic Worker in Washington, DC. After meeting him and seeing the extreme need there, I promised to return for a year in August. Coincidentally, a friend, Eileen Shea, planned to go to the nation's capital as a member of the Jesuit Volunteer Corps (JVC). She expressed uneasiness about my relocating to DC because of an earlier suggestion of mine that we should consider becoming "more than friends" and also because she felt my going to a tougher neighborhood than the one she headed for stole her thunder. Silly person. Fourth and P North West, the locale of Saint Benedict's and Mary Harris houses, was so beaten down in 1982 that nothing happening there would ever be heard of by anyone. The black guests of Saint Benedict's told me that the only white people on Fourth Street were cops, clerics, or corpses.

Eileen was right though about my presence being a romantic nuisance. I came over to the JVC house, just south of Logan Circle, often during my first week. I also went down to Saint Francis Catholic Worker house on Sixth Street and heard from Marcia Timmel about a young volunteer named Claire Schaeffer who worked parttime at *Sojourners* magazine. I went there to inquire about work for myself and met Claire. She claims that my first words to her were, "So, are you going to be sucked into the vortex of resistance?" Ridiculous. As a pitifully inexperienced peace activist only eighteen months older than she, I hope I was less arrogant than that. At any event, Claire and I met, and she invited me to join her on a journey to Jessup, Maryland, where her community went once a week to salvage borderline produce from the dumpsters of a massive food distribution center. I went along and enjoyed the early morning conversation.

A couple of days later as I pestered Eileen, I mentioned Claire, whom Eileen had seen at a demonstration.

"Oh, she's beautiful," Eileen crooned, not bothering to hide her desire to redirect my ardor.

"What are you talking about?" I replied, "She's too thin, and I could never date a redhead."

How little did I know myself. In short order, I was spending hours every day with Claire at Saint Francis House, at Mass, or on the pay phone from Saint Benedict's. We had highfalutin talks about Dostoevsky and Tolstoy, Mother Teresa, and Saint Francis. She was a 1982 University of Virginia grad with a degree in political and social thought, not bad complements to my religious studies degree. We were fresh out of college and full of crap and idealism in equal measure. They both can take you a long way.

Under Michael Kirwan's sway, reinforced by Franciscan aspirations, Claire and I embraced a nearly insane fidelity to voluntary poverty and openness to the poor. I filled every inch of space at Saint Benedict's with guests, slept on the hallway floor to make more room, and nearly died from bronchitis. Claire gave away all the money in the Saint

Francis Catholic Worker account to a swindler from Florida with a preposterous sob story. We did not apologize for the foolishness of our actions. Like the Catholic Worker Movement's cofounder, Dorothy Day, we earnestly wished we could be as foolish as Jesus seemed to be.

On a night I spent at Saint Francis House sleeping on a couch adjacent to another on which a guest named Picky snored, I woke in the middle of the night to find Claire crouching near my face in the darkness. She startled me with a kiss, something she had been thinking about doing for hours. I was surprised but not at all displeased. Would that I could always wake up to such a treat. I guess I could fall in love with a redhead.

Not long afterwards, Claire moved into Mary Harris house, and we became coworkers as well as romantic partners. Faith-filled, idealistic, progressive, intelligent, brave, good-humored, compassionate, and attractive, Claire was the hard-headed woman Cat Stevens sang about. Her love challenged me to become a better person.

In the midst of those heady days, I was hired at *Sojourners* to split a full-time position as receptionist with Claire. We answered the phone and took messages for the magazine's staff. We made enough money to pay our college loan bills, quite affordable in that more enlightened age, and tossed the rest of our income into the common pot at our houses.

Late one afternoon in early October, I went to *Sojourners's* office near Catholic University to walk Claire home from work. Rain threatened, so I loaned her my blue, hooded sweatshirt and donned a black trash bag. We had not gone far down the street, when, under a ginkgo tree just starting to shed its yellow leaves, I turned to Claire, a woman I had known for only seven weeks, and asked, "Will you marry me?"

A stranger crossed our path at this moment and, instead of answering me, Claire said to him, "This man just asked me to marry him. What do you think?"

Nonplussed, the fellow replied, "Well, a lot of marriages end in divorce."

"That's true," I agreed, "but what do you think?"

He pursed his lips and asked, "Do you love each other?"

"Yes," we answered in unison.

"Then, go for it," he concluded before going on his way.

I suggested that we buy a package of Tastykake Butterscotch Krimpets and eat them on the swing set of an adjacent park to celebrate. And so we did.

Our engagement continued through the fall and winter. And then, in May of 1983, Claire and I went on a trip to climb and meet some of my family. I had reached the summit of New Hampshire's Mount Washington five previous times and assumed that an early May climb would not be a problem. It surprised me then that the steep and rocky trail from the Appalachian Mountain Club building in Pinkham Notch quickly turned into a cascade of ice. We ascended only by grasping tree trunks and branches and pulling ourselves up the muddy sidelines. By the time we reached Tuckerman Ravine, where we planned to spend the night in a lean-to shelter, it was clear that there was considerably more snow on the mountain than I expected, something we were certainly not prepared for. Also, the night was so incredibly cold that we combined our sleeping bags and squeezed together inside them for greater warmth. All night long, we heard howling wind punctuated by what sounded like enormous explosions that we later learned were avalanches off the ravine headwall.

Claire, a generally well-spoken Southern Methodist with a growing appreciation for Catholicism and not much given to profane speech, told me through alternately clenched and chattering teeth, "I am so FUCKING cold!"

The next morning found the sun shining into blindingly white snow piled up all around us. A climber came by on his way down, the only one we had seen since our departure the previous day, and told us, "You should go back. The dangers are many, and the rewards are few."

But I "reasoned" that our foot gear was inadequate for going back down on the icy trail, leaving us only one option: reach the summit and come down via the auto road. In other words, we had to go up to get down. The hiker took pity on us, gave us his ski poles, and off we went.

On one particularly dangerous and snowy section of the Lion's Head Trail, I said to Claire, "We should probably rope up in case one of us falls."

She looked at me like I was the Devil, and I said no more.

The snow was so deep that we could only rarely see the cairns of stones marking the trail, so we more-or-less headed to the summit by dead reckoning. To our surprise, we made it and then trudged wearily down the winding auto road to the highway. Unfortunately, we had parked the car we borrowed three miles farther south, and no one would give us a ride. An altogether unhappy outing.

A day later, after watching family slides at my brother Michael and sister-in-law Charlotte's house in western Massachusetts, Claire announced that she was breaking up with me. Despite my track record, I hadn't seen it coming and was an immediate mess. Our bus ride back to DC the next day was marked by a pathetic cavalcade of tears and fruitless pleading that she reconsider. But Claire was done with me. Period. She had many reasons, probably all of them valid.

By this time, we had two coworkers at the Catholic Worker, Kathy Hochanadel and Carl Siciliano. In short order, both of them lost patience with my sob story. Claire remained similarly unmoved, so I took a different approach to my quandary. I stopped whining and went cheerfully back to work only to ask Claire, each and every day, in an offhanded way, to marry me. Claire would ask what were our tasks for a given day, and I'd say, "We could do laundry, fix the broken window, or get married." I proposed so often that not only Claire but also Carl, Kathy, and all our guests simply ignored it. I might as well have been saying, "How are you?" for all the impact it had, so I upped the ante. I painted "I LOVE CLAIRE!" on the front step to Mary Harris House. When that went unremarked upon ("Just ignore him" seems to have been the watchwords of that time), I painted a much larger proclamation on a six-by-eight sheet of plywood that I leaned against a beat-up fence. Without comment, someone flipped it, message-side down. At the time, I thought I was just being charmingly persistent while today I realize that my behavior smacked at least of harassment if not stalking. Thank God this happened before cell phone cameras, YouTube videos, and easily obtained restraining orders.

Through all my antics, Claire never once wavered. When she didn't completely disregard my overtures, she urged me to find one of those other proverbial fish in the sea. Clearly, she had no idea how unsuccessful all my previous fishing trips had been.

Finally, I took Claire at her word and asked a woman named Jan for a date. Claire seemed delighted. In truth, I only asked this friend to go out in order to prove to Claire that dating others was not for me. I borrowed a car, met Jan in Baltimore, and promptly confessed to her that I was still hopelessly mired in unrequited love for Claire. I said I was still willing to go out that night with her as long as she understood where I was coming from. Appreciating my candor, she accepted my terms. We went off to a neighborhood bar that sold white T-shirts emblazoned with the words, "BEER: Ask for it by name. Accept no substitutes."

We sat in rocking chairs and talked about our families, work, likes, and dislikes. After a bit, we walked along the harbor and snuck a visit onto the deck of a rich person's yacht. We got along pretty well and even fell into each other's arms at the night's end. I had never had a less self-conscious date. I spent the night on a couch at her place and assumed that she'd make excuses in the morning for why she couldn't see me again, but that wasn't the case. I told Jan that I wanted to go on another date with her but wanted first to share the good news with Claire. I called Mary Harris House, told Claire how well the date had gone, and thanked her for suggesting it. To my surprise, there was a long silence on the other end of the line.

"Could she be jealous?" I wondered. "No way," I thought, "This is the woman who told me 'No' a thousand times."

An hour later when I pulled up on Fourth Street, I found Claire sitting on the stoop in her usual bib overalls with her hair tied back and tucked under a kerchief, but she wore a pair of earrings. I had never seen Claire wear earrings in DC. Was she "dressed up" for me?? Impossible.

On the extremely slim chance that my date with Jan had somehow reopened Claire's heart to me, I said to her, "I had a great date last night but told Jan that I love you. She wants to go out with me again, but, if I do that, I don't want to give her divided attention, so I'll ask you one last time if we can be together again. If you say 'no,' I will never ask you again."

Claire considered and then said, "Let's go out tonight and see what happens."

Wicked cool! Me, who hadn't had a date in a jillion years, had two in a row. And I had a wonderful time, too. She and I kissed on a park bench in Southeast DC, a virtual public display of affection. Amazing.

I called Jan the next day and told her what happened. She was remarkably supportive. No hard feelings. No messy complications. I was free to bask in the sun.

Not six weeks later, on a peace mission to war-torn Nicaragua, Claire asked me to marry her, which I did on June 22, 1984, the feast of Saint Thomas More, in DC's Saint Patrick's Church.

Can a loser ever win? I tell you with all certainty, beyond his wildest imagining, he can indeed.

Scott and Claire Schaeffer-Duffy on their wedding day
"Be joyful always, for this is God's will for you."

—1 Thessalonians

The Thrilling Three

My wife, Claire, and I read aloud to all four of our children from their infancy until they were sixteen and sometimes older. In 1992, when our firstborn, Justin, was seven, he and I spent a great deal of time reading books from Alfred Hitchcock's *Three Investigators* series. Like *The Hardy Boys*, only spookier and more fun, the Hitchcock mysteries were my favorites back in the late sixties. Our son not only enjoyed them but also interrupted me often to say, "I know what's going to happen next" or "I know the solution to the mystery."

One day, after being "I knowed" so frequently that I could barely finish two consecutive sentences, I blurted out, "If you know so much about mysteries, why don't you become a junior detective yourself?"

His whole face lit up with a kind of "Great idea, Dad!" look. Minutes later, he was dictating a letter to explain his hopes and qualifications. After putting this resumé into an envelope addressed to "Alfred Hitchcock, Hollywood, California," I said, "Let's see what happens."

That should have been the end of the matter, especially when one considers that Hitchcock died a dozen years earlier, but Justin's enthusiasm inspired me to reach outside the limits of the great director's mortality. I secretly typed the following letter to my son:

> Dear Justin,
>
> I'm so glad you are interested in becoming a detective. I'd be happy to give your name and address to people in your area who have mysteries that need solving. I will forward cases that are appropriate for clever children like yourself. I suggest you recruit some partners and give your agency a name. Best of luck!
>
> *Alfred Hitchcock, Jr.*

Does such a person even exist? I had and still have no idea.

Impatient to get the adventure rolling, I mixed my letter with the rest of the next day's mail to convince Justin that it was genuine. Thankfully he did not notice that it wasn't postmarked or wonder how he could have received a reply from California in so short a time. When you are an excited seven-year-old, all things are possible.

Immediately after getting the green light from the junior Hitchcock, Justin went to work assembling his team. Eight-year-old Victor and seven-year-old Dan said they were game. Calling themselves The Power Boys, a name shoplifted from *The Power Boys and the Haunted Skyscraper*, another mystery Justin had read, they awaited their first case.

Needing an accomplice, I called my friend, Dawn McCabe, whose husband is Masood Abolfazli. The Persian name seemed like an exotic choice for a first client. She agreed to use her spouse's name while posing as a client. She also agreed that her house could be used as a location for the yet-to-be-concocted mystery. I then forged the following letter to The Power Boys from Mrs. Abolfazli:

Power Boys Detective Agency

Dear Sirs,

I have been informed by Alfred Hitchcock, Jr. that you are members of a junior detective agency. I would appreciate it if you would consider taking my case.

The mystery began a week ago when my husband returned home early from work only to find the dining room window open and the screen torn. A ball of red yarn and some walnuts from a bowl on the table were missing as well as a suitcase and family album that had been in our bedroom. Nothing of great expense was taken. We were planning to use the suitcase, though, for an upcoming vacation to the Mediterranean island of Malta. The photo album was important to us as well, especially since we do not have negatives for all the pictures.

While we debated calling the police, the doorbell rang and I found both the album and the suitcase abandoned on the stoop. This seemed very strange. Stranger still was the receipt, the next day, of the two enclosed letters, which read, "A brush of paint makes the truth appear" and "Things are not always what they seem to be." I have no idea what to make of them.

If you decide to take the case, please call me at ********** and send written reports of your progress to ********.

Mrs. D. Abolfazli

When I showed her this letter, Claire cautioned that I was sailing in dangerous waters by weaving such a tangled web for the Boys.

"Trust me!" I chortled. "This is going to be lots of fun. And besides that, they'll be learning how to write reports, do research, and think analytically."

Without a smidge of hesitation, The Power Boys accepted the challenge. Together they considered the facts and examined the evidence at hand. Obviously, the Boys concluded, this was no ordinary thief or thieves. After scrutinizing the anonymous letters, Victor suggested that there might be a hidden message in them, but nothing revealed itself when he held the sheets up to the light. Dan despaired that any clues could be gleaned even by handwriting experts since the author used nondescript block letters. And then, when I worried that the puzzle I had left for them was too arduous, Justin saved the day by crowing, "There could be something here in invisible ink!"

"Yeah," said Dan, "I heard spies use lemon juice."

"Maybe the message 'A brush of paint makes the truth appear' tells us what do to," suggested Victor.

They dug up a set of watercolors and brushed black paint onto the first letter's surface. The following message, written in wax, leapt out: "DANGER! JOHN B. TRAVELS

WITH YOU." When the same coating was given to the other sheet, it proclaimed, "BEWARE THE LIMPING MAN!"

"Cripes!" Victor shouted.

"Mrs. Abolfazli's in danger!" Justin concluded.

"We've got to warn her!!" the Boys yelled in unison.

The game was indeed afoot.

After calling their client and writing up their first report, they made a plan to go the next day to the scene of the crime. I volunteered to act as chauffeur/chaperone but promised to leave all the sleuthing to them.

I had already begun thinking in terms of episodes I needed to plan, so that night I called my friend Mike Boover who agreed to take on the role of the limping man. I picked up a cloth suitcase at a thrift store and left it at Dawn's house along with some red yarn and walnut shells I scattered on the ground outside her window, leaving a trail to an oak tree. I shimmied up the trunk and deposited bits of yarn and shells. I scheduled a time when Dawn would be out of her house because Justin knew her by sight as my friend. Michael Boover, also familiar to Justin, promised to disguise himself.

About midday, The Power Boys, who had also decided to wear disguises as a precaution against tipping off any crooks who might already know their identities, rode up to the Abolfazli house.

It didn't take long for the Boys to deduce that the window screen had been torn by a thief to gain entrance so he or she could steal the suitcase and photo album. They still could not explain the return of said items. The Boys successfully traced the "theft" of the nuts and yarn to squirrels and eliminated that circumstance as unrelated to the real crime in question.

And then, as we headed back to the car, Dan pointed to a strange man half-hidden behind a tree a block away. In spite of the eighty-degree heat, he suspiciously wore a dark trench coat, black hat pulled down low, and dark glasses. A heavy brown beard further obscured his face. Any doubts about his identity, though, evaporated seconds later when he began moving towards us with a profound limp.

The Boys' eyes popped like those of rubber squeeze toys.

"Oh, my God! It's the limping man!" Dan cried.

"Run for it!" they shouted as one, nearly knocking me over in their rush to get in the car.

Meanwhile, the limping man hurried back to his own vehicle. Seeing this, Justin rightfully concluded, "He's onto us. We've got to lose him!"

Although their excitement was at a fever pitch, I couldn't resist the devilish temptation to pretend that our car wouldn't start. While the Boys frantically urged me to hurry, I checked the rear view mirror to be sure Michael was well under way before I peeled out. After all, what mystery is complete without an old-fashioned car chase? We turned left. He turned left. We turned right. He turned right. The Boys pleaded with me to go faster.

From the back seat, Victor exclaimed, "This is just like TV, only it's real!"

69

With my expert driving skills augmented by a pre-arranged decision that Michael would get left behind at a traffic light, we lost our pursuer.

In the aftermath, Justin, Dan, and Victor gathered on our front porch to write their report and keep a lookout for the limping man's car. They were very excited as well as more than a little scared.

Claire wagged her finger at me, challenging, "You made this mess. Now you have to clean it up!"

"Maybe she's right," I thought.

During the car chase, The Power Boys rode a tightrope, balanced between elation and coronaries. But I didn't want to call it quits. Their faces, concentrated on the case, had been indescribably full of life. They were not just little kids but detectives on a serious job. I could almost see them growing in stature right before my eyes. Besides, I too was enjoying the ride. The next episode would have to allay some of Claire's and the Boys' fears.

So, I typed another letter from Mrs. Abolfazli informing the Boys that she had received an anonymous phone call telling her that the limping man was named Stanley Fortuna. On such short notice, the first name that came to me was that of the wonderful musician who had been a novice with me in the Capuchin-Franciscans. In reality, Stanley neither limps nor steals suitcases.

At the next morning's meeting, I encouraged the Boys to consider all the clues.

"Isn't it strange," I suggested, "that the first two warnings were written in wax and now, Mrs. Abolfazli is getting unencoded warnings over the phone? What could this mean?"

With light prodding, the sleuths proposed that the wax had been used because the author needed to protect the message from prying eyes whereas now the informant was free to speak openly, even if he still chose to remain anonymous. They kicked around various circumstances that might fit these scenarios until settling on the likelihood that the first two letters had been written in jail, where mail is subject to scrutiny by the guards. If that were the case, then the author must have been released, or he would not have been able to call Mrs. Abolfazli directly.

The Boys agreed to test their hypothesis by calling the county jail. At their direction, I took down the phone book and read out the number, which Victor dialed.

A deep bass voice answered, "Worcester County Jail and House of Correction. Can I help you?" To achieve this stunt, I had to coerce a friend named Jim Briggley, better known as Briggs, to answer all calls to his phone that way. Unbeknownst to the Boys, the number I gave them belonged to Briggs.

"I'm with a junior detective agency called The Power Boys," Victor explained. "We were wondering if you would help us with an ongoing investigation."

"I've heard of you guys," Briggs replied. "What can I do for you?"

Cradling the phone against his sweater, Victor whispered with happy amazement, "He's heard of us!"

Uncovering the receiver, Victor asked if the jail had an inmate named Stanley Fortuna.

"Oh yeah, we had Stanley, but he's out now," Briggs answered.

"Can you tell us anything about him?" Victor asked.

"Sure. Stanley is a petty art thief and smuggler. He's been here many times."

After I prodded Victor to ask if Stanley was dangerous, Briggs laughed, "Oh no, he's a big chicken, afraid of his own shadow. He never carries a gun and runs at the first sign of any trouble. He's a powder puff. He's always boasting about the next big heist he's going to pull off when he gets out, but we don't take him seriously."

"Thanks a lot," Victor concluded.

"No problem," replied Briggs, and then, before hanging up, "Call us any time you Boys need help."

Justin, Dan, and Victor's faces told me that this ruse had flushed their anxieties right down the drain. Before I could bask in my ingenuity though, Justin suggested that we go over to Mrs. Abolfazli's to examine the suitcase and photo album. He had an idea but refused to disclose it until he could check those items out. This close-to-the-vest modus operandi was characteristic of Jupiter Jones, the chubby leader of Hitchcock's Three Investigators. I was astonished to see the Boys not only tackling the case but picking up eccentricities of other well-known gumshoes as well. I would not have been surprised if one of them turned up with a deerstalker cap, magnifying glass, and Meerschaum pipe.

Once I verified that Dawn was out for the day, we drove to her house and found the stolen/returned objects. Justin noticed that a photo appeared to be missing from the album. The Boys concluded that the blank space in the middle of a series of close-ups of Dawn and Masood made it highly likely that the stolen photo was also a portrait. The suitcase proved even more interesting. On the surface, nothing seemed awry, but a close examination revealed that the lining of one interior wall was of a slightly lighter shade than the other.

Justin felt around the edges and then dramatically peeled back a secret panel held in place with Velcro, a good effect, easily arranged beforehand.

"It's all beginning to make sense to me now," he purred. I told Claire that reading all those mystery novels would come in handy someday.

With Justin at the helm, the Boys brainstormed. To my delight, they concluded that Stanley Fortuna planned to steal a painting and needed someone to help him smuggle the artwork out of the country. After learning somehow that the Abolfazlis anticipated going to Malta, he broke into their house to borrow the photo album and suitcase. He added the hidden compartment to the luggage and removed a photo of the couple from the album. He sent the picture to an accomplice in Malta who would otherwise have difficulty identifying the Abolfazlis. Apparently, Stanley thought he could extract and return the items before Dawn or Masood discovered them missing. Failing this and hoping they would not be scrutinized, he abandoned them on the doorstep.

"So much for what's already happened," I said. "But what now?"

"My guess is that Stanley hasn't stolen the painting yet," Justin smiled. "Otherwise he would already have placed it in the suitcase. But, once he's snatched it, I'll lay money that he'll try to sneak it into the Abolfazli's suitcase."

"Without even knowing it," Dan mused, "our client will be smuggling art out of the country."

"Yeah," said Victor, "and Stanley's accomplice in Malta will simply steal it from the Abolfazli's hotel room."

"They might have gotten away with it, too," said Dan, "except for those letters in invisible ink."

"That's right," Victor concluded. "Those letters must have been written by a cellmate of Stanley's who was trying to warn the Abolfazlis. He had to hide his message not only from the guards, but also from Stanley."

"Which leads us to our last clue," triumphed Justin, brandishing one of the wax letters. "'John B. travels with you!' must be a reference to the identity of the painting Stanley means to steal. If we find it first, we can trap the crook."

By unanimous assent, the boys planned an expedition for that afternoon to the Worcester Art Museum. Although Justin had visited many times, neither Victor nor Dan had been before. The Boys started their search on the second floor, where they carefully examined every painting. Dan took notes on any likely candidates for the moniker "John B." They scrutinized works by Monet, Pissarro, Renoir, Whistler, El Greco, Goya, and, one of my particular favorites, a masterpiece by Rembrandt of Saint Bartholomew contemplating the instrument of his martyrdom. I was pleased to see them dwell on each piece, often commenting on the subject and technique. I made a mental note to tell Claire how I had managed to convince the Boys, who would otherwise be watching TV or playing basketball, to spend hours looking at art.

I also contrived our search to culminate in a gallery where a painting by Andrea del Sarto had just been added to the museum's collection. Amazingly, this work was discovered hidden away in someone's attic. No one guessed its value. Thankfully, it was donated to the Worcester Art Museum and not sold at a yard sale.

After gazing at del Sarto's brilliant use of color, Dan spied the inscription below and then cried, "John the Baptist! This must be it!"

"You're right," concurred Justin. "It's the same size as the Abolfazli's suitcase."

At that very moment (a product of excellent planning, if I do say so myself), Stanley Fortuna appeared in the gallery's doorway.

With no fear of the criminal whatsoever, Justin commanded, "Get him, men!"

They raced across the marble floors, down stairs, and past the Roman mosaic in the main entry's great hall. As fast as his limping form would allow, Stanley (a.k.a. Michael) headed for his car. Although we did not catch him on foot, we were soon in hot pursuit by auto. This car chase appealed much more to the Boys than our first.

"Get his license plate number!" Justin told Dan, who dutifully entered it into his notebook.

Stanley, meanwhile, shot through a yellow light, and I braked hard.

"Sorry, Boys," I apologized, as Stanley got clean away. "Good detectives obey traffic laws."

"Not to worry," Justin soothed. "We've got his plate number. His goose is cooked."

And so it was.

The Power Boys wrote complete descriptions of the case for the chief of police, museum director, and Mrs. Abolfazli. I "mailed" all three letters before proceeding to devise a closing chapter.

Ruth Cook, a friend who worked at the museum, agreed to present the Boys with certificates of award in the gallery where the del Sarto painting still hangs. I made up the certificates and apprised Ruth of what to say. She proved an excellent accomplice.

In their finest attire, The Power Boys stood at attention as Ruth said formally, "On behalf of the Worcester Art Museum and all those who believe that great art should remain available to the public, I would like to present each member of your detective agency with these small tokens of appreciation. Because of your diligence, the theft of a great work of art has been prevented and the would-be thief sent to jail. We hope that each of you will visit the art museum often in the future."

Dawn McCabe (a.k.a. Mrs. Abolfazli) also contributed to the wrap-up by sending Justin, Victor, and Dan a postcard of thanks from Malta, where she really did vacation with her husband. I added my own twist by having business cards printed that read: "The Power Boys - Junior Detectives • We cracked the case of the limping man!" The card featured a drawing of Stanley in his hat, beard, and glasses as well as a phone number to contact the Boys for future cases.

Saint John the Baptist
Andrea del Sarto • oil on panel c. 1517

It could have all ended there, but Justin did not wait long to start pining for a new case. How could I let him down? Besides, aren't all parents supposed to live out their own fantasies vicariously through their children?

Apparently not. Dan's mother put the kibosh on his participation in any future detecting. The exploits of The Power Boys registered a nine out of ten on her worry scale.

Undeterred by Dan's departure, Victor and Justin recruited a new member named Kate. Since a coed detective agency couldn't very well be called "The Power Boys," they agreed upon a new name: "The Thrilling Three." I promised to make them new business cards when they solved a case together. As it turned out, it did not take very long.

Their first adventure came to be called The Mystery of the Cursed Ring. While the educational subtext of the initial adventure was art appreciation, this one qualified as making history come alive. It began in late September a month or so after putting away the Limping Man. I recruited a new accomplice, Luisa Heffernan. Using the pseudonym Mrs. Upham, Luisa approached The Thrilling Three for their help. They agreed straight away to take her case, the details of which she promised to reveal at a meeting that evening at her home.

It was a dark and stormy night, literally, when we pulled up to a colonial mansion on Worcester's tree-lined Massachusetts Avenue. The house actually belonged to Luisa's parents, but she insisted we meet there for a spookier ambiance. Little did I know how deeply she planned to immerse herself in the role I had concocted.

Kate, Justin, and Victor walked onto the unlit porch and rang an old-fashioned bell. Mrs. Upham came to the door wearing a long black gown with a cameo broach adorning her collar. She had pinned her hair up in a spinster's bun atop her ramrod-straight back. The only light in the house flickered from a candelabrum she carried.

"The Thrilling Three, I presume," she said with puritanical severity as she simultaneously gestured for us to enter the pitch-black hall behind her.

Once the door closed heavily behind us and she triple bolted it, Mrs. Upham said, "I apologize for the dimness, but our power is out. Tempestuous nights like this seem to prefer the darkness."

Victor gave his partners a look that seemed to say, "If she takes us any deeper into spooky-town, I'm outta here."

But no one backed out, and moments later, we all sat at a long, highly polished wooden table. After putting down the candelabrum, Mrs. Upham excused herself. There wasn't a sound to be heard save the howling of wind outside and the morbid ticking of a grandfather clock inside. Luisa let the Gothic atmosphere sink in a bit before she returned to explain her quandary.

"My family has lived on or near this location since 1673," Mrs. Upham began. "As you might expect, this house holds many secrets. One of them came to light under a floorboard in the attic last night."

With a grand flourish, she produced a piece of yellow parchment with ornate writing in faint black ink. The paper was actually cut from the margin of a Declaration of

Independence facsimile. I had inscribed it's 332-year-old message less than two hundred minutes earlier. She placed the document on the table in front of her and gazed at it as if it were a vile thing. Then she dabbed her eyes with a lace handkerchief and sobbed, "Read it for yourselves!"

Apparently fearing it would crumble in her hands or burst into supernatural flames, Kate very cautiously slid the parchment closer to the candles, and read:

> Grievous sin be upon the breast of the Uphams from this generation onward until the cursed ring be recovered and penance accomplished. All Quinsigamond is shamed by the foul deed on Wigwam Hill. These praying cousins were no kin of the dread Philip. Ye shall find the proof five paces south of the praying rock. May the God of Justice have mercy on thy souls.
>
> *Reverend Gookin*

As Kate shakily pushed the parchment away, Mrs. Upham cried, "Our family has had its share of misfortunes over these many years. Maybe this curse has been the cause. Please, I beg of you, discover its meaning and lift the pall that hangs over us."

Although lesser mortals might not have, Kate, Justin, and Victor took the case. It involved numerous trips to the Worcester Historical Society and Clark University library.

Some possibilities were easily unraveled. Their research taught them that Indians gave the name Quinsigamond to the first English settlement in Worcester. Gookin was an extraordinary Puritan missionary who not only had visited but often lived with the native peoples. Settlers called an Indian village that Gookin frequented Wigwam Hill. It also wasn't hard for The Thrilling Three to learn that a native named King Philip led a rebellion against the colonists in 1675. Although Philip managed a number of daring raids, the English made sure that the natives paid fourfold for every white death. Indian converts to Christianity, though, refused to join Philip's uprising because of their conviction that their new faith called them to be peaceful. These praying Indians, as they were called, surrendered themselves and their families to the mercy of Puritan leaders in Boston. In gratitude for their not joining Philip, the Puritans herded the defenseless refugees into a kind of concentration camp on Deer Island, where most either froze or starved to death. It was a grim chapter in a long chronicle of Native American suffering at the hands of white settlers.

Armed with their detailed research, The Thrilling Three sought out a historical marker for Wigwam Hill. They assumed that an Upham or those under his command had attacked the place Gookin referred to in the parchment. Historical records showed a Captain Upham active in King Philip's War. After discovering the monument adjacent to a patch of woods, the children planned an expedition to locate the praying rock.

With a camera, compass, and two shovels, the junior detectives plunged into the woods. It didn't take them long to find a large flat boulder where Victor posed in a kneeling position. Kate counted five paces to the south where they began digging. To my relief, none of them commented on how loose the soil was.

Justin and Victor on the trail of The Cursed Ring

"Go easy!" Kate shouted, "I think we've found something."

Justin carefully removed a wooden box from the hole, brushed away the dirt, and placed it on the leaf-strewn ground. He opened it to reveal a silver ring lying on a bed of cinders. Another piece of parchment stuck to the lid of the box. It read:

The Upham ring lieth here on the ashes of my congregation's village, where the captain dropped it. Too late, I arrived to stop the massacre, but I pray that thou wilt now lead the Uphams to repentance. Thy humble servant,

Reverend Gookin

"Let's take this to Mrs. Upham," Kate said.

But before they could gather up the tools, The Three noticed two Worcester police officers approaching them through the brush.

"What's going on here?" one of the cops asked sternly.

Completely unruffled, Justin said, "It's okay, officers. We're The Thrilling Three wrapping up a case. The chief knows all about us."

"Good grief!" I thought, "This is the end of the road for sure."

"We got a call from a neighbor who reported seeing a man carrying a shovel walk into the woods with three children," the second policeman said to me.

"Didn't you ever look for buried treasure when you were young?" I asked, hoping to get away with revealing only a fraction of the truth.

As it turned out, my explanation was unnecessary. The Three had proceeded in businesslike fashion to pack up and walk toward our car.

Kate, who carried the box, said to the policemen, "If you'll excuse us, officers. We have to get this evidence to our client."

Dumbfounded but more or less reassured that whatever had been going on wasn't criminal, the police followed us to the street in silence. I breathed a sigh of relief when they drove off.

The case concluded later that day when Mrs. Upham told The Three that their revelation would inspire all surviving Uphams to reach out to Native Americans in Worcester County and beyond. To show her gratitude, she gave them gift certificates to Angela's Italian restaurant.

At Angela's the next day, a waiter approached the table with a bottle of sparkling cider and said, "Compliments of the management for The Thrilling Three." (Easily arranged in advance.) A hearty, satisfying toast followed. As their glasses clinked, Victor proclaimed, "To another case closed!"

As a peculiar side note to this mystery, the silver ring found by The Three actually does have a kind of curse on it. It belonged to my friend Chris's former girlfriend, who gave it to Chris in a vain attempt to lure him away from the woman he eventually married. Rather than mislead his old sweetheart, Chris gave the ring in turn to me along with other bribes, like a bottle of champagne and a bouquet of flowers. I gave the booty to my wife, Claire, save the ring, which ended as you now know. I was kind of disappointed when Chris's former girlfriend finally gave up.

Although the run-in with Worcester police officers made me nervous, I was not about to quit my side job as scriptwriter for The Thrilling Three. Since Halloween had just passed, I reasoned, "Why not a ghost story?" And so, The Case of the Phony Ghost got under way.

As always, I easily procured a co-conspirator. A friend named Henry Ritter readily agreed to act as the new client. After I spelled out broad outlines of the mystery, Henry called The Three to beg their assistance with a supernatural problem. They set a meeting for the next afternoon.

Kate, Victor, Justin, and I pulled up to Mr. Ritter's Elm Street address, a six-story apartment building with an ornate front like a Venetian palazzo. After marveling about this striking architectural feature, we entered the small front lobby where Justin pressed the appropriate buzzer.

"Yesss?" asked a disembodied voice.

"The Thrilling Three to see Mr. Ritter," Justin nervously replied to the wall of buttons.

"You may proceed," the voice intoned as a door clicked open.

I could tell that the kids were a little spooked as we climbed the stairs to the second floor apartment, but nothing prepared them or me for how Henry set the stage.

Kate knocked on Henry's door, and almost immediately an African American man peered out from a crack in the door held by a gold burglar chain. Strange music filtered through the crack. The man removed a pair of sunglasses, looked us over with suspicion, and then, apparently satisfied, unlocked the chain and opened the door just wide enough for us to squeeze through. He closed and double locked the door so hastily that he almost caught my arm in it. We could now see that he was clad in black from head to toe and once again wearing dark glasses. Background music played the theme from the Jamie Lee Curtis movie, *Halloween*. Like Luisa Heffernan, Michael Boover, and Dawn McCabe before him, Henry went over the top for his role in the mystery.

"Please excuse the dark glasses," he opened, "but I've been a little nervous about being recognized since my troubles began."

Taking out his pad, paper, and pencil, Victor asked, "And just what are these 'troubles,' sir?"

"Come this way, and I'll show you," he said, leading us to a telephone on his bedside table. "I've been getting strange phone calls from someone claiming to be my Uncle Mark, who used to live here with me."

"What's so strange about that?" asked Kate.

"My uncle died five weeks ago. He was killed in a car accident."

After a moment of stunned silence, all three investigators asked overlapping questions: "Does this caller say he's your uncle?" "Does his voice sound like your uncle's?" "What does he say?"

Henry raised a hand to stop them.

"You can hear it yourselves," he said, as he rewound his answering machine. "I captured one of the calls on tape."

When Henry pushed "play," a slow, wavering voice implored, "Hennnry. Hennnnreee! There is danger for you on Elm Street. Go away from that apartment. I beg yooooou! When it is safe for you to return, I will reach out to you from beyond the grave. If you doubt me, come to the woods behind Fairlawn on Wednesday night, where I will show myself to you. I will not rest until you are safely away from Elm Street. You must beeeeware!"

A pitiful moaning topped it all off.

Once again, I was impressed by the way the children did not chicken out. Justin asked "Mr. Ritter" to play the tape again so they could listen closely for clues. Victor claimed that he could hear the faint sound of traffic in the background, proving that the caller was very much in the smoggy land of the living. Kate tried to console Henry by stating emphatically, "There is no such thing as a ghost."

"What should I do then?" Henry despaired. "These calls keep coming, and they upset me terribly. I'm at my wit's end. Maybe I should just move out like he says."

"No," Justin replied, "don't do that, at least not yet. The ghost says he wants a meeting. The Thrilling Three will meet him. We'll teach this phony ghost a lesson and find out what he's really up to."

Bravo, Justin. Way to lead the team!

And so it was decided that Kate, Victor, and Justin, with me in reserve, would "stake out" the woods behind Fairlawn Hospital on Wednesday night. Clad in rain gear and carrying flashlights and a camera, we split ourselves into two groups on opposite sides of the only path through the trees. It had rained quite a bit earlier and still threatened to do so again, leaving us without benefit of the moon or stars for light. My partner Victor insisted that we crouch painfully low to the ground while we waited.

No more than thirty minutes into our vigil, although it seemed like thirty hours to my aching knees, we heard a moaning sound wafting out of the darkness farther down the trail. Eventually, we could just make out a white figure drifting towards us. A friend named Martin Andes took the spectral role and seemed to relish it every bit as much as all the other adults who helped make the mysteries credible.

When the ghost was no more than twenty-five feet away, The Three simultaneously jumped out of the undergrowth, turned on their flashlights, and shouted, in the deepest voices they could muster, "Hold it right there!"

In a very unghostly tone, Martin cried, "Yikes! Cops!"

At this point, my script called for Martin to turn and run, as the Three captured sufficient evidence on film to prove he was a fake. They had agreed not to chase him. Justin knew Martin quite well, so it was essential that my friend escape without giving away his identity. Unfortunately, the ghost slipped in the mud and fell flat on his face. As the children sprang towards him, Martin, muddy, soaked, and tangled up in a sheet

Justin and Kate react to Scott wearing the "ghost's" abandoned sheet

that he left behind, cursed while desperately struggling to crawl away. Amazed at how lustily they had taken off in pursuit, I figured they would catch him. But Martin dug down deep inside to tap that last ounce of energy necessary for him to reach safety. A very close call indeed!

I was exhausted, but The Thrilling Three hardly wanted to quit for the night. They located a clear footprint in the moist ground and made an excellent plaster cast using materials in their supply kit. While waiting for it to set, they took several pictures of me wearing the ghost's mud-stained sheet. Kate also discovered a small notebook near the spot where the suspect had fallen. This proved to be the best clue of all.

The notebook, a journal, revealed how its owner had become familiar with Henry's Uncle Mark, who apparently had no faith in banks. The uncle planned to write a will leaving his fortune to Henry along with instructions as to where to find the cash hidden in the apartment. Unfortunately, Mark suffered an untimely death, providing a window of opportunity for the thief. Getting Henry out of the apartment for a few days would buy sufficient time for the ghost to find the cash and spirit it away. For an unexplained reason, the would-be crook noted the absolutely crucial necessity that he remove the money before the weather turned bitter cold.

Despite the late hour, The Three insisted on calling Mr. Ritter to apprise him of the night's events. Afterwards, he agreed that they ought to conduct a thorough search of the apartment the next day.

At ten sharp, Justin, Kate, and Victor reported for duty. They searched all the heating vents first, since those locations would provide perilous hiding places during the heating season. Afterwards, they turned their attention to the fireplace. Henry told them that he never used it before Thanksgiving, only two weeks away. The information jibed with the crook's sense of urgency.

The Three approached the dark opening in silent anticipation. Kate flashed a light up the chimney and exclaimed, "There's something up there all right!"

She reached inside and pulled down a paper bag and carried it over to a glass-topped coffee table. She opened the bag, turned it over, and poured out dozens of wads of dollar bills.

"Money!" said Kate.

"A lot of money!" added Victor.

In fact, it was five thousand dollars. Quite a few friends had emptied their bank accounts for the day so I could hide their money up Henry's chimney.

The sight of Justin, Kate, and Victor posing for photos with the money was unforgettable. Just like them, I had never seen so much cash.

With a huge smile of gratitude, Henry said, "I cannot thank you enough. If it weren't for you, I would have lost my inheritance to that crook. I might even have burned it up. Let me give each of you a small reward." He gave them each ten dollars.

Victor, Kate, and Justin display some of the cash they discovered

As they exited Mr. Ritter's building, the junior detectives smiled and gave each other high-fives to mark another mystery successfully cleared up.

By now, you can well imagine that the private eye adventures required significant planning, time, and sometimes money. These factors contributed to my taking a four-month hiatus from ghostwriting until their incessant complaints wore me down. "When will we get another case? Why are clients not calling us?" they lamented. The latest mystery came to be called The Case of the Spider Web Gang.

By now I was practically a professional forger. In no time at all, I concocted a letter to The Thrilling Three from Worcester's Chief of Police. It described how a notorious group of jewel thieves called The Spider Web Gang had been smuggling stolen gems out of the country. Numerous undercover detectives had followed them to discover their secret drop-off point, but, each time, the crafty criminals managed to give them the slip. Perhaps The Thrilling Three would be more successful because they were children.

"After all, what thief would expect a group of kids to be working for the police?" the chief asked.

"You don't need to catch them either," he went on. "We just need to know where they leave the bag of jewels. Follow them anywhere they go. Don't worry about expenses. The police department will reimburse you."

The chief closed by telling the young sleuths where and when they could expect to begin following the crooks. His only advice on how they should identify the gangsters was to say, "They will be kind of shifty looking."

As always, I had no trouble finding actors to fill the necessary parts. A school teacher friend named Brian Keeney volunteered to lead the Spider Web Gang. Brian took down the details and assured me that he'd bring along a credible partner.

The chase was set to begin behind Worcester's City Hall. Forgoing disguises, The Thrilling Three milled around nonchalantly making a conscious effort to act like kids as they kept their eyes out for two characters fitting their profile of jewel thieves. At exactly noon, Victor spotted a short and slender fellow alongside a heavily bearded, tall, stout man cradling a briefcase under his arm. Their black hats, suit jackets, ties, and sunglasses made them look for all the world like The Blues Brothers.

"That's got to be them," Justin said.

For the next twenty minutes, Kate and Justin alternated between strolling innocuously behind the thieves and hiding in doorways where they documented the chase by sneaking photographs. Victor was less eager.

Staying well back from his comrades, Victor told me, "I'm a little bit scared, but I'm still gonna get 'em."

After noticing how the two suspects lingered now and then, Kate concluded, "They're waiting for us. They're nice crooks."

Moments later, when Justin and Kate sauntered out into the open, I asked Victor, "Vic, don't you think you should cover their backs?"

"Well . . . ," he said, reluctantly nodding his assent, "but not because I want to."

Except for the cat-and-mouse routine, the case didn't seem very eventful until our prey suddenly jumped into a waiting cab. They had been instructed to do so only if another taxi was available behind theirs. Without a moment's hesitation, The Three and I jumped into a second cab.

As I had hoped, Victor instructed the driver, "Follow that car!"

Justin handed the cabbie one of their new business cards explaining, "We're on a case for the Worcester police."

Since the driver was a complete stranger, I wasn't sure how he'd react. I held my breath for a second and then, to my delight, he nodded and said, "No problemo. Hold on tight!"

By then, the other taxi was almost out of sight. We shot after it so quickly that I was thrown back against the seat. We weaved in and out of traffic at horrendous speed. Just as we started catching up, the lead cab squeaked through a yellow traffic light. Rather than stop, our lunatic driver cried, "Hold on!" He laid on his horn and shot through the red light. Hardened by previous car chases, the children took this in stride, whereas it was white-knuckles time for me. Thanks to whatever guardian angels protect junior detectives, we made it safely through that busy intersection as well as another red and two "pink" lights.

Once we were less than thirty yards behind our prey, Justin concluded, "They're heading for the airport!"

"What are we going to do if they fly somewhere?" wondered Kate.

"The chief said to follow them no matter where they go," I reminded her as we pulled up to Worcester Regional Airport, "Remember it's on the police department's tab."

The Spider Web Gang emerged from their taxi, glanced this way and that, and then dashed into the terminal. After paying Dale Earnhardt Jr. for breaking the inner-city speed record, I too raced inside on the heels of the fearless trio.

The crooks stood in line for tickets on the American Airlines shuttle to Newark. Fully anticipating being airborne soon, Kate, Victor, and Justin also joined the line, several patrons separating them from their quarry.

Victor then uttered words that have probably never been said with so much enthusiasm, "We're going to New Jersey!"

But alas, this was not to be. Just as their turn came at the counter, the duplicitous duo fled the line and hurried outside to another waiting cab. Before long, we were once again sailing over speed bumps and ignoring all manner of traffic laws in our pursuit.

While we sped along, Kate confessed, "For a while there, I was afraid we were going to Hawaii with no suitcases or anything."

We circled through downtown Worcester for fifteen minutes without any sign of slowing, which prompted Justin to say, "Boy, this guy must have three gas tanks!"

Eventually, the Spiders came to a stop at the train station.

Since there were no trains at the platform, The Three took a moment to catch their breath. After gathering their wits, Justin asked the cabbie to park beside the building out of the thieves' view. Kate volunteered to go inside the station and eavesdrop. She returned momentarily saying, "They're asking about tickets to Boston."

But no. It was yet another ruse. Before Kate could finish her report, the crafty criminals jumped back into a cab and sped on their way again.

With some difficulty, we tracked the gang to the Greyhound bus terminal, where the elusive pair spent several minutes looking over their shoulders. Having apparently satisfied themselves that no police officers lurked, the crooks stowed their briefcase in a locker and, with expressions of smug self-satisfaction, walked away. The Thrilling Three made note of the locker number for their report to the police chief.

On the ride home, Kate confessed, "Before the case happens, I don't want anything to do with it, but, when it's over, I'm not afraid at all."

Minutes later, using a Smith Corona typewriter and lots of Wite-Out, Victor typed, "We have cracked the case of the Spider Web Gang." He characterized the criminals as "tricky" but made it clear that locker 466 was the long-sought-after drop-off point. By mutual agreement, Victor concluded, "We would like to meet you at the police station as soon as possible. Give us a call when you nab the crooks because we'd like to see the jewels and stuff."

Although I couldn't imagine where to get a convincing collection of gems, I did think an event at police headquarters was within reach. Consequently, I wrote a letter to Chief Edward Gardella, who arranged a meeting with Detective Sergeant Goddard. Like Watergate, The Thrilling Three conspiracy reached high levels of law enforcement. The children accepted junior detective badges and a tour of the station, including a visit to a row of empty cells. The Sergeant assured them that their investigation had led directly to the apprehension of The Spider Web Gang. Unfortunately, the jewels had been returned to the homes of the various billionaires from whom they were stolen.

For a while afterwards, I contemplated putting together an ambitious case set in Manhattan. Two friends who lived in New York City, Amy Moose and her husband Tim Nolan, had pleaded with me to find them roles, but I was too pooped and impoverished to make it happen. As the children became more involved in other activities, they asked less and less often why clients had not contacted them with another case. I finally resolved to be satisfied with what had already occurred.

A question lingered though: "Was The Thrilling Three a good idea?" Would the kids be psychologically scarred once it came out that I contrived the entire thing? Like Steve Martin in the movie *Parenthood*, I worried that Justin would one day become a sniper on top of a water tower shooting strangers and shouting, "This is for all the adults who lied to me!"

But was it a lie? Didn't Kate, Victor, and Justin really solve those cases? Weren't they genuinely clever and brave? I don't know if I would have had the guts when I was only seven to hide out in the woods at night waiting for a ghost. In a strange way, the entire affair was a great big role reversal. The children acted as adults, and the grown-ups shamelessly portrayed characters from their juvenile fantasies. As a witness to everyone's enthusiasm, I couldn't help but feel thrilled at the universal and completely innocent human capacity for adventure and fun.

And so, on January 4, 1999, I choked back my anxieties and admitted to Justin, by then a high school freshman, that I was the mastermind behind The Thrilling Three.

He was silent for a tense minute before he said, "It did seem a little weird that all that money was up a chimney." Then Justin smiled broadly and, to my everlasting relief, added, "You should do the same thing for Patrick!"

Case closed!

Kate, Justin, and Victor high-fiving after solving a case

Saints Francis & Thérèse Catholic Worker

"Isn't April Fool's Day a bit early for a cookout?" I wondered as I turned onto Preston Street.

Wait a minute. That's no cookout. Someone's house is on fire.

Holy guacamole! It's our house!!

Indeed, the Saints Francis & Thérèse Catholic Worker was only eight months old and already burning down.

Fire may be every CW house's destiny, but shouldn't we have had a waiver for at least the first few years?

Nothing doing. Flames engulfed the gray triple decker at the corner of Jaques Avenue and Preston Street before fire trucks arrived. By nightfall, it lit up the skyline and burned to a wreck by morning. In short order, we went from sheltering the homeless to being homeless ourselves.

Two years earlier as Claire and I moved out of Washington, DC, we would have told you that we were done with the Catholic Worker. Determined to continue as peacemakers, we planned to live in our own apartment on Castle Street in Worcester, Massachusetts. I even painted the living room floor bright yellow. That's not something anyone would do if he intended to offer hospitality.

Claire cleaned houses. I worked at a nursing home. We prepared for the birth of our first child. We went to Gilreins Pub to hear the blues and dance. We went to cheap movies. We vigiled weekly against nuclear weapons and did some civil disobedience as well. That's what got us off the *Ozzie and Harriet* track.

During a short jail sentence, I met a man named Kenny scheduled for release just before Christmas with nowhere to go. I called Claire, and we agreed to let him stay in our apartment when he got out. Hosting him reminded us both how much we missed that aspect of the Catholic Worker. So we put out feelers to see if any friends wanted to start a new CW community. Our best man and former coworker, Carl Siciliano, opted in as did a prayerful friend of his named Sarah Jeglosky. A neighbor named Dan Ethier also expressed interest. Dan had worked as a computer programmer at Data General in Westborough near where we vigiled against nuclear weapons. He eventually joined that vigil, left his job for human services, and moved to Worcester. He, Carl, Sarah, Claire, and I met for months to discern our CW vision.

Worcester already had the Mustard Seed Catholic Worker, but, since it was rebuilt after a fire, it operated only as a soup kitchen. We figured we could meet a different need by offering shelter. We also wanted to publish a newspaper, do peace work, sponsor speakers, and have communal prayer life. In July 1986, we moved into a five bedroom, first floor apartment we called Saints Francis & Thérèse Catholic Worker. We welcomed one, and then two, guests. We published the first issue of a paper we called *The Catholic Radical*. We expanded a cottage industry Claire and her friend Barbara Horn had begun called "The Bread Not Bombs Bakery." Although Carl left us to work in New York City (Worcester was just too small for him), we were off to a promising start.

founders of the Saints Francis & Thérèse Catholic Worker, from left, front:
Carl Siciliano, Sarah Jeglosky, and Dan Ethier; back, Claire Schaeffer-Duffy with Justin Duffy, and
Scott Schaeffer-Duffy

And then the house burned down—on April Fool's Day no less. We had five dollars in the bank. After a night in a hotel thanks to the Red Cross, we scattered all over the city staying with friends. Shortly thereafter, I was sent to jail for thirty days. When it rains . . . .

While I spent time in the slammer, Claire and our one-year-old Justin found refuge with the Little Franciscans of Mary. Claire put word out in *The Catholic Free Press* that we wanted to find a new house. Monsignor Edmund Tinsely suggested one on Mason Street, a two-family home with an unfinished basement and attic. Because of our Catholic Worker opposition to usury, we could not go to a bank for a loan and probably would not have qualified for one anyway. The house listed on the market for $115,000. The owners, greedy Gordon Gecko types, had bought the house a year earlier for $65,000. I used my jail time to fundraise. I wrote letters to national and local newspapers. I penned appeals to friends and strangers and even a few celebrities like Ron Darling, a pitcher for the New York Mets, and the actor Martin Sheen. Lo and behold, with hundreds of donations and an interest-free loan from a friend, we bought the house for $85,000. The greedy owners would not drop the price below $90,000, but the Realtor admired what we wanted to do so much that she gave up her commission. After we turned the deed over to a land trust, we did what renovations we could and began offering hospitality again.

drawing by Grace Duffy

Saints Francis and Thérèse Catholic Worker
52 Mason Street, Worcester, Massachusetts

Unlike in DC, we hosted both men and women in the same building but never more than eight and usually six at a time. We added a nine o'clock curfew and a no smoking rule but kept with the free spirit of Saint Benedict's in other regards. For example, we took the locks off the front door. We have never locked Saints Francis & Thérèse house since it opened in 1987.

We've hosted an enormous diversity of people—folks with substance abuse, mental health challenges, or a lack of documentation as well as ex-cons, refugees, new immigrants, victims of abuse, and those left homeless by fires. Many experienced homelessness for the first-time—folks laid off or fired. Others had slept on the street for years. Everyone gathered together at five each night for a communal dinner along with Claire, our growing family, an assortment of live-in volunteers, and me.

For six months, we welcomed three Central Americans, Angela and her four-year-old son, Leo, from Honduras along with Esmerelda from El Salvador. The lives of all three were at risk in their homelands. Angela and Leo fled a right-wing death squad whose members murdered her husband for his work as a labor organizer. Esmerelda escaped left-wing guerrillas who blew up a bomb at a Christmas party killing her military father, mother, and siblings. All three entered the country illegally, and US immigration detained them. A human rights lawyer secured their release pending action on requests for political asylum in the US and in Canada. Before either result could come to pass, Esmerelda ran away with the circus. No kidding. Barnum and Bailey performed in town, and she had once been a wire walker. Angela began receiving anonymous letters telling her, in the most formal and polite Spanish, to come home so she and Leo could be murdered. If they did not return, the shadowy thugs threatened to begin killing her cousins "one by one" until they did. This so infuriated Quaker friends of ours that they went to Honduras, rounded up Angela's extended family, and got them safely to Canada, where Angela and Leo ultimately found sanctuary.

Angela on the day she and her son Leo flew to Canada for asylum

We had a gracious and very appreciative guest, Ali from Iran, who once insisted on making an elaborate Persian meal for everyone. This older man told stories of the great wealth he had to leave behind after the Islamic revolution ousted the Shah.

When I asked Ali how he got to the US, he replied, "I came over with the Shah."

"Don't you mean 'at the same time as the Shah'?"

"No," he continued. "I was part of his entourage."

Remembering that the former dictator had come to the States for cancer treatment with only his closest family and staff, I asked, "Just what did you do for a living in Iran?"

"I was the head of an organization you've probably never heard of called SAVAK."

A chill ran through me. As a former member of Amnesty International, I knew SAVAK well. It was the Iranian Gestapo, a terrifyingly brutal secret police force, described by *Time* magazine as Iran's "most hated and feared institution" prior to the revolution of 1979 because of its practice of torturing and executing opponents of the Pahlavi regime.

But we knew this modern Himmler as a kindly old man in need of shelter. Where else but at the Catholic Worker could you experience such contradictions?

One night, I got a phone call from a man at New York City's Port Authority bus station looking for a temporary place to stay. I asked him why he would call us in Worcester instead of seeking help in the Lower East Side at Saint Joseph's Catholic Worker. He explained that he had been staying there but had worn out his welcome and started calling other CW houses, one at a time, in an ever-widening circle. If we couldn't help, he planned to call Boston's Haley House next and then Philadelphia and Pittsburgh and so on.

All of our beds were full, but one of our guests worked third shift. His bed was empty every night. If we changed the sheets each day, we could host the New York guy, at least for a little while, so I said he could come.

An hour later, Tom Cornell called from the Catholic Worker Farm in Marlboro, New York, to warn us not to welcome the man because he was a volatile white supremacist.

"You're too late, Tom," I told him. "He's already on his way. And, get this, he'll be sharing a bed with a black man."

And so it went. During his short stay, we juggled things in such a way that neither man ever saw the other.

Although I do see many movies, I hardly ever see television shows, but I did see an episode of *LA Law* that included a person with Tourette Syndrome. The condition renders its sufferers incapable of controlling verbal outbursts. I had never heard of it and suspected that the television show sensationalized the disease for dramatic/comedic effect.

But in a case of uncanny synchronicity (I say "hippopotamus," and I see one), we promptly acquired not one but two guests with Tourette's. What are the odds of that? The first man's symptoms were relatively mild: brief, wordless exclamations and physical tics, but the disease overwhelmed the second guy to such an extent that he apologized for it immediately upon his arrival. He suggested we situate him in an as out-of-the-way place as we could manage. Despite his request, he seemed like someone hurting for normal human contact.

"We're very happy to have you," I said to him.

"Thank you," he replied softly and then shouted, "YOU FUCKING LIAR!"

After shaking off the outburst, I introduced him to my coworker, Dave Maciewski, the most sincere person I have ever known.

"This is Dave. If you have any questions, he'll be able to answer them."

"Great," he replied before turning his head to the side and blurting out, "PRETENTIOUS BASTARD!"

It reminded me of the scene in *Annie Hall* with subtitles for Woody Allen and Diane Keaton's conversation for the audience to translate it more honestly.

In 1989, we had a guest named Betty who bathed only three times during her yearlong stay. She liked to keep the window open in her room at night long after the heating season began. I repeatedly asked her not to do it. She ignored me. I nailed her window shut, and she pried it open.

I finally appealed to her with a calendar in hand, "Betty, it's long past summer. Please keep the window closed at night."

"Whoever told you fall begins in September," she retorted, "was a nut!"

When I tried to show her the calendar, she rushed out the door. I didn't catch up with her until we were three blocks away.

"Betty," I pleaded. "Look at the calendar. You're acting crazy."

Pointing to my stocking feet she said, "You're running down the street without shoes and calling me crazy."

A guest named Steve who had stayed with us many times before came into the house one night and got into the attic bed he used to use only to discover that it was now Dave's bed. Since Steve was drunk and we had no other bed for him, I offered to drive him to a friend's house.

Along the way, Steve told me, "Dave, Claire, and you are good people. You help people. Didn't you go somewhere?"

"Yes, Steve," I replied, "I just came back from Bosnia."

"That's what I'm talking about," he continued with alcohol-induced sincerity, "You are good people, and I'm not going to forget you. Others might take your help and forget you, but not me. I'll never forget you, Dennis."

Often, our guests say the darnedest things. On a night when we served pasta stuffed with ricotta cheese, Ray said, "Could I have more chicken? That was delicious. No bones or anything."

When I asked Kenny if he wanted to join us for dinner, he replied, "No thanks, I'm incognito today."

Ron, who described himself as "a homeless inventor who is not Catholic or a worker," told us, "*The Three Stooges* used to use Albert Einstein as a consultant for their shows." At another time, he said, "I told Joey he couldn't stay anymore because he didn't go through the prescribed hassles."

John said, "Priests and sisters are one hundred percent to Jesus. I'm only thirty percent to Jesus, but you folks are seventy percent to Jesus."

A different John instructed us, "Tell my parents not to call me (at Saint Vincent psych ward) until October 10. October 9 is John Lennon's birthday, and I need some quality TV time."

Herman announced at dinner, "This was the first vegetarian meal I've ever had, and it wasn't half as terrible as I'd expected."

Freddie confessed to our coworker Mike Benedetti, "When I first came here, and you answered the door, I was scared because you look like Jeffrey Dahmer the serial killer."

Andrew said, "Scott's sick. He needs help. That's why so many people help him."

Sam claimed, "I shot rats as large as cows in my basement where I was growing marijuana. A plague of leeches grew on the carcasses, which the police exterminated with a horde of locusts. That's the standard thing."

After a rant against Buddhists, gays, and all non-Catholics, Angelina looked at the stunned faces around the table, turned up her hands, smiled, and said, "I'm just an Italian woman. What can I say? That's amore!"

Bruce Russell stayed with us briefly in the early 1990s and has come to dinner most Sundays since. He is a colorful rock n' roll guitarist and horror movie fan who calls himself The Snow Ghost of *Scooby Doo* fame. For years, he'd greet everyone with the question, "What's the first thing you know?" to which you were supposed to reply, "Old Jed's a millionaire" (a line from the theme song of the television program *The Beverly Hillbillies*). In 2008, alongside our coworker Mike Benedetti, Bruce hosted a cable access television show. I appeared as a guest in an episode on *The Three Stooges* and another on the relevance of nonviolence during a zombie apocalypse. I treated the interviews as a lark, but was surprised to see them appear for years as the top listing when someone Googled my name.

Claire and our children add their voices to the mix as well.

the Schaeffer-Duffy family in 1997:
clockwise from left, Aiden with Scott,
Grace, Claire, Justin, and Patrick

photo by Patrick O'Connor for Worcester Magazine

When we went to the Easter Vigil Mass at our local parish, four-year-old Patrick asked me what was happening during the baptisms. I told him, "These people are becoming Christians. They go under the water as a sign of dying with Christ." I was going to add, "And they come out of the water as a sign of sharing his resurrection," but before I could say this, Patrick looked up at the church's large crucifix and said, "Thank God, I'm not a Christian." Years later, Patrick would emerge from his first confession and proclaim, "Wow, that was even better than Christmas!" He's nothing if not emphatic.

Four-year-old Grace offered this prayer, "Hail Mary, mother of Grace, pray for our sinners and that flowers will grow in Africa. Amen." When asked how often she had to practice music, Grace replied, "Two months a week." She also said, "My grandma and grandpa live in Virginia, and they speak the same language as us."

When Patrick was seven, he asked Claire, "Can I give you a hug, Mom?"

"Sure," she replied. Afterwards she asked, "What was that for?"

He shrugged, "I had nothing else to do."

After seeing a letter carrier, he asked me in all seriousness, "Dad, when you grow up, would you like to be a mailman?"

In the tub one night, he asked Claire, "Can you still go to college if you skip the third grade?"

Four-year-old Aiden said, "Let's play chess, Dad. We can be on the same team. We can both win the game. We can make that rule. There'll be no checks." Later that year he said, "I got a million, jillion, pillion candies for Halloween last year. This year I'm going to get infinity. That's a wicked lot."

Sometimes Claire and I wondered if the Catholic Worker environment would be too chaotic for our children, but I was reassured when Justin at five years old said, "I learned not to take myself too seriously from Yogi Bear."

Ultimately, children help us keep our feet on the ground. One day, as eight-year-old Patrick and I left the YMCA, a clerk said to me, "You're doing really good work. Keep it up."

"Thanks," I replied.

Patrick, who had lived his entire life at the Catholic Worker, turned to me and said, "Good work? What the heck was he talking about?"

Have we ever had a scare vis-a-vis hosting strangers alongside our children? Thankfully, only once. A young guest came into the first-floor kitchen one night with two slightly older men we assumed were his friends. While our guest used the bathroom, I chatted with one of the strangers, a rather friendly black man. The other fellow seemed impatient and irritated. Before long, this guy pushed by me, strode up to the bathroom door, and began hammering on it with his fists. Justin and Grace slept in the front room not fifteen feet away. I was concerned he'd wake them and also that he'd break down the rather flimsy door. Then, our guest started pleading with us to protect him from the men to whom he apparently owed fifty dollars.

Claire, Dan Ethier, Paul Giaimo, our friend Patrick Kiritsy, and I insisted that this matter could not be settled in our house and that we would not tolerate any violence.

The black man left with an apology for the disturbance, but the angry dude didn't leave before poking me, Claire, Dan, and Paul in the chest. When he came to Patrick, who is very much not a pacifist, Patrick glared at him and warned, "Me, you do not want to mess with."

I was a bit embarrassed that I had not been as macho as Patrick, so I followed the man out the front door and scolded, "Don't you dare ever threaten anyone in this house again!"

This caused him to turn around and say, "I'll be back later to burn your house down." So much for my having the last word.

Visions of a Molotov cocktail smashing through a front window into Justin and Grace's bedroom prompted Claire to move them permanently to safer quarters in the back while Dan, Paul, Patrick, and I stood watch on the front porch all night long. Nothing ever came of the threat, but I did learn that a prideful desire to have the last word only escalates violence.

At this writing, all our children are doing very well, thank God. Aiden is preparing for a semester abroad at the Siena Art Institute for his junior year at Holy Cross. Grace got her masters at Clark University and works at the Regional Environmental Council. She is happily married to the irrepressible Anthony Sliwoski. Patrick graduated from Harvard, became a teacher, and is engaged to marry his charming classmate Jun Shepard. Justin, who earned a BA at Wesleyan and a masters at Pace, is in Egypt for three weeks helping establish some of the finest science and technology schools for girls in that country, where he and his adventurous wife, Patricia Kirkpatrick, lived for a year, and where our lovely granddaughter Scotti May was born.

Sometimes at the Catholic Worker, the meaning of events is cloaked in mystery only to be revealed later on. For example, at Christmas 1992, Ephraim Perez came by and left on his bicycle balancing two pieces of apple pie on the handlebars. He returned the pieces of pie uneaten two hours later without explanation. On February 10, Ephraim reappeared to say, "I hope you aren't mad at me because I brought that pie back to your house. My girlfriend, Carol, and I had a fistfight over who should get the biggest piece. The police came and told us we'd better get our act together, so I returned the pie. If we were going to fight over it, no one should have it."

We all lose it sometimes. Mike Benedetti lost his temper at a guest who called me a dago, even though I am an Irish/English/Swede and not an Italian. After hearing conservative radio talk show host Rush Limbaugh contend there is no rational reason to try and save obscure species from extinction, Claire shouted at the radio, "Web of life, asshole! Web of life!" To Claire's amusement, I ranted and raved when I mistakenly believed that someone had stolen the dipstick from our car.

While the Catholic Worker reveals our frailties, it also reminds us that the poor have their gifts. We've hosted guests who've been helpful, creative, and very interesting. Aguido rebuilt our back porch. Sharon clipped our cat Thérèse's claws. Lee painted a picture of our kitchen table/altar. A guest named Dan, an Irish tenor, insisted on singing for his dinner. We tried without success to decline his offer. Dan's rendition of "Somewhere

94

Over the Rainbow" was so beautiful it left us speechless. Another guest did magic tricks, amazing everyone, especially our children, with his sleight of hand. Many tell jokes. More tell their stories.

We hear tales of hardship, broken families, lost opportunities, injustice, and adventure. We often learn a great deal about other countries and cultures. We are constantly reminded how blessed our own lives are and how easily misfortune could have changed them.

Not every guest has been easy. We've had to take more than a few to detox or the emergency room. Many guests have tested our patience. The Catholic Worker's co-founder, Peter Maurin, said that when welcoming the stranger, we are "entertaining angels in disguise," but sometimes our guests seem more like devils sent to torment us. It helps that the Catholic Worker's other co-founder, Dorothy Day, didn't romanticize nor sugarcoat working with the poor. She often quoted a line from *The Brothers Karamazov*: "Love in dreams is easy, but love in action is often a harsh and dreadful thing." Like Claire did for me in Washington, DC, Dorothy also reminded us that "We have to put up with others the way God puts up with us."

And thankfully, just when tempted to quit, we run into a guest so needful that our compassion is renewed. We had a Vietnamese guest in 1993 named Hang who told us: "1972 was a very bad year for the war. My aunt lost five sons that year. She couldn't cry any more."

Some guests are especially remarkable. An older man named Kurt came to us after being evicted when the bank foreclosed on his apartment building. Kurt had been a journalist in New York City during the September 11 attacks on the World Trade Center. Caught up like many New Yorkers in a desire to do something to help, he volunteered to write for the US Army. Modeling himself on the WWII war correspondent Ernie Pyle, Kurt went to Iraq to pen stories about ordinary soldiers, "to make them hometown heroes for a day." In 2007, Sunni insurgents kidnapped and tortured him and his Army translator, a young woman. Kurt suffered broken ribs, smashed kneecaps, burns, and other injuries. They beat and raped his translator. US Special Forces rescued them after nine days, but they spent a long time in medical rehab and continued to suffer traumatic stress afterwards. The translator killed herself in 2012, while Kurt found hope to carry on. He had the phrase "Choose Life" tattooed onto his hand and applied to return to the Middle East with the Peace Corps. His triumph over adversity both humbles and inspires us.

Of course we want those we shelter to go on to happier, more secure lives, but that isn't always the case. We had two guests die in our house, one from a heart attack. The other, Ephraim Perez, choked to death in his sleep from a medication overdose. Good hearted Ephraim jokingly referred to me as "the man with the pitchfork," aka the Devil. A woman guest attempted suicide by slashing her arm. I found her unconscious on her bed with her bleeding arm resting on several neatly folded towels on the floor. Although I was certain she had died, the EMTs revived her. After a young man named Jeff relapsed on heroin in our second floor bathroom, I took him to the city shelter where he took his life three days later. Thankfully, he was the only person we know who had so much despair. More often, people leave us, fall down in some way, and come to us again for help. If we have space, we always welcome them. Who among us has not tried without instant success to become better?

Thankfully, most guests leave in better spirits than when they arrived. Two, one from Haiti and the other from Africa, delivered babies with Claire's assistance. She is godmother to these little angels, whose families are doing very well. Quite a few former guests come back to visit. Some send us letters thanking us for our hospitality. More than we deserve tell us, "You saved my life."

Beyond hospitality, we try to contribute a bit to Peter Maurin's vision of a "Green Revolution." To that end, Claire and our coworker Dave Maciewski created a wonderful community garden on land we do not own but have the owner's permission to use behind our house. They harvest peppers, cherry tomatoes, kale, broccoli, carrots, peas, lettuce, eggplant, garlic, oregano, and basil. From their little plot, we enjoy pesto and bruschetta well into the fall.

While Claire and Dave chose to grow edibles, I took over a trash-strewn lot on our block to transform it into a flower garden. I planted tiger lilies, roses, petunias, impatiens, snap dragons, marigolds, and daisies in beds encircled by stones and paths covered in wood chips.

Dave liked to point to the vegetable garden and say, "The world will be saved by food," while I preferred Dorothy Day's favorite Dostoevsky quote, "The world will be saved by beauty."

One morning while I weeded on my hands and knees, a mother and her small son stopped on the sidewalk. He gawked at me amidst the splendor of flowers and asked, "Are you a fairy?"

among Catholic Worker projects: cloth bags

Actually, a Catholic Worker wears many hats. Our community, for example,
- ran summer peace camps
- organized nonviolence training sessions
- led a successful campaign to remove lead from Worcester water
- convinced a grocery chain to introduce cloth bags
- conducted an unsuccessful campaign to prevent the introduction of Junior Reserve Officer Training Corps to the public schools
- helped prevent the opening of a slot machine parlor in Worcester
- aided a local soda company in beating off a frivolous law suit by Coca-Cola
- joined peace walks

- organized Mother's Day peace marches and rallies
- fasted for an end to violence against children and, another time, for lifting of the Israeli blockade of Gaza
- painted several murals
- supported nurses and Verizon workers in winning strikes
- marched in the Saint Patrick's Day parade, and
- defended the right of the poor to beg on street corners, as well as the right of the organization Food Not Bombs to feed the poor on those same street corners.

We organized an international gathering for Catholic Workers to mark our movement's seventy-fifth anniversary. Claire has written hundreds of published, freelance articles while volunteering at the Center for Nonviolent Solutions. I coached soccer for a dozen years and cross country for the past five. We both have become long distance runners.

We have had our fingers in many pots.

We could not accomplish anything, though, without a broad community at Saints Francis & Thérèse Catholic Worker house. After Carl, Dan, and Sarah, Claire and I have been blessed to live and work with Dave Maciewski, Dan Lawrence, Chris Allen-Douçot, Mike Benedetti, Brenna Cussen, Cinnamon Sarver, Christine Lavallee, Hazen Ordwell, Meg Brodhead, Elizabeth Detweiller, Timothy and Christa Aikens-Hill, Robert Peters, Bridget Dignan, Hannah Landsel, and Jennifer Hoffman.

Many others, especially Ken Hannaford-Ricardi, Jo Massarelli, Marc Tumeinski, Dave Williams, Dave Besnia, Mike Cahill, Vinnie Sullivan-Jacques, Sue McCune, Teresa Wheeler, Kate Carew, David Maher, John and Anne Marie Thornton, and Michael True, have been invaluable parts of our hospitality and peace work.

Add to them the hundreds of individuals who come in to volunteer from time to time, who send us letters and donations by mail, or who join us for Mass or Evening Prayer. Without this multitude, we could never have repaired our roof, painted our house (several times over), gotten out our newsletter, or attended to the myriad of other needs that arise so often.

Lastly, the Saints Francis & Thérèse Catholic Worker is sustained by bread, quite literally. Claire, Barbara Horn, and Sarah's early cottage industry has grown to be a common work for all our community members. The Bread Not Bombs Bakery is a weekly operation out of a kitchen at Blessed Sacrament Church's Phelan Center. On Fridays and Saturdays, we get up long before dawn in solidarity with millions who do it every day to hand bake oatmeal raisin, honey wheat, Italian, buttermilk white,

Brenna Cussen listens to a guest at the Catholic Worker house in 2009

97

and Irish soda bread as well as carrot raisin bran muffins and cinnamon swirls. We take our products to a different Catholic church each weekend to offer along with our paper, *The Catholic Radical*. We do not set a price. People give however they feel inspired. And yet, this work provides nearly half our income. It also connects us to people all over our diocese and helps us distribute our message beyond a mailing list of already-sympathetic readers.

Although many hands support our efforts, there are times when the entirety of what we hope to accomplish seems in peril of imminent collapse. We have emergencies that tax our imaginations and tempt us to give up this precarious lifestyle. After all, it is our own choice that bars us from insurance, retirement funds, salaries, tenure, tax exemption, government or corporate grants, personal property, and other things that regular folks rely on in adversity.

But during such emergencies, I recall the morning after the Jaques Avenue fire when our ragtag group gathered in the chilly air to salvage what little we could from the ashes before the firefighters boarded the wreck up. We had no money or plan for relocation. I, for one, was in shock. But then, our friend John Shields, an old-time peace activist with great Irish wit, suggested we say the Morning Prayer on the street corner and open it with the song, "Rejoice in the Lord Always."

As Job proclaimed, when everything dear to him was taken away, "Naked I came into the world, naked I shall leave it. The Lord made heaven and earth. Blessed be the name of the Lord."

The lawyer who handled the deed for the Mason Street house pleaded with us to sign up for fire insurance. "The Catholic Worker House of Ammon in Hubbardston had a fire. The Mustard Seed had a fire. You have just had a fire," he said. "This is a no-brainer. You are going to have another fire. Take out fire insurance."

"As Catholic Workers," I replied, "we shouldn't set aside a penny today in fear over what might happen tomorrow. If we have another fire, the same God who raised up this new house for us will do so again."

As Saint Luke says, "Fear is useless. What is needed is faith."

This faith is not some pie-in-the-sky hope. The continued existence of the Catholic Worker Movement, disorganized as it is, flies in the face of reason and testifies emphatically that miracles still happen. To attribute our successes to our own efforts is ridiculous.

We are simply not that talented.

How did we feed and shelter so many people?

How did our children manage to go to Wesleyan, Columbia, Harvard, and Holy Cross without loans?

How did we publish more than two hundred thousand copies of our newspaper and send them out first class mail?

How did we survive with an open door in the poorest section of New England's second largest city?

How did all our bills get paid?

How did we manage to return unscathed from peace campaigns in Bosnia, Iraq, Haiti, Darfur, Israel/Palestine, and Afghanistan?

How did we survive repeated jail sentences for civil disobedience?

How did I run five marathons in fourteen months, for crying out loud?

Our own merits? Nonsense.

When I was a senior in high school, a bunch of my friends climbed New Hampshire's Mount Washington. We had just crested a steep rise on the Lion's Head Trail towering over Tuckerman Ravine when a fierce wind nearly knocked us over. My friend Briand Lessard stood at the cliff edge with his legs spread, arms outstretched, and black hair whipping. In a voice booming over the tumultuous wind, he quoted Psalm 8: "When I consider Your heavens, the work of Your hands, the moon and the stars, which You have set in place, what is man that you are mindful of him, the son of man that you care for him?"

He raised his hiking stick as high as he could and bellowed, "And yet you have made us little less than gods!!"

When we set out to do good, I believe that Briand and King David were right. There's nothing we can't do.

Civil Disobedience

Revealing no more to us than, "We're going for a ride," my father often piled my three brothers, three sisters, and me into our 1968 VW bus on weekends. The mysterious trips over curvy, tree-lined New England back roads terminated at places of historical, literary, or geographical significance—Charlestown's Bunker Hill Memorial, Salem's House of Seven Gables, the Hammond Castle in Gloucester, the crook in the Millville road where, "under a spreading chestnut tree," Longfellow's village smithy stood, and, more often than not, Walden Pond with its recreation of Henry David Thoreau's hut.

Perhaps it was on one of these trips to Thoreau's hideaway that I first heard the term civil disobedience. I had a vague familiarity with it from newspaper headlines about Dr. Martin Luther King, Jr. and Vietnam War protests, but I wasn't emotionally touched by the idea of deliberately breaking the law until I read *A Man for All Seasons*, Robert Bolt's play about Sir Thomas More. I was swept away with admiration for the witty, courageous, and faith-filled English martyr who proclaimed himself "The king's good servant but God's first." Bolt convinced me nothing is more glorious than taking a stand for one's ideals and being thrown into a dungeon for it. I memorized segments of the play and can still quote them. Later on, when I saw a movie version starring Paul Scofield as More, Robert Shaw as Henry the Eighth, and Orson Welles as Cardinal Wolsey, there was no turning back. With the closing credits of Scofield's film, I was completely formed as an idealist waiting impatiently for the time when I could sacrifice my freedom for a noble cause.

But by the time I entered Holy Cross in 1976, the Vietnam War had ended, the draft was discontinued, and civil disobedience seemed passé. You were considered a campus radical if you wrote a letter to the editor. Until campaigns very late in my college days to remove Reserve Officers' Training Corps and to divest from South Africa, I had little to squawk about, much less get arrested while protesting on campus. I seemed to be condemned to the lesser heroism of holding more progressive views than the majority of my peers. My biggest sacrifice involved spending a few bucks now and then on magazines like *Mother Jones*.

That's when I became familiar with nuclear weapons. One can't rationally go to the mat for small "e" evil, but the threat of nuclear Armageddon certainly qualifies as big-time EVIL. Better yet, in 1979 I found a flyer put out by the Justice and Peace Commission of the Archdiocese of Boston specifically condemning the cruise, MX, and Trident missiles. The commission described the Trident submarine as the world's largest with twenty-four Trident missiles carrying more than three hundred individually targeted nuclear warheads each with explosive yields many times the impact of the Hiroshima bomb.

The commission quoted Seattle Archbishop Raymond Hunthausen, who called the Trident "an oven without walls." As luck would have it, General Dynamics Corporation manufactured these insidious nuclear nightmares in nearby Groton, Connecticut, where civil disobedience would take place during the April 7 christening of the first Trident to be completed, the USS Ohio.

Inspired by the peace and justice committee's call to action, I recruited two friends, Joe Borkowski and Pat Tam, to go to Voluntown, Connecticut, for required nonviolence training a day before the planned mass demonstration. Prior to leaving Holy Cross, we decided to visit the college chaplain, Father Bob Manning, SJ. Famous for going to Hanoi on a peace mission during the Vietnam War and a professor of the left-leaning theology of liberation, the chaplain would surely give us an enthusiastic blessing.

To our surprise, after he heard our plan, Father Manning said, "I forbid it!" He went on to explain, "College is the nest where ideals are brought to maturity. You don't spread your wings and fly away until afterwards."

Joe and I were at a loss for words, but the more typically shy Pat said, "Father, I have prayed long and hard before making this decision. I believe this is something God is asking me to do. If I say 'no' to God now, how much easier will it be to keep doing so for the rest of my life?"

Before the chaplain could say a word, Pat walked out of the office. Joe and I just followed in his wake.

A group called the Community for Nonviolent Action ran the training at the A. J. Muste Center on a farm in Voluntown, Connecticut. Attended by several hundred prospective arrestees, the training opened with an impressive talk by author and scholar Marta Daniels on why the Trident is a destabilizing weapon. Ms. Daniels explained that the Trident missile like the MX, boasts pinpoint accuracy and high-explosive yield.

To prevent nuclear war, the United States and Soviet Union relied on a policy of Mutually Assured Destruction (MAD) wherein both sides maintained the nuclear capacity to destroy the other's major cities. The two superpowers avoided nuclear war because neither side could win.

MAD did not require high-yield or pinpoint-accurate nukes. An atomic explosion on any street in Moscow or Washington, DC, constituted an equal deterrent. Weapons like the Trident and MX, on the other hand, targeted specific missile silos and command centers buried deep underground. To prevent retaliation, a nuclear first strike would destroy such targets. The Reagan administration called the MX missile The Peacekeeper, but actually, it and the Trident provoked the Soviets to adopt a launch-on-warning, hair-trigger strategy. During a crisis, the Russians would end up in a use-them-or-lose-them fix. The prospect so alarmed the editors of the *Bulletin of Atomic Scientists* that they moved the hands of the doomsday clock closer to midnight, the symbol of nuclear annihilation.

A talk on the philosophy of nonviolent protest, its history in Connecticut, and the tactics we would employ the next day followed Dr. Daniels's presentation. Trainers answered questions and orchestrated role-playing of arrest scenarios with a special emphasis on the feelings of people expected to attend the launch: Trident workers, invited guests, and the police. To mitigate any self-righteousness we might harbor, trainers encouraged us to take on the role of Trident supporters. The plan included our march to the gate of the General Dynamics Corporation Electric Boat factory in Groton for a silent blockade of the entrance. We heard an outline of prospective legal consequences, in the likely event of our arrest before we went to a Methodist church in New London to eat dinner and roll out sleeping bags for the night.

In a side room off the main sanctuary, Father Dan Berrigan, SJ, famous for his part in the destruction of Vietnam War draft files as one of the Catonsville Nine, offered Mass by candlelight. Jim Dugeon, a young and talented musician, played guitar and sang quite beautifully. After reading the Gospel, Father Dan reflected on his experience watching cancer patients die at Saint Rose's hospice in Manhattan and how a nuclear war would compound that horror beyond measure. Joe, Pat, and I felt welcomed into an intelligent, creative, and compassionate community of deeply spiritual activists.

The next day's demonstration surpassed our wildest expectations. Five thousand people marched in silence down Groton's Main Street to Electric Boat. Five hundred of us sat or knelt on the asphalt in front of the main gate. The only sound was the rhythmic chanting and beating of drums by Buddhist monks. When launch ticket holders approached from the opposite end of Main Street, they seemed affected by the spectacle of so many people putting their bodies between them and the Trident. A single woman screamed a shrill unanswered insult and then all was silent. I felt like I was in an amazing play creating a somber mood that no one could ignore.

For what seemed like a very long time, police did not attempt to remove us, so strong was the spell of the action, but, finally, the chief took out a bullhorn and warned us to end the blockade or be arrested. Minutes later, local and state police officers began placing us one by one under arrest for disorderly conduct and into plastic handcuffs. No one resisted, but, at the same time, no one facilitated his or her removal. We went limp, and the officers carried us to police vans. After several hours in custody, the police released us with our promise to appear for arraignment.

You might think that Joe, Pat, and I had regrets once we returned to campus. After all, disorderly conduct carries the possibility of a thirty-day jail sentence, something that would have negated an entire semester's studies. But we felt strangely confident that the same divine presence that called us to take the risk would see us safely to its completion.

And so it was. The court continued all the charges without a finding. Our foray into civil disobedience had cost us only a couple of missed classes.

The following year, the US Navy planned to celebrate the Ohio's commissioning, the occasion when the crew actually boards the submarine for active duty. Organizers announced a coinciding protest, and I was eager to join it. This time, though, I wrote a letter to my parents explaining why I felt compelled by conscience to risk arrest. My father and I both admired Thomas More, for whom primacy of conscience was sacrosanct, but my dad had become a very conservative Republican swept up in anti-Communist rhetoric by daily editorials in the Manchester *Union Leader*. His response, delivered by my mother, came swift and stark. If I joined this protest, I would cease to be his son.

Bummer. Especially when I considered that a decision not to protest would probably diminish his respect for me as well. So, I went to Groton again. This time, my arrest appeared on the evening news. My paternal grandmother saw it and remarked with characteristic understatement, "The things you see on TV these days."

True to his word, my father didn't speak to me for five years. He returned my mail unopened and did not attend my college graduation or wedding nor the baptism of my first two children. On the one occasion I tried to force the issue by visiting him unannounced, he met me at the door saying, "I'm going to get my gun!" The two college comrades with me refused to wait and see if he'd really shoot me dead. But even a square-headed, Irish Swede like my dad runs out of steam over time. My grandmother brokered my return to the family, and my father became an affectionate albeit quirky grandfather to my children.

Since those two protests, I have been arrested many more times, mostly in opposition to nuclear weapons and war but also against abortion, apartheid in South Africa, and genocide in Darfur. Most of those protests occurred in small groups. Less than half of them resulted in jail sentences. Some were well organized. Others were hopeless screw-ups. I tried to learn from experience but was often surprised at how poorly I predicted any outcome.

Scott arrested by New York City police during a 1982 Ban-the-Bomb protest

photo by Tom Lewis

At one rainy day protest during the winter of 1985 at a General Dynamics facility in Norwich, Connecticut, Claire, Terri Allen, Daniel Sicken, Peter Holliday, Dan Lawrence, Cal Robertson, and I expected to be arrested quickly, so we didn't hesitate kneeling on the ground in prayer. Unfortunately, the cops left us shivering in our we-will-not-be-moved stance for more than an hour. By the time we appeared in court for arraignment, everyone started feeling sick, and when the judge set bail, which we refused in conscience to pay, things got even worse. He sent us to jail to await trial, the men to the county jail in Montville and the women, including my pregnant wife Claire, to the state prison for women in Niantic. The men's jail was so overcrowded that we had to sleep on the concrete floor of a large cell that doubled as a day room. By the next morning, I had a fever and vomited into an open toilet with dozens of inmates gathered around me chanting, "Go, go, go!"

Meanwhile, Claire and Terri endured meager food with only slightly better conditions than Montville. After noticing that Claire was pregnant, a heroin addict described how she had been taken to the hospital in shackles to deliver her son and how, due to her addiction, the child was taken from her. Looking for something to humanize this grim account, Claire asked, "What did you name him?"

"Justin Peter," the woman replied.

The next day, while lying in her bunk, Claire felt our first child move in her womb and decided to call him Justin as well.

To all of our surprise though, after we spent twenty-eight days in jail awaiting a trial date that hadn't even been set, the judge, who seemed surprised that we hadn't posted bail, released us with "time-served" but not before Dan got pneumonia, Cal was hospitalized for seizures, and Daniel accused me of trying to kill him by breathing on him in the lockup after we were arrested and packed together like sardines. On top of it, Peter railed daily about how torturous it was to take a shower in a place where, any time someone flushed a toilet, he got scalded.

* * *

My concept of pacifism extends beyond opposition to all war. I also oppose the death penalty, euthanasia, and abortion. I recognize that very few people choose to take a life lightly and many support doing so because they see no alternatives. I have never employed civil disobedience as some kind of judgment of others nor as a means to make them feel guilty and myself morally superior. Instead, I view civil disobedience as a sacrificial act of personal integrity that I hope initiates a spark in the intellect and conscience of others. Along these lines, Claire and I held a small sign in the hallway of an abortion clinic for an hour, and after talking with us, Worcester police officers refused to arrest us.

My only arrest at an abortion clinic had nothing to do with abortion. When Chris Allen-Douçot, who would later help found the Hartford Catholic Worker, was a junior at Holy Cross, he and I wanted to investigate a group called Operation Rescue. For a time in the late 1980s, these folks blocked entrances to abortion clinics and went to jail. Their protests were organized from the top down with the location of the civil disobedience kept secret from the press and all participants until the very last minute.

On October 28, 1989, Chris and I met with Operation Rescue organizers to say that we'd only attend one of their demonstrations if we could hold a sign proclaiming, "Ban the bomb, not the baby." We figured they were not really pro-life, as in pacifist, but merely anti-abortion. To our surprise, the woman coordinator welcomed our sign even though Operation Rescue generally forbade all signs save their identifying banner.

So, that night, Chris and I attended a rally/revival meeting at a Catholic church in Framingham, Massachusetts, and then joined a caravan of cars that led us circuitously to Providence, Rhode Island. While the mostly middle-aged Operation Rescue people blocked doorways, Chris and I stood aside, held our sign, and observed. It amazed us to see such evidently straight-laced folks enduring very rough police treatment without a word of complaint. It astonished us even more to see those who had been dragged away, some by their hair, from the doors, get back up, and return time and time again until the cops handcuffed and locked them in transport vehicles. Within minutes of our arrival, an angry counter demonstration formed. That crowd, including several peace activist friends of ours, waved coat hangers and chided police for not being even more aggressive. I found it disturbing, since I wouldn't encourage the police to beat anyone.

After an hour, a police captain announced that the clinic had closed for the day and asked us all to leave. Chris and I turned to do just that when we ran into another police officer, who said we could not cross the street to get back to our car. I explained to him that a captain had just asked us to go home, but the young officer replied, "I don't know anything about that." When I suggested that he ask the captain, the cop said, "I don't ask questions. I just follow orders."

Chris shot back, "Well, that's just like the Nazis."

In a flash, the cop handcuffed Chris and tossed him into an empty police van. A much calmer, more senior officer took the volatile cop's place in front of me.

I said to him, "That was not right."

"Probably not," he agreed.

"Can you let him go?" I asked.

"No," he sighed, "but if you want, I can put you with him."

I couldn't let Chris go to jail alone, so I offered my wrists to be cuffed. To my horror, while we waited to be transported to the police station, our peace activist friend Sheila Parks pressed a coat hanger and her face against the van's window while singing the Monty Python song, "Every Sperm is Sacred." She assumed we had blocked the clinic, when all we did was try to go home.

In a case of the most serious underestimation of risk, my friend Tom Doughton told me that, during the early 1970s, he joined a pro-democracy protest in Francisco Franco's fascist Spain. The demonstration was very modest. Tom and a group of Spaniards held signs on the steps of the presidential palace in Madrid. The Spaniards were arrested and then summarily executed. Because of his US citizenship, Tom was only beaten and then expelled from Spain. His story has always made me a little leery of doing civil disobedience overseas, but sometimes the draw is just too strong.

From 1991 until 2001, the US enforced comprehensive sanctions against Iraq, which UNICEF said were directly responsible for the deaths of over eight hundred thousand Iraqi children. The American rationale for the sanctions relied on the claim that Iraq was secretly building weapons of mass destruction (WMDs), weapons President George W. Bush insisted could never be tolerated in the Middle East. But, despite the fact that international weapons inspectors never discovered WMDs in Iraq, crippling sanctions remained, and the US threatened war.

Ironically, as the US sanctioned Iraq for WMDs it did not possess, we sent aid and arms to another nation in the Middle East proved to have them. In 1986, a former Israeli nuclear technician named Mordechai Vanunu gave photographic and other evidence exposing Israel's extensive nuclear weapons program to *The Sunday Times* of London. In September, just before the *Times's* article appeared in print, Israelis kidnapped Vanunu and kept him in solitary confinement for twelve years.

In 1998 as part of a campaign to secure Vanunu's release and to promote a nuclear-free Middle East, I joined Israeli, American, and English activists for "a citizens' weapons inspection" of the Israeli nuclear weapons site in the desert town of Dimona. David Polden from London; Sam Day, the former editor of the *Bulletin of Atomic Scientists* from

photo by Art Laffin

Barry Roth, left, and Scott during a "Citizens' Nuclear Weapons Inspection" in Dimona, Israel in 1998 resulting in their arrest with other Americans and internationals

Chicago; Felice Cohen-Joppa, an editor of *The Nuclear Resister* from New Mexico; Art Laffin from the Dorothy Day Catholic Worker in Washington, DC; a young Israeli activist named Ruth Haviv; Eurydice Hirsey and her husband, Barry Roth, of Boston, and I walked towards the reactor dome in Dimona and where police arrested us. Once in custody, we experienced the most dramatic good cop/bad cop interrogation I have ever known. The first Israeli officer came in screaming in broken English that he could beat us and have us sent to a midnight "trial" without a lawyer to represent us unless we signed a document apologizing for violating Israeli security and promised never to do so again.

Unlike the first, the second officer, originally from Indiana, asked us in perfect, soft-spoken English, "Can I get you any coffee or something cold to drink?" He apologized for the delay in getting us released and then asked us to sign the same form as the angry cop did. The performance went on for several hours as conditions softened with each visit until they asked us merely to promise to stay away from the reactor for the rest of that day. Since we had already made our point, it seemed like a demand we could agree to without moral compromise, especially after we learned that Ruth was a diabetic who would need her medication before too long.

As we talked the situation over, the angry guard came in and grabbed a couple of us by the sleeve. He shouted, "No more waiting. You are going to jail!"

David took out a pen to sign the promise, but Ruth stayed his hand, insisting that we refuse on principle.

From his place standing in the background, the good cop stepped forward, opened the outside door, and said, "You are all free to go." A limousine waited outside to take Ruth to the studio of one of Israel's prominent television stations for an hour-long program on Israel's nuclear weapons policy, the first such interview in Israel's history. Civil disobedience is often like this, a roller coaster of emotions, anxieties, and struggles with conscience.

In contrast, some demonstrations are whimsical. In 1986, when the War Resister's League asked us to protest the sale of war toys on the day after Thanksgiving, the busiest shopping day of the year, I donned a Santa Claus costume and went to Toys "R" Us in Auburn, Massachusetts. I armed myself with a letter from the North Pole. It read:

> Dear Shoppers,
>
> It has come to my attention that Toys "R" Us is advertising the sale of war toys under a heading "Smart Santas shop at Toys "R" Us." Since when did I or my elves authorize the sale of war toys? Mrs. Claus, a longtime member of the International Women's League of Peace and Freedom, has been after me for years to take a stand on this issue, and I think it's high time I did . . . . Try giving nonviolent toys this Christmas. How about Mr. Potato Head?
>
> *Santa*

107

Auburn police officer arrests Santa Claus

I strode into the store singing "You better watch out . . ." and positioned myself in a row of toy guns, some of them startlingly realistic. The store manager came and told me I'd have to leave.

I asked her, "Will the war toys be leaving the store?" When she answered in the negative, I said, "Ho, ho, ho! I can't leave either."

I continued caroling and distributing letters to shoppers until a police officer came. When he threatened to arrest me, I took a lump of coal out of my pocket and said, "Don't make me use this." He handcuffed me and walked me out the back of the store where supporters and the media waited. I beamed and sang as the policeman, father of two small children, pulled his hat way down over his eyes to avoid being identified as the cop who arrested Santa Claus. At my trial, I was convicted and then sentenced not to dress up as Kris Kringle again until the next Christmas.

Some demonstrations turn out unintentionally funny, like the one wherein multiple protesters insisted on giving their names as Dr. Martin Luther King, Jr. The judge refused to arraign them under pseudonyms, so he sent them to jail. He brought them back to court every few days to see if they would admit their actual identities. After the shuffle went on for several weeks, the exasperated judge finally exclaimed, "For crying out loud, none of you are even black!"

GTE Corporation security confronts Carol Bellin and Scott during their
Saint Valentine's Day protest

At a Saint Valentine's Day protest in 1986 against nuclear weapons, Carol Bellin, a film producer from Somerville, Massachusetts, and I poured our blood on GTE Corporation's corporate sign and then displayed a large heart, encircled by white doilies and proclaiming "Love Disarms." Afterwards, *Worcester Magazine* lifted a line from our leaflet for their headline—"Protesters arrested 'in act of love.'" Ouch!

On another occasion, Michael Cahill and I held a banner at the Pentagon proclaiming "WAR is a SIN." After a colonel tore our banner in half, I suggested to Mike that we could still hold the remnant depicting the word "War" dripping blood. Twenty minutes later, another officer approached and asked earnestly, "I don't want to tell you how to hold your protest, but just what does your banner mean?" Only then did we discover that we were holding a sheet that cried, "WA."

Surprises and screw-ups notwithstanding, over time I've developed my own philosophy on civil disobedience. Many of my values were gifted to me by Tom Lewis, a member of the Catonsville Nine with Dan Berrigan and the godfather of Claire and my oldest son, Justin. Tom used to say, "There is spiritual value in a person being in jail for conscience even if no one knows it." He showed us the importance of using traditional religious imagery to oppose violence. For Tom, the stations of the cross, rosary, sacraments, bishops, popes, saints, and, most especially, the Bible were integral to peacemaking. The liturgical calendar, especially Good Friday, Easter, and the Feast of the Holy Innocents when Herod killed all the children in Bethlehem, provided key times to protest for Tom, much more important than election day or the Fourth of July. He also taught us to work closely with Buddhists, Jews, Protestants, agnostics, and atheists. He inspired a number of us, Christians and Jews, to protest the launching of a Trident submarine on Yom Kippur by donning prayer shawls and yarmulkes for a blockade marked by Hebrew chant and sounding a shofar.

I had the privilege of spending my first weekend in jail with Tom. His good humor and steadfast religious faith transformed it into a retreat. He told the guards who delivered thin coffee and stale doughnuts to our bare cells, "Thank you for breakfast in bed."

Most importantly, Tom stressed that civil disobedience should never be a first resort to resolve conflict. He believed in employing the least confrontational method necessary to change hearts. Before kneeling in a federal building to pray for an end to the war in Afghanistan, our group vigiled outside the building six days a week for almost six weeks. Prior to the start of every vigil, we went inside to talk with the US marshals. By the time we did civil disobedience, we knew each other pretty well. Even after more than twenty local police officers arrived on the scene, the federal marshals held up our arrest until we completed a rosary and sang the "Salve Regina." In some cases, we have leafleted or held a weekly vigil for months or even years before risking arrest.

I should also stress that the point of civil disobedience is not to be arrested but to change hearts and minds. If the goal can be accomplished without risking arrest, so much the better. There are a hundred times more protests when no one is arrested than when someone is.

And it also happens from time to time that police choose not to arrest someone who expected to be. It happened to Gordon Davis, Robert Peters, and me on Valentine's Day 2013 when we challenged a Worcester ordinance against panhandling by begging near the police station. Perhaps the police agreed with us that the poor should not be harassed. Maybe they just didn't want to arrest a blind man like Gordon, a Buddhist mendicant like Robert, or a person dressed like Saint Francis of Assisi, as I was. You never can tell. As the press quoted me, "Any day I don't get arrested is a good one."

Civil disobedience has many aspects, but the one that strikes me most forcefully is the sense of taking a leap of faith, of stepping out of conventionality, and of breathing astonishingly fresh air. It is a kind of freedom that can only be understood by experience. It's what Rosa Parks felt when she refused to move to the back of the bus and Tom Lewis felt when he burned draft files. It's not just about marching to a different drummer. It's doing what we can to persuade others not to march over a cliff. Given its emotional and spiritual impact, not to mention its importance as a remedy for governmental and industrial outrages, civil disobedience is worth doing at least once in one's life.

panhandlers Robert Peters, left, and Scott on Saint Valentine's Day, 2013

The Mountain Warriors

My uncle Bob should have died that day. It was March 1971, and Bob led my friend Steve Archambault and me up Mount Washington, the highest peak in the northeastern United States. We had clear sky, brilliant sun, and very little wind, all quite rare on the notoriously fickle peak. I've climbed it a dozen times since then only to encounter wind so strong you can hardly stand much less climb, or fog so thick you can't see more than eight feet in front of you. What we did have was snow, lots of it. After we passed the tree line, snow was so deep and hard-packed that we walked on top of it.

By eleven in the morning, we had spread ourselves out across a huge, steeply sloping sheet of white. The trail had long since disappeared below us. We climbed by dead reckoning. Amazingly quiet and a little disconcerting, the snow sheet extended hundreds of feet before and behind us. If we slipped and fell, we would hurtle down with increasing velocity until a field of jagged boulders would tear our limbs off and fracture our skulls—kind of a hairy prospect for two seventh graders like Steve and me. None of us had snowshoes, an ice pick, rope, or crampons, the spiky attachments serious climbers put on their shoes to give them better purchase. We did not carry flares, and no one had yet dreamed of cell phones. Primarily, my uncle's wild photographer's promise drove us: "I'll get some great shots."

Whenever we demurred about any risky venture, Bob asked, "Are you men or candy asses?" What the flip is a candy ass? He then asked in a deep voice, "Are you game?" He cocked his head, raised an eyebrow, and added, "I'm game." I think he could have persuaded Steve and me to go over Niagara Falls in a barrel.

The sound of a roaring river and Uncle Bob's shouts for help suddenly interrupted our nervous but steady ascent. At first, I couldn't see him at all. He seemed to have disappeared. But then Steve spied Bob's hiking stick straddling an inky black hole in the snow. Bob's gloved hands clung to the one-inch-diameter stick over the abyss where he dangled. Apparently, we had been climbing on top of the iced-over Ammonoosuc River. The snowpack was so thick, we hadn't heard the torrent, but we sure as all heck could after Bob broke through it. Semi-competent Boy Scouts, Steve and I crawled on our bellies toward the hole. I grasped Steve's ankles, and he snagged Bob's hand. We nervously eased him to safety as snow began to crumble along the lip of the hole. Had we acted less quickly, my uncle would have fallen to his death in the fast flowing, icy river. His body would not have been recovered until the spring thaw.

With extra caution, we continued our climb with our hiking sticks held horizontally across our shoulders to brace us in case anyone else "broke on through to the other side," as Jim Morrison so aptly put it. We were very grateful to finally reach rocky ground and the summit.

Perhaps the memory of this and other good times in the White Mountains with Bob and his crazy friends (a former Green Beret named George ate live June bugs with a Bowie knife) gave me the idea for a mountain climbing club for my younger sons.

More likely, I was motivated by my distress over how much time they spent watching TV. Not hundred-percent couch potatoes, they all played youth soccer and took music lessons. We read out loud to them well into their high school years. To varying degrees, they grew into avid readers themselves. But unlike Justin, who enjoyed two years as a junior detective, Patrick and Aiden seemed to have few adventures. Reading mysteries or seeing action films doesn't equal experiencing the uncertainty of real life, testing their mettle in circumstances where choices have serious consequences, learning to trust companions with their lives. Where in America outside the military can you get that kind of experience?

I certainly enjoyed mountain climbing with my Uncle Bob. On one expedition in New Hampshire, he convinced my friend Richard Bates and me to jump twenty feet into the Swift River's Rocky Gorge, a place plastered with No Swimming! signs. When I plummeted deep under the icy surface of the very well-named river, I thought I would drown, but minutes later I scrambled onto a boulder and shouted, "That was wicked cool!"

And so, when I considered how best to energize my sons, I naturally looked to the mountains. I broached the idea of a climbing club with twelve-year-old Patrick and nine-year-old Aiden. They agreed and recruited their friends Josef Ameur, Conor Cappe, Evan Johnson, and Kieran O'Sullivan, who collectively came up with the macho name The Mountain Warriors. On June 15, 2004, we took a day hike up nearby Mount Wachusett in Princeton, Massachusetts. We easily reached the 2,001-foot peak in forty-four minutes, but not before seeing an eastern newt, a black-throated blue warbler, a woodpecker, a turkey vulture, green frogs, and goldfish. We had fun climbing, and I knew we could handle an even bigger challenge.

Kieran, Aiden, Patrick, Evan, and Conor, from left, on the summit of Mount Wachusett in Princeton, Massachusetts, in 2004

So, two weeks later, we journeyed to Jaffrey, New Hampshire, to tackle Mount Monadnock, the second-most climbed mountain in the world after Japan's Mount Fuji. It took us two hours to attain the rocky 3,165-foot summit where Patrick declared, "Suddenly, I feel very religious." When we returned to the bottom, Conor exclaimed, "My legs! The pain!"

They did not give up. After climbing Massachusetts's highest peak, Greylock at 3,491 feet and then Stratton at 3,940 feet, in Vermont, the Warriors felt capable of really raising the bar. In summer 2004 on August 11, we tackled Mount Washington at 6,288 feet, the same mountain that almost claimed Uncle Bob in the winter of 1971. It took us four hours and thirty minutes to reach the top of New England, the place where a world-record wind of 231 mph was recorded in 1934. Unfortunately, the summit was socked in with clouds.

Nonetheless, Conor called it "the most beautiful mountain I've ever seen."

"I liked the halfway house and the clouds too," Kieran said.

"It felt like needles stabbing into my legs," Aiden added.

Aiden, Patrick, Kieran, and Conor, from left, atop the highest peak in the northeastern US, Mount Washington

"This was an incredible journey to remember," Patrick concluded.

What more could we do?

First, I recruited my daughter Grace to make a logo (Grace had and still has no interest in hiking, although she and her friend Ruth did summit Mount Washington once). Then I put together a booklet called "The Mountains of New England" with stats and photos about their climbs. The boys chose the motto, "It's all about the altitude." The Mountain Warriors' Team Philosophy pronounced:

Mountain climbing is fun. Every member of this team, regardless of age, physical strength, injury, or exhaustion is essential. No one is left behind. The group continues together or not at all. Rests are taken whenever a member needs one. The slowest hiker often leads the team in order to set a pace that he can cheerfully maintain. We climb in all weather. Food is shared. No one gets put down. Everyone is encouraged when they feel like giving up. Time is set aside to investigate wildlife and to take photographs. We leave nothing behind but footprints. We respect nature, mountains, ourselves, and our comrades.

logo by Grace Duffy

Over four years, these boys and sometimes girls, women, and other boys climbed twenty-six of the forty-seven peaks higher than four thousand feet in New Hampshire's White Mountains. They grew from children who often begged me to carry their packs (I once shouldered three at a time) into remarkably hardy young adults. They spent the night on a mountain during their conquests of Carter Dome and Wildcat. They learned what to wear, carry, eat, and drink to make them into more efficient climbers. They contended with insects, heat, cold, rain, snow, sleet, mist, and wind. By painful trial and error, they improved their ability to cross raging streams. They traded notes with other hikers, some of them attempting to complete the entire Appalachian Trail.

They had to read maps, identify landmarks, and follow trails. They had to treat small injuries. There was nothing theoretical about their experience. If they continued climbing, they reached a summit. If they quit, they did not. No one ever quit. That's not to say that there were not sections of trail so difficult or frightening that individuals weren't tempted to turn back nor times when summits seemed so eternally far away that it was impossible to reach them. As the Warriors became more confident, they began to relish the most difficult climbs, epic assaults on the heavens.

One such climb came on an attempt to summit three peaks in a single day—Mounts Haystack, Lincoln, and Lafayette. Climbers attain the feat by first ascending the Falling Water's Trail, a steep path crisscrossing two brooks that feed into the Pemigewasset River in Franconia Notch. My sister Chris calls it the Falling Bodies Trail.

As we often do, we stopped en route at the White Mountains Visitor Center in Lincoln to check on the weather and trail conditions. Even though it was June 5, 2005, the temperature above four thousand feet could still be quite cold, and even snow is not out of the question. Ice often lingers into summer. People ski in Tuckerman Ravine on Mount

Washington well into July. Risk of thunderstorms presented particular concern on this day. The triple climb constitutes a big circle with a 1.7 mile stretch along exposed ridges linking the mountains. At that altitude with no cover, hikers face the extreme danger of being struck by lightning during thunderstorms. Unfortunately, the ranger could not give us a conclusive forecast. We would have to reassess our plan should storm clouds roll in.

Thankfully, clear skies and hot sun prevailed for the first relatively flat mile through pine and birch forest. As we made the arduous ascent up to Little Haystack's highest point at 4,760 feet, we were grateful that it had become partly cloudy and a bit cooler. We lunched on the summit and discussed what to do next. Ominously gray and black clouds lurked in the west, but no one relished the idea of climbing down the way we had come up. It's always easier to ascend cliffs and boulders than to descend them. Weighing options, we decided to press on.

After dropping two hundred feet and then rising five hundred more, we reached Mount Lincoln. Since we were well above the tree line, we clearly saw Mount Lafayette a mile away across another ridgeline dip. Although the slate gray sky threatened showers, we remained optimistic that we could make it safely to the Greenleaf Appalachian Mountain Club (AMC) Hut located at the tree line, a mile below Lafayette's summit.

Patrick enjoys a rest

At 5,260 feet, Lafayette is the sixth highest peak in the White Mountains. Weather permitting, it affords a panoramic view of the entire region. Snow covers its bald, windswept top at least five months a year. We could see a few white patches on it as we set out onto the ridge over a spectacular stretch dropping steeply on both sides. The trail towers over Cannon Mountain and the now lost Old Man of the Mountain profile. In different weather, we might have lingered to take pictures, but gray clouds gave way to black ones, so we dared not dawdle.

The sound of approaching thunder prompted Kieran to predict that lightning would kill us all. He hiked in silence for five or six minutes and then repeated his dire concern.

Low rumbling prompted him to prophesy, "We are doomed."

Clouds rolled in above and around us. Visibility dropped. My wife, Claire, who accompanied the Warriors on this climb, became anxious. While looking down into a valley is pretty scary, it's actually worse to have fog obscure the precipice. For all we knew, a tumble to our right or left would send us careening for thousands of feet.

Luckily, our only misfortune was getting rained on. No one fell to his or her death. Zeus did not strike us with a thunderbolt. We reached the Greenleaf Hut in one piece, where we enjoyed hot chocolate. Each AMC hut, scattered throughout the Whites, is a rustic oasis where hikers warm themselves, use a bathroom, refill their water, and, for a hefty price, eat a meal and spend the night. A few are open all year round. All have acted as lifesavers for ill-prepared or unlucky hikers.

As I hefted my backpack to leave the hut, a fit young woman AMC volunteer staffer asked, "Would you be willing to bring a radio down to my coworker? Her battery gave out. She's a half-mile down the trail attending to an injured hiker."

"Sure thing," I answered.

We found the volunteer and injured climber sitting on a jumble of boulders just below the tree line. The victim was a woman with an apparently broken ankle. Her husband stood by with the radio-deprived volunteer. I gave her the fully charged radio, which she promptly employed to initiate a rescue. As we continued down into Franconia Notch, we passed at least a dozen volunteers racing up to help carry the injured woman to an ambulance waiting at the trailhead. We learned that it takes at least six people at a time to carry a stretcher, but, because of the rockiness of steep trails hemmed in by trees, progress moves at a glacial and exhausting pace. The stretcher-bearers need either rest or replacement every fifteen minutes. The descent that took us four hours would take them ten or more.

We found the experience all the more sobering since we realized that one false step could have injured any one of us as badly as or worse than the woman with the hurt ankle. The Mountain Warriors, Claire, and I gained great respect for the women and men who are on call for such emergencies.

The Warriors encountered snow on six of their climbs but none as formidable as they trudged through on November 10, 2006, during their ascent of North Kinsman. In keeping with their philosophy about climbing in all weather, the boys set out in thick fog mixed with cold drizzle. They encountered slushy snow at a surprisingly low altitude. The only view they had was of pine trees pressing in on all sides. Everyone slipped and fell. More than a few got snow down their boots and up their jackets. Stream crossings added to the general misery. And yet, when they reached the thankless, fog-shrouded, 4,293-foot summit and I asked them if they were willing to hike three more hours to reach South Kinsman at 4,358 feet, they unanimously agreed. Bagging the extra peak was worth it to them. These boys had become pretty resilient climbers more likely to carry me along than vice versa.

The following November, the Warriors tackled Mount Zeland 4,260 feet. In order to make the long hike from the AMC's Highland House, reach the summit, and get back

Kieran, Aiden, Josef, and Patrick atop Mount Zealand

before sunset, we set out at five in the morning. With headlamps and flashlights, we picked our way along the trail until we reached the Zealand Hut, where we saw the sun rise over the Presidential Range to the east. Lots of snow had fallen fresh on the trail and trees at the higher altitudes. Unlike the miserable slush on the cloud-covered Kinsmans, this fluffy stuff sparkled in the bright sun. The boys rejoiced to see the first snow of that winter while, down below, it was still fall.

On one dry summer day, the Warriors took on Mount Jefferson, at 5,712 feet New Hampshire's third highest peak. Although conditions were near perfect, my brother Michael warned us before the climb that a series of rocky steps called the Caps Ridge had some fairly steep, rough sections. Each of the Caps Ridge rock walls not only blocked our view of anything ahead but also challenged our endurance and creativity. Unlike worn smooth rocks we had encountered previously above the tree line, these boulders were jagged and sharp. At first glance, some of them looked insurmountable. But then another climber with

Aiden and the rock wall

a small dog came up behind us. To our amazement, the little Welsh Corgi found a way to charge up the rock face. When he reached the top, the dog looked over the edge at us and barked as if to say, "What are you waiting for?"

As much as the terrain, the Warriors kept an eye out for wildlife. Although they did see a moose, the boys were a bit disappointed not to see any other large animals save a fleeting glimpse of a red fox. But on Columbus Day weekend in 2005, while climbing Mount Garfield, they had a close encounter with birds. My brother Tom, an avid hiker in his own right, told us the night before our climb that, if we stood still for a few minutes, gray jays would land on our outstretched hands. The boys found it true. The fearless birds perched on their palms, and we took photos.

In contrast, on a different climb, Nori Needle joined the club. We heard him exclaim, "Is it raining?" Immediately afterwards, Aiden saw a bird poop on Nori's hat. My coworker Robert Peters tells me that he was out riding a bike once, when a huge shadow came over him. It was so large that he assumed it was a low-flying airplane, but when he looked up, a pelican crapped on his face. Nature is at once beautiful and cruel.

The various ascents were not without their trials. Outdoor adventures include bug bites, blisters, sunburn, frostbite, scrapes, and bruises as well as interpersonal conflicts, especially under physical duress. We had dustups over the climbing pace. Although it is a safety issue to have anyone out of sight up front or in back, no group hikes at the same speed all the

*Aiden and Josef on the summit of
Mount Garfield*

time. Holding rabbits back or urging turtles on is not popular with either group or easy to accomplish. Conflicts arose over which trail to take as well as estimated arrival time if we took said trail. Machismo and competition both sustained and aggravated our climbs.

Guidebooks are another matter. They often underestimate or misrepresent trail conditions. On their best days, the boys laughed off a path labeled "moderately difficult" as they ascended arduously hand-over-hand. On other occasions, I fought to keep one Warrior or another from throwing the offending guidebook over a cliff. We learned to take published descriptions with a grain of salt. A guide might poetically describe a slope as "sweeping gracefully upward" when in fact the damned trail rears vertically like a jagged stone wall.

On our first attempt to climb Mount Garfield, we followed a book closely until we realized we were four miles off course, so far that we had to abandon the summit until another day. In fairness, part of the problem with guides is that they are written at particular times. New England winters, not to mention avalanches, easily alter terrain, landmarks, and trails. Trees fall. Brush obscures signs. Especially in springtime, even rivers change course. An old guidebook may be particularly deceptive. Also, what is easy for some authors may be challenging for other climbers.

On Mount Tripyramid, a guidebook instructed us to "scramble up the steep granite slabs" of the North Slide and warned that the trail is "unsafe if wet or icy." Since the day was warm and sunny, we went up the slide only to discover that it was still sliding. Every few minutes, rocks as big as cinder blocks rebounded from above and below. We spread ourselves far apart to reduce the risk of dislodging a boulder onto another member of our party or losing the entire club in an avalanche. It was a no-brainer deciding to take the longer and safer Scaur Ridge Trail down.

Aiden in the Alpine zone on Mount Franklin

Josef and Patrick chillin' on a natural water slide after
climbing Mount Eisenhower

We did find some guidebooks more accurate than others. *The 4000-Footers of the White Mountains: A Guide and History* by Steven Smith and Mike Dickerman is particularly good. Nonetheless, some of our best experiences came when we went off the reservation, bushwhacked a trail, slid down smooth rocks till our pants nearly ripped, or swam in mountain streams. We had particularly good times riding natural water slides in the same Ammonoosuc River that once threatened to kill my Uncle Bob.

Water and food can also be sources of friction because these necessities have to be carried, and every ounce on a person's back makes climbing harder. Some Warriors foolishly sacrificed hydration and nutrition for shoulder and back comfort, not smart since thirst and hunger are mighty unpleasant in their own rights. Experience helped mitigate all these problems. The boys learned, like Boy Scouts, to be prepared for the worst. It never hurt to carry extra of what could not be procured on the trail.

Choosing the right clothes and shoes is important as well. We learned the hard way that cotton kills and that synthetic fibers wick moisture and breathe better. Crappy shoes promote blisters. The temptation to overdress at the outset lessens with experience. You have to pick the right amount of clothes to keep comfortable while exerting yourself, which is an entirely different amount than what you need to wear when you first get out of your car.

We learned these and other lessons together. We hiked hundreds of miles. We ate a lot of gorp (raisins, nuts, and chocolate) and peed on trees that sprouted before Abraham Lincoln was president. We laughed, sang, farted, and burped (too much of the latter two, according to Claire). We reached the summits of twenty-eight beautiful peaks, something each of the Mountain Warriors is proud to have accomplished.

Ultimately, the busier schedules of high school and some increasing pain in my knees brought our climbing to a halt, but I am pleased to say that two of my sons have made additional climbs with their friends, once in the dead of winter. Patrick and Aiden also lobbied for an August climb with me in 2013. Like my uncle Bob, I passed on an enthusiasm for mountain climbing and shared a few adventures.

Kathy M. Newman, an associate professor of English at Carnegie Mellon University, said in a March 16, 2014, *Boston Globe* op-ed entitled "Power Play":

> Parents today—myself included—are afraid to let our kids so much as run to the neighbor's house, and schools are cutting back on recess to focus on test prep. It's not hyperbolic to suggest that the decline of wild, unsupervised outdoor play—the play the vast majority of us grew up with, whether we were born in the 1940s or the 1970s—has reached crisis proportions. We are raising a generation that is more anxious, depressed, and narcissistic, and, without a doubt, less inspired.

In June 2014, National Public Radio reported that the predominant exposure to the outdoors for today's youth is summer camps. Parents spend a great deal of time and money to get their children into a one- or two-week-long camp.

In 1995, Claire and I considered ourselves lucky when a friend invited our firstborn to Camp Applejack in upstate New York. Sleeping in cabins around a pristine lake with counselors organizing games and other activities sounded pretty good. But Justin did not enjoy himself. Some of the other campers, who came from money, were snobs. The staff highly orchestrated the entire time with nothing left for the children to figure out. No risks were taken. And Justin missed us, as we did him.

Why in the world do parents pay thousands of dollars to send their children away to the woods rather than spend far less to go climbing with them? Nothing is more valuable than time together accomplishing something challenging. Claire and I are so close to our children because we share challenging experiences. We would never consider time apart from them better than time spent together.

We will have stories to share by the fire when we are old and frail. We will look at photos and enjoy more than a few laughs. Between daycare, preschool, summer camp, and all the other child-rearing done by strangers, it's small wonder that many adults can't communicate with their offspring. My advice to new parents is, instead of sending your sons or daughters on an organized field trip, set off with them on a disorganized adventure. And let it unfold as it will.

Patrick, a Mountain Warrior, only a little less than a god

Holding Court

Tom Lewis, a self-described artist-activist, taught me that civil disobedience has five distinct parts: planning, execution, litigation, consequences, and evaluation. Each phase has its own challenges and charms, but the trial, especially a jury trial, is my favorite. There's something exhilarating about laying one's reasoning out before a group of peers and awaiting their judgment. It provides intellectual challenge as well as an important check on self-righteousness. It's a dramatic game with moral and political stakes.

I believe trial by jury is one of the most precious institutions of our government, one that would be even more potent if citizens understood the extent of their own power. Too often, jurors are so cowed by years of docility in the face of all authority figures that they cannot believe the fact that they, and they alone, render an unimpeachable verdict. Too many people lean forward in the jury box like witless pets waiting the commands of their masters during a judge's final instructions. They practically shout, "Tell us what to do, O black-robed Deity, for we are not worthy!" But, once in a while, I've seen an individual juror or even an entire panel display the kind of independence that our colonial forebears cherished. The promise of appearing before jurors like that fills me with hope when I go to court.

Most of my jury trials have been grounded in an ancient legal doctrine called the necessity defense. In a nutshell, it holds that when a person breaks a lesser law in order to prevent a greater crime, he or she is excused from the lesser charge. Sir Walter Scott said, "Necessity creates the law: it supersedes rules, and whatever is reasonable and just in such circumstances is likewise legal." Instances of necessity stretch all the way back to the Book of Jonah where sailors threw cargo into the sea to prevent their ship from sinking.

In US law, the oldest cases, *The William Gray* (1810) and *United States v. Ashton* (1834), involved violating an embargo act and justifying mutiny to prevent a ship from sinking. Other cases have justified shooting of protected game, removal of a child from school due to illness, lowering a dam to prevent flooding, and political civil disobedience. The most common illustration is the case of a burning building where a child is screaming for help. With no other immediate and effective means of saving the child, a person is justified to carry out the rescue personally without fear of being convicted of trespass. Necessity justifies breaking the law in the presence of imminent harm when alternative means of preventing the harm are unavailable or ineffective and the means a person employs can reasonably be considered effective. Such stipulations prevent misuse of necessity as an excuse for wanton lawbreaking.

I see the necessity defense as a bulwark against absurd enforcement of the law and a reminder that individuals retain ultimate responsibility for preventing evil. Without necessity, potential heroes would stand idle, waiting, perhaps in vain, for designated professionals to arrive or, worse yet, feel satisfied to file petitions to those professionals while people die. When faced with the destitute, Ebenezer Scrooge asks, "Are there no prisons? Are there no workhouses?" Pilate washes his hands of Christ. Both refuse personal responsibility for people whose lives hang in the balance. Necessity encourages us to do better.

While any defense is usually mounted by a lawyer, my experience is that representing yourself at trial is vital. Going *pro se* or representing oneself also gives a defendant a better opportunity to make a personal appeal and, if one prepares properly, can be very empowering.

My first experience with a necessity defense stemmed from civil disobedience at a GTE plant in Westborough, Massachusetts. At that time, GTE had a five-hundred-million-dollar contract to design the command, control, and communications system for the MX missile. They called it C3 and boasted that this computer system would withstand a nuclear attack and continue directing American nuclear missiles, even in the absence of human operators. Tom Lewis called it "the eyes, ears, and brain of nuclear war."

On August 3, 1984, only two months after Claire and I were married and three days before the thirty-ninth anniversary of the United States atomic bombing of Hiroshima, a group of us demonstrated at the GTE plant, including Claire; a former Trappist monk Dan Lawrence; a teacher Ernie LeBeau, and me. We walked up GTE's driveway, knelt by the main entrance, and prayed for nuclear disarmament.

On November 7 at our trial in Worcester, we planned to argue that GTE's work presented an imminent threat of nuclear war, that alternative means to abate that threat had been tried without success, and that prayer has the power to abate the harm. After Judge Thomas Fallon denied prosecutor Harold Johnson's motion to limit the scope of the trial, we brought military experts to testify to the likelihood of nuclear war and clergy to testify to the efficacy of prayer to reduce that risk.

During cross-examination of Worcester's Catholic Bishop, Bernard Flanagan, Mr. Johnson asked, "Do you condone going onto someone else's property to make a statement?"

"It has to be left to the consciences of the people involved," the bishop replied, "whether they feel justified in breaking a lesser law, as it were, for a greater good."

"Isn't it true," Mr. Johnson asked, "that prayer would be just as effective off the GTE property as on it?"

Taken aback, the Bishop answered, "I guess so."

The district attorney should have left it there, but instead he asked the same question to our next witness, a Methodist minister named Steven Harvester. "Absolutely not!" Rev. Harvester replied, "In my pastoral experience, prayer is more efficacious in proximity to the sick."

Bishop Flanagan rose up from his seat in the gallery to say, "I agree!"

Unfortunately, after deliberating several hours, the jury found us guilty, and the judge gave us thirty days in jail.

On March 5, 1986, Harold Johnson prosecuted Carol Bellin and me in Westborough District Court for a Valentine's Day protest at GTE. In her testimony, Carol told Judge Paul LoConto that her actions at GTE followed a three-year peace walk across the US and Soviet Union. "My intention was to call out to the hearts of the GTE workers on a day that often trivializes love," she testified.

"I am a Roman Catholic, struggling to be a good Christian," I testified. "Our protest is a minor misdemeanor in light of the work being done at GTE . . . . What the company is about is the shedding of blood, the taking of life. The work done there could potentially incinerate everyone in the courtroom . . . . The money they spend on the MX," I testified, "could be used to feed the poor."

"Does the state have a recommendation for sentencing?" Judge LoConto asked after finding us guilty.

"Yes, your honor," Mr. Johnson said. "The maximum: thirty days in jail on the charge of trespassing and sixty days on the charge of disorderly conduct, to be served consecutively."

Holy cannoli! Harold had loaded both barrels.

Then the judge said something I had never heard before or since: "What does the defense recommend?"

Carol proposed, "A guilty finding, your honor."

"Would you pay a fine or accept community service?" Judge LoConto asked.

"No, you honor," I replied. "We could not pay a fine in good conscience, and we believe that our actions at GTE were a community service."

The judge sighed and called for a recess. We full well expected him to return and say something like, "While I sympathize with the defendants, since they refuse lighter sentences, my hands are tied. In a sense, they are forcing me to send them to jail."

The packed courtroom was silent with everyone expecting the worst when Judge LoConto returned to the bench. But then, without elaboration, he said, "Guilty finding. You are free to go."

Poor Mr. Johnson was flabbergasted. Our friends, family, and supporters cheered and swept Carol and me into the lobby where everyone joined hands for a prayer of thanksgiving. Judge LoConto stunned us by coming out of the court and standing just outside our circle with his head bowed. His courage serves as a powerful reminder that anyone can take a stand for peace.

My next foray with necessity arose out of a blockade of the entrance to Westover Air Force Base in Chicopee, Massachusetts. After Iraqi President Saddam Hussein invaded Kuwait in August 1990, President Bush began deploying US troops to Saudi Arabia through Westover. He called it Operation Desert Shield, insisting its purpose was to dissuade Iraqis from invading their oil-rich neighbor. By October, nearly ninety thousand US soldiers had passed through Westover on their way to the Persian Gulf. Military experts reported that once US forces in Saudi Arabia exceeded a hundred thousand, logistics would require that they either advance into Kuwait or be withdrawn before winter sandstorms commenced in March. Deployment of additional troops in October guaranteed that Desert Shield would become Desert Storm.

In fact, the predicted outcome occurred, and, as peace activists feared, the human cost of driving Iraqis out of Kuwait grew enormous. During his last televised press conference after the US invasion, General Norman Schwarzkopf, who had commanded US troops, was asked if he knew how many Iraqis had been killed in the war. I will never forget hearing him reply, "One hundred thousand, two hundred thousand. I don't know, and frankly that's not a number I'm very much concerned about."

On October 20, 1990, as the point of no return leading up to this slaughter approached, 130 anti-war activists used their bodies to block all entrances to Westover Air Force Base. The commander told the press that the protest effectively shut the base down.

On May 13, 1991, thirteen *pro se* defendants went to trial by jury in Springfield, Massachusetts. We beefed up our expert witness list and prepared a lengthy brief on necessity. Judge Michael Ryan allowed our defense to go forward *de bene*, a kind of provisional approval that he would affirm or deny at the trial's end, thus permitting or disallowing the jury's consideration of the necessity defense. The case lasted a week and included testimony from experts and all the defendants.

Our first witness was Paul Walker, Ph.D. He is a US Army veteran, arms analyst, author on arms control and military policy, former faculty member at Harvard and MIT, and consultant for the US Department of Defense and US Arms Control and Disarmament Agency. Dr. Walker testified to the inevitability of war once the hundred-thousand-US-troops mark passed. He detailed the threat to civilians posed by weapons the US deployed and later used.

Alan Miller, a Vietnam veteran, testified to the effect of an anti-personnel weapon nicknamed The Daisy Cutter. This fuel-air explosive, used in Vietnam and Iraq, is so heavy that it has to be rolled out of a plane rather than dropped through bomb bay doors. We asked Mr. Miller what one could see on the ground after one of these bombs was dropped. In a barely audible whisper, he replied, "There's nothing to see . . . . An area the size of several football fields is completely incinerated."

US Army Captain Harlow Ballard, an active duty military doctor who applied for conscientious objector status in the fall of 1990, testified to civilian casualties in Iraq as well as physical and psychological harm done to US troops sent to the Gulf.

Ted Conna, M.D., child psychiatrist, and assistant professor at the University of Massachusetts Medical School, testified to psychological harm done to American children by deployment of US troops to the Gulf. Even children without relatives in the military experienced increased anxiety. Dr. Conna also testified how studies showed that this anxiety was greatly reduced for children whose parents resist war. Apparently, children feel reassured by association with adults who try to prevent harm.

Meyer Weinberg, PhD, professor of Afro-American studies at the University of Massachusetts, Amherst, testified to the historic effectiveness of civil disobedience in opposing racism. He began with an account of slaves in colonial Georgia breaking the law to teach each other to read and culminated with his experience working with Dr. Martin Luther King, Jr.

Michael True, English professor at Assumption College, a longtime activist, an author and lecturer on the history, theory, and practice of nonviolence in America as well as a dear friend, testified to the effectiveness of civil disobedience in the history of the American labor, women's, anti-nuclear power, and peace movements.

Joseph Gerson, Peace Education Secretary for the New England Office of the American Friends Service Committee, testified to the link between US intervention and the risk of nuclear war.

An immigration lawyer and representative of the American-Arab Anti-Discrimination Committee named Susan Akram testified how US deployment in Saudi Arabia instigated violent attacks in the US against Muslim Americans.

Sister Jane Morrissey, SSJ, Director of the Office of Justice and Peace for the congregation of the Sisters of Saint Joseph in Springfield, Massachusetts, and professor at Elms College, testified to the religious necessity of Christians to oppose all wars, most especially those that indiscriminately harm civilians.

The judge rejected testimony of Tess Sneesby, director of Abby's House women's shelter in Worcester, who intended to offer evidence that the Gulf War had diverted federal funds away from the American poor. Nonetheless, with three military veterans, four PhDs, two medical doctors, and an attorney, we felt we had made a case that ours was a serious and necessary action.

The defendants, five women and eight men as young as nineteen and as old as seventy-four, then testified as to what we did and why. The jury, seated only eight feet away, was as close and personal as one could imagine. We looked straight into their eyes and poured out our hearts.

Ironically, some of the trial's best moments for the defense occurred under cross-examination by the prosecution. After seventy-four-year-old Frances Crowe, a fantastically dedicated Quaker peace activist, gave her testimony, Assistant District Attorney John O'Neil tried to get her to admit that, instead of civil disobedience, she could have continued protesting on public property near the base's main gate.

"When was the first time you protested at Westover?" he asked.

Frances thought for a minute and replied, "1961."

Even Judge Ryan had to laugh.

After the defendant and World War II veteran Alden Poole's testimony, the prosecutor asked, "When did you first realize you were a pacifist?"

"When I saw my first dead German soldier in 1943," Alden said.

> He had a rosary and a belt buckle that said 'Gott mit uns,' 'God with us.' I was surprised that those heathens believed in God. I looked in his wallet and saw a picture of his wife and kids and realized that he was a slob just like me, trained to be a killer by the lure of medals, flags, and uniforms. I knew I was a pacifist then. I just didn't have the guts to live it out until later on.

Tom Lewis introduced his paintings of homeless men and women to underscore his belief that ending war was essential to ending poverty. During cross-examination, the prosecutor sauntered up to Tom, pointed toward one of the portraits, and asked in a friendly tone, "What is the name of this person?"

Tom leaned out of the witness box to peer at the canvas and said, "Dave."

Alden Poole, World War II veteran and peacemaker

Mr. Ryan gestured to another portrait saying, "And who is this?"

"Sally," Tom replied.

And then, quite suddenly, the prosecutor spun around and bellowed, "AND HOW DO YOU THINK DAVE AND SALLY WOULD FEEL IF OUR COUNTRY WERE INVADED????"

"Well, to be honest," Tom answered calmly, "these folks are so downtrodden, that, if there was an invasion, I'm afraid they would join it."

The entire courtroom, jurors included, burst into laughter. Undaunted, Tom pressed on, "I'm serious. These people have been thoroughly crushed."

In her testimony, US Congressional candidate Lisa Baskin moved the jury to tears when she concluded:

Tom Lewis and his portraits of the homeless

photo by Christopher Navin for *Inside Worcester*

> I felt that if I had been a German citizen in 1939 or 1940 that I had a responsibility to question at great risk and to open my mouth and to protest the government and not be a good German and not to go along with my government's workings if I felt that it was immoral and devastating . . . . And the harm that I felt I was going to do by sitting in the road and helping to shut down the business of war for just a few minutes would be something I could say to my grandchildren who turn to me and say, 'Did you do anything to stop those children from being killed? Did you do anything? Were you silent? What did you do?'

Despite our best efforts, the judge ruled that we had failed to bring sufficient evidence to raise a necessity defense. Since we had stipulated to all the physical facts, we were essentially standing naked in front of the jury. I had the unenviable position of concocting a closing argument. If I referred to nuclear weapons, the Gulf War, or the defense of necessity, the judge would declare a mistrial and we would face a repeat trial.

Shooting, so to speak, from the hip, I said:

In a few minutes, the judge is going to instruct you in matters of the law relevant to your deliberations. He will read the model jury instructions which say that your decision must be unanimous and is final. It is your decision and yours alone.

The judge will read the statute we are charged with violating, which says: "Whoever, without right, enters or remains in or upon the . . . land . . . of another . . . after having been forbidden to do so by the person who has lawful control of said premises, whether directly or by notice posted thereon . . . shall be punished by a fine of not more than one hundred dollars or by imprisonment for not more than thirty days . . . ."

The key phrase for us is "without right." Massachusetts Chief Justice Paul Liacos says the jury is "the conscience of the community." And what is conscience? It involves morality, ideals, our concept of what is right. You will have to decide, on the basis of all the evidence you have heard, whether we had a right in conscience to do as we did.

I urge you to remember that only three Americans enjoy national holidays: George Washington, Abraham Lincoln, and Dr. Martin Luther King, Jr. Washington led a rebellion against the unjust laws of Britain, Lincoln was elected in large part by abolitionists who broke many laws to free slaves, and King was arrested many times to oppose segregation. I suggest that, in the context of all that we knew on the day of our arrest, we not only had a right to act as we did but a duty to do so. I pray that you agree and return a verdict of not guilty for all thirteen of us. Thank you.

Mr. Ryan, who had a US Air Force captain sitting next to him throughout the trial, closed by acknowledging that we had been following our beliefs but asked the jury, "What about the beliefs of the servicemen fighting in Iraq?"

"This case is not about war," he continued, "it's about law. They have a right to protest, but no right to break the law." He told the jurors that the case was open and shut.

To everyone's surprise, the jury deliberated for two days. The jurors returned guilty verdicts for us all but not before the forewoman read a statement saying, "If we had been allowed to consider the defense of necessity, we would have acquitted the defendants."

We appealed the verdicts and convictions to the Massachusetts Court of Appeals. The brief I wrote ran to forty-four pages and cited sixty-five cases. I argued it before the three-judge panel. After Ben Goldstein, an advising lawyer, read the brief and heard my argument, he told us he was optimistic about our chances.

The attorney for the state came woefully unprepared. When a justice asked her what case she relied on for an aspect of her argument, she fumbled with her papers in embarrassment. I felt so bad for her, I whispered, *Commonwealth v. Brugman.* No matter. Four months later, the court denied our appeal without comment.

Thankfully, we have had other opportunities to sharpen our argument. On November 1, 1989, All Saints Day at a trial stemming from another protest at GTE, a jury in

Worcester Superior Court found Tom Lewis, Hattie Nestel, Ken Synan, Jennifer Hoffman, and me not guilty.

At the opening day of that trial, Judge Austin Philbin sighed audibly and said, "I was a college activist who knew the day would come when I would be the authority figure looking down at other activists."

Nevertheless, he promised to run the trial by the book and show us no favoritism. When the jury acquitted us, Judge Philbin stepped off the bench and told me, "I am so relieved! I didn't sleep at all last night worrying about how I'd feel sending you all to jail." An even bigger surprise came outside the court when a juror approached us. He was the only man on the jury, a Massachusetts state trooper whom we would have rejected during jury selection, but we had already used up all our peremptory strikes.

The clean-cut, middle-aged trooper told us, "You deserved a jury of your peers, but you didn't get one. You are all so much better than us."

We replied that this was not true and that what the jurors did was very courageous.

"For a while," he said, "I stood as the sole proponent of acquittal until the women came to agree."

I couldn't help but think of Henry Fonda in the movie *Twelve Angry Men*, only ours was a jury of six with five angry women.

The case set a minor precedent. It was widely reported and is archived at the Meikeljohn Civil Liberties Institute in California. The government eventually scrapped the MX nuclear missile, and the GTE plant in Westborough served first as an office supply store and then a community college. Sometimes, not that often, but once in a while, activists do more than spit into the wind. Sometimes we actually save lives.

Another necessity case arose out of genocide in Darfur, Sudan. In December 2004, Brenna Cussen, Chris Allen-Douçot, Grace Ritter, and I formed a Catholic Worker Peace Team that went to Nyala in southern Darfur. We delivered aid in massive camps of internally displaced people and witnessed horrific effects of mass killing, abduction, and rape by government troops and allied militias.

When we asked Sudanese human rights activists what would be the most effective thing we could do to stop the genocide, they told us that civil disobedience at the Sudanese Embassy in Washington, DC would send shock waves through the government in Khartoum. So, upon returning to the states, we wrote to the ambassador,

photo by Brenna Cussen

*defense exhibit D51,
women in Dereig camp for
internally-displaced persons in
Southern Darfur*

reported our findings from Darfur, and asked for a meeting to discuss how the Sudanese government must stop the killing.

After receiving no reply, Brenna and I, along with Tom Lewis, Brian Kavanagh, Ken Hannaford-Ricardi, Harry Duchesne, and Liz Fallon blocked the entrance to the embassy while holding enlarged photos of victims in Darfur. When the US Secret Service, the police charged with protecting embassies, arrived, we knelt and prayed until they handcuffed and arrested us. They transported us to the Fifth Precinct and offered

photo by Kathy Boylan

Harry Duchesne, Tom Lewis, and Scott, from left, front
blocking the entrance to the Sudanese Embassy with Brenna Cussen

the chance to post and forfeit fifty dollars. Essentially, it amounted to a payoff to go free without the arrest appearing on our records.

We knew that most people arrested previously at embassies accepted the terms, but we did not want to do civil disobedience as kind of theater, so we refused to pay. We spent the night in the central cell block. The court arraigned us the following afternoon.

Although our charges did not warrant a jury trial, we took the case very seriously. The prosecutor, a decent fellow named Anthony Gagliardi, agreed in pretrial conference not to contest a defense of necessity if we would stipulate to all major facts, something we planned to do anyway. Judge Rufus King III seemed amenable. A pretrial conference set the stage for us to put genocide in Darfur on trial on May 25, 2005. To accomplish it, we once again brought many experts to testify.

Our first expert, Professor Eric Reeves from Smith College, the world's foremost authority on genocide in Darfur, testified.

> Four hundred thousand people have already died in the Darfur genocide. Mortality is now running at a rate of fifteen thousand human beings a month, five hundred a day . . . . I think it's extremely important we realize both the scale of the genocide in Darfur and the recalcitrance of this regime . . . . This is a regime that feels no significant pressure to stop the genocide . . . . In light of that failure, it is incumbent, I believe, upon citizens such as yourselves to make it clear that we have not only a moral but a legal responsibility to take action . . . . Given the scale and urgency of genocidal destruction, it is very difficult for me to see other means that can be as efficacious as those which make it very, very clear that in this city those present will not accept a business-as-usual arrangement with the government of Sudan.

Mwiza Munthali, information director at TransAfrica Forum, a global justice organization focused on Africa, the Caribbean, and Latin America, testified how TransAfrica had sponsored civil disobedience at the South African Embassy as part of the successful campaign to end apartheid.

Barbara Wien, co-director of Peace Brigades International, said we had done "a tremendous humanitarian service to stop the genocide."

Bishop Thomas Gumbleton, auxiliary Roman Catholic Bishop of Detroit and former president of Pax Christi USA, described us as people who acted

> out of a perspective of faith and a profound regard and respect for human life, and the need to protect that human life, especially when it's being attacked in such a ferocious way. Something like they did is so very important because it's hard to get attention to what's going on over there, and our own government has failed to respond adequately. And we're in danger of having a second Rwanda and that was eight hundred thousand people.

After all seven defendants testified, Judge King asked how we could consider our small act of civil disobedience an effective means to abate so large and distant a harm as genocide in Darfur.

I answered,

> If your honor draws attention to the case of *New York v. Gray*, which is cited in our brief, you'll find substantial legal argumentation on what they call "the hammer blow theory." When a carpenter hammers in a nail, he strikes a single blow at a time. Well, each blow that the carpenter strikes is a part of the effective force necessary to drive in the nail. The first blow may not drive the nail all the way home, but the last blow is not the only effective blow, because without the previous blows the nail would not go home. So each link in the chain is equally sufficiently effective.

The judge then asked if it wasn't a violation of the law "to block the access to a building, not because of anything going on in the building but in order to achieve notice to an issue which, for the sake of this argument, we can say, is an urgent issue and requires media attention."

I replied,

> Well, Your Honor, before I went to Sudan I would probably say that an action at the Sudanese Embassy, or at any other government institution in the United States, would hopefully be helpful but not necessarily the most effective means [to abate the harm of genocide in Darfur] . . . . But having been in Sudan and having been told by people there that actions at that embassy in the United States would be the most effective and would resonate in Khartoum, I feel differently. Sudanese human rights activists said a demonstration in Khartoum would last a minute and would appear in no Sudanese press. We would be deported, and no one would hear about it.
>
> But a demonstration at the embassy in Washington would be front-page news, and it would give hope to people and would hold back the hand of that government from sending planes again to bomb more villages and to take more lives. And we could only do what we reasonably thought we could do to save those lives. If we were in Nazi Germany and someone told us blocking train tracks could save lives in Auschwitz and we had evidence to corroborate that and we had seen for ourselves that other things had failed, then even though blocking the tracks could be a criminal act, we might have done that as well.

Judge King posed another question: "Taking that example, would it make any difference to you if the train you were blocking had, as its cargo, prisoners bound for a concentration camp as opposed to a train serving normal passenger traffic as noncombatants?"

I answered,

> There has to be a direct link between our action and the harm sought
> to be prevented. The link between a civilian train and the Nazi regime is
> tenuous. But a government office, a Nazi office, a chancery of the German
> Reich is similar to this chancery of the Republic of Sudan. That is part of
> a government guilty of humankind's most grievous violation of law. The
> employees are part of that government. So there is a very, very close link.

Judge King recessed for two hours and then concluded,

> Having considered the arguments, the very well-presented arguments
> and exhibits which make a clear case that the defendants acted in good
> faith and with integrity pursuant to deeply held beliefs, the court is
> nevertheless constrained to find that the Government's case has been made,
> and the defense of necessity has failed to negate or excuse it, so I find the
> defendants guilty.

We appealed the verdict to the DC appeals court, no mean feat, and after failing there went on to the US Supreme Court, a task I wouldn't wish on my worst enemy. Our best efforts did not prevail. The justices refused to take up the case: they agree to hear fewer than one percent of the cases that come to them. Out of legal options, we returned to the Sudanese embassy and blocked the entrance once again. If at first you don't succeed . . . .

In twenty-five trials, my co-defendants and I have sometimes been sent to jail, more often received probation or community service, and been acquitted only twice. However, victories are not so easily measured.

When Tom Lewis stood trial in 1968 for burning draft files in Catonsville, Maryland, the judge interrupted Tom's testimony to ask, "If these men were not sent to Vietnam, other people would have been sent who would not otherwise have been sent, would they not?"

"But why, your honor, why this?" Tom replied. He continued,

> Why does it have to be like this? You are accepting the premise that if
> these men are not sent, other men will be sent. You are not even asking
> what can be done to stop this insane killing, what can be done to stop
> the genocide, what can be done to stop the conditions in Latin America.
> You are not dealing with these things. You are accepting this as in Nazi
> Germany people accepted the massacre of other people. This is insane. I
> protest this.

In a similar way, I challenged an African-American judge named Kevin McKenna in Providence, Rhode Island, who, on Martin Luther King Day 1989, sentenced demonstrators, one after another, to three days in jail. Judge McKenna acted completely without emotion, not even looking up as defendants made statements. He shuffled papers as court officers led each one away to the Civil War-era jail in Cranston.

The Sudan Seven: Tom Lewis, Harry Duchesne, Brian Kavanagh,
Liz Fallon, Brenna Cussen, Ken Hannaford-Ricardi, and Scott

When I came before him, I ended my statement by expressing my sorrow that a black judge could show so little regard for protesters on the day honoring a man who won the end of segregation through civil disobedience.

He looked down at me and said angrily, "I am not obligated to give you only three days you know. I can just as easily send you to jail for a month."

"That's right, your honor," I retorted. And then,

> You have the power to be even more severe. But what you are not seeing is how many other ways you can respond. I once stood before a judge who continued my case without a finding and then gave my co-defendant and me twenty dollars each. You could really listen to us. You could choose this to be a day when you take a stand for justice as Martin Luther King did. This doesn't have to be just another day. It could be a great one.

In the awkward silence that followed, I braced myself to get whacked, but, after an obvious inner struggle, the judge swallowed his anger and repeated, "Three days in the house of correction." Maybe, as Tom did, I gave the judge something to think about.

Civil disobedience comprises not only an act of conscience but also a plea for sanity, a call for individuals and institutions to break with convention to protect lives. In some cases, as in that of Franz Jägerstätter, the only known Catholic conscientious objector to serving in Hitler's military, the personal consequences are quite severe. Jägerstätter's family, friends, neighbors, parish priest, and even his bishop advised him not to resist the military. Jägerstätter told them he had a recurring dream that everyone in Germany and Austria had boarded an enormous train speeding towards Hell, a train he would not board.

The Nazis beheaded Franz Jägerstätter on August 9, 1943. If he and so many others throughout history could be so very brave, how could I, an American risking so much less, not stand in front of the Hell-bound trains of my day?

Over the years, I've come to believe that the important thing in life is to live with integrity regardless of the consequences. I think the road to Hell is paved with indifference, conformity, hypocrisy, and fear. As soon as someone stands up at personal risk to save lives, we all achieve victory. A criminal conviction and jail sentence do not diminish that victory.

As Father Dan Berrigan said on October 9, 1969, after he and his co-defendants received a three-year jail sentence for their draft resistance as the Catonsville Nine, "We would simply like to thank the court and the prosecution. We agree that this is the greatest day of our lives."

Running

I was never physically fit as a child. I know because my gym teacher administered the President's Physical Fitness Test each spring, and I always failed spectacularly. In order to pass, you had to be proficient in calisthenics, gymnastics, and track and field. I was a skinny boy who had about as much strength and coordination as an earthworm. I couldn't do one chin up, much less the required ten. It always bothered me that the girls only had to hang from the bar for ten seconds, while I had to heave my chin up and over the damned thing ten times. The only event I could actually compete in was the six-hundred-yard dash—the marathon of elementary school sports. I realized early on that long-distance running didn't require anything more than determination. Although I couldn't hit a baseball, lift weights, or do a hundred sit-ups, I could keep running after most of my classmates had quit.

This realization led me to join the cross country team in high school. Back then, when Richard Nixon still presided over the United States, I "ran" for Alvirne High in Hudson, New Hampshire. I was the second slowest member of the team. This proved lucky, because the screaming coach brutalized the boy who always came in last and berated him for not trying harder. I am ashamed to admit I felt mostly grateful that I wasn't in his shoes when he tearfully protested that he had done his best. My guilt deepened when he was diagnosed with brain cancer. During the summer when I sat next to him at a lake and mentioned an upcoming event, he replied matter of factly, "I'll be dead by then."

How could I possibly respond to such a statement? I knew one thing. If I ever became a coach, I would never scream at a runner or doubt when runners said that they had done their best.

I also had to come to grips with the realization that the only person I ever bested had a terminal illness. It did not bode well for my future in the sport.

In 1974, my hometown of Pelham, New Hampshire opened its own high school, and I ran there until I graduated in 1976. I worked very hard, never missed a practice or walked during a race, but I just didn't get faster. In those days, high school competitions ran for two and a half miles. Stars covered the distance in twelve minutes. I usually came in five to seven minutes later, although I did finish once around sixteen minutes because it was so cold that, like all my teammates, I sprinted through the finish directly into the warm school bus. Surprisingly, the team elected me co-captain along with the number one runner in the state, Ray Demers. The honor made me very proud. Little did I know, it would qualify as the first and only election of any kind that I would win in my lifetime.

With every intention of running at Holy Cross College, I met the coach early on. He asked me my pace for ten miles. Having never run that far, I assumed it would be no worse than my high school best, so I told him seven minutes, a ridiculous pace I can only dream of achieving for ten miles. He seemed pleased, which pleased me too. Unfortunately, he came into the field house a day or two later while I trained and said, "You run like a duck," effectively killing my desire to run for him. I quit the team.

After graduation, I ran on and off until I was twenty-five, racing an occasional 5K (kilometer) and Charlie's Surplus, Worcester's legendary ten-mile race over Bancroft Tower Hill, but I gradually left the sport behind. Thankfully, my metabolism still burned calories like a blast furnace. Until I was thirty-five or so, I could eat five meals a day and not gain an ounce. I often wolfed down a pound of pasta for lunch, a large pizza for a snack, and an entire box of Cocoa Krispies with a quart of whole milk in a huge salad bowl before going to bed. Kraft Macaroni and Cheese, Twinkies, pretzels, beer, and even jellybeans had no impact on my weight.

But then, all of a sudden as if by magic, my body started to expand. By thirty-five, I was kind of chubby. At forty-two, I climbed Mount Washington with a couple of friends and nearly collapsed. My housemate Dave Maciewski started calling me Chumly, after the walrus in the *Tennessee Tuxedo* cartoons of the seventies. Strangers asked, "When's the baby due?" And worst of all, I began to feel like a hypocrite when giving talks about simple living. My belly became so large, I could almost use it instead of a podium to hold my notes.

The final straw came in 2008 when Claire started running. She read somewhere that physical activity helps prevent the onset of Alzheimer's, a condition her father suffered before his death in 2007. Claire became so dedicated to running that she did it year round

photo by Grace Duffy

at 190 pounds, Scott, right, running his first 5K in
thirty years with Claire

140

in all kinds of weather. I was simultaneously impressed and humiliated. My dismay came to a head when, on February 10, 2009, I climbed on a scale and with shock saw 199 pounds on the display. It was like reading my own obituary. I had weighed 60 pounds less on my wedding day. Claire could still fit easily into her wedding dress. I had gone from a loose 28-inch waist to tight 40. My doctor told me I had borderline high cholesterol. She warned that I was marching toward obesity and heart problems. The message was clear: change or die.

So on February 11, I started running. It wasn't easy or pretty. I huffed and puffed to the end of my street and back. To say that it hurt would be an understatement. No runner's high. Just misery.

I also changed my eating habits. I knew from earlier participation in political and religious fasts that I could drop weight quickly if I wanted but that afterwards I would eventually gain it back and then some. I didn't need a diet. I needed a lifestyle, something I'd embrace forever, a permanent change. The approach I adopted was probably not the healthiest but it appealed to me. I resolved to eat only twice a day, once in moderation and the other time without restraint. Nothing in between. I also began drinking more water, which I like with lemon juice. The combination of exercise with less consumption did the trick. I began gradually to lose weight, a pound or two a week.

To seal my deal, Claire and I signed up to run a race in April. We chose the Jay Lyons 5K that starts and ends conveniently at Blessed Sacrament Church, four blocks from our house. The weather on race day was unseasonably hot, near ninety. Nonetheless, I showed up in a cotton shirt with cargo shorts and an Australian hat. Although I had been running outside for months and weighed ten pounds lighter than my peak, I still looked like a bleached and beached whale. Six minutes into the race, a man passed me pushing a double stroller. He chatted away like he was sitting on a beach chair sipping Coolattas while I was in agony. I didn't know him but hated him nonetheless. Claire and I stayed together for two and a half miles. I picked up the pace a bit and finished at 31:03 with Claire not far behind. More than a hundred people came in behind us. The results appeared online at a site called Cool Running. The experience left me hooked on racing.

I started timing practice runs and making charts of my progress. I signed up for more races. Knowing nothing about proper training, I ran every day and tried my hardest to go faster each time. For a while this scheme seemed wise. I lost more weight and dropped my 5K time down to twenty-nine, twenty-eight, twenty-seven, and then twenty-six minutes. At the Jack Kerouac 5K in his birthplace, Lowell, Massachusetts, I won a small medal for coming in fifth in my age group.

Of course, my relentless overtraining resulted in a typical runner's injury to the iliotibial band and pain in my forefoot that sent me to a podiatrist.

He pointed to x-rays of my feet and announced grimly, "You have early osteoarthritis. The cartilage between your bones is almost nonexistent."

"If you keep running," he predicted, "you will be in a wheelchair by next year."

Bummer.

At such times, a second opinion is a good idea. My regular doctor referred me to a sports injury clinic where I met a genius named Michelle Wellen. She scoffed at the idea that I should stop running. After inspecting my feet, legs, and shoes, she gave me an orthotic insert to wear and a large Styrofoam roller to stretch my upper thighs as well as other strengthening exercises.

"If you follow my instructions," she assured me, "you will not only keep running, but you should get faster too."

Woohoo!

Scott losing faith in the "runner's high" as he pushes to the finish line

She was right. In the six years since Dr. Doom predicted I'd end up crippled, I have run more than six thousand miles and competed in hundreds of races, including four half and eight full marathons. I got my weight down to 149 pounds and became faster. I ran several 5Ks below twenty minutes. I have earned fifteen trophies and many more medals. I even won two races. I routinely finish in the top ten to fifteen percent. To my delight and astonishment, I became considerably swifter than I ever was in high school. As far as I'm concerned, the jury is still out about how fast I may eventually become.

While competition and speed are important parts of my attraction to running, I cannot stress enough how wonderful the experience has been socially. Claire and I joined the Central Mass Striders (CMS), a running club whose die-hard members gather each Monday night all year round at a pub for a crazy, self-timed race in heavy traffic followed by a potluck supper. I started going to weekly races at Worcester State University and in Holyoke, where my older brother Michael has raced for years. I became familiar with dozens of new people, some of whom I now count among my best friends. Something about sharing the experience of racing bonds you with others who do it. Runners push their bodies and challenge their minds to go beyond the limits of normalcy, to keep going when reason screams "Stop!" Runners share a kind of insanity that bonds complete strangers.

This is not to say that I am a soft and fuzzy runner. Hardly. I have a solid reputation as a trash talking, super competitive jerk. I find that needling my competition ratchets up the importance of the outcome. I get people so riled up that many of them want to beat me more than anything else. I told my wife that if I were hit by a car during our weekly pub run, my last words would be, "Did I beat Scott Stevens?"

For Christmas, I gave Mr. Stevens a snow globe embedded with a photo of me defeating him in the Freezer Five. Near the finish of the Canal Diggers 5K, as my friend

Vin Garofoli ran by, Stevens yelled from the sidelines, "Way to go, Vin!"

When I passed, five seconds later, Stevens yelled at me, "Epic fail!" Indeed, I lost to Vin by two seconds.

Mr. Stevens came to a race in Holyoke just to beat me on my birthday. As I sprinted for the finish, my children yelled, "Go Scott, go!" I wanted to tell them to say "Dad," but it was too late. Scott Stevens passed me inches before the finish line, a defeat I not only endured at that moment but over and over again online, since the race director films and posts the finishes.

I sometimes limp to a starting line, massaging a thigh and telling competitors, "It's your race to win" or "I'll be lucky just to finish." But once the race begins, I experience a miraculous healing.

photo by Patrick Duffy

Claire "thanks" Scott for convincing her to run a difficult race

At one such contest when I passed Vin, he turned to me and sneered, "Injuries, my ass!" On another occasion, during my pre-race psych-out, I produced a letter from a doctor at the Cains Mayo Clinic certifying that I was a "broken-down piece of junk."

During my first renewal year of racing, I took on America's most common distance, the 5K. At 3.1 miles, it initially seemed to me to be a very long-distance race, well beyond that six-hundred-yard dash of my childhood, but to most runners, I soon learned, it is a very short race, virtually a sprint. At my third or fourth 5K at Worcester State, a cold rain poured down. As I looked out the window from the sign-up area in the lobby of the university's gym, I shared my dread with two veteran runners.

Scott Stevens's sign posted on Coolrunning.com

One of them shrugged and said, "It's only a 5K" as if the damned thing would be over before I could get cold and wet.

"What are you going do?" the other said. "We have to run anyway."

First of all, a 5K seemed eternally long to me and secondly, I most certainly did not have to run. I could go home and curl up on the couch with a good book and a cup of hot chocolate if I so desired. Nothing forced me to run. What the heck were these people talking about? Not being as macho as they are, I decided to brave the deluge, but, unlike the hard cores , I would ward off pneumonia by donning my blue, hooded sweatshirt.

I felt warm and cozy at the starting line. Unfortunately, my cotton apparel soaked up water like a sponge. By the race's end, the hoodie weighed more than fifteen pounds. I was drenched, frozen, and hunched over like Quasimodo. I never ran in a hoodie again.

Interestingly, I have come to a complete understanding of how the experienced runners felt. In time, running changes from casual to habitual and finally to essential. Weather is never a roadblock, just a factor. Since that downpour at Worcester State, I have run in temperatures over a hundred and below zero, in gusts up to fifty miles an hour, and in rain, snow, sleet, and hail. Claire and I along with other Striders did a winter run by the light of a full moon on the West Boylston Rail Trail. For crying out loud, I ran during Hurricane Sandy and in Kabul, Afghanistan! Only the wrath of my daughter, Grace, kept me from running on Christmas Day. To say it becomes an obsession is to understate its draw.

But, I still had a great deal to learn. By my tenth race at Worcester State, I began to notice that my first mile looked a lot better than my second, which looked better than my third. A gifted runner, Carol Hurley, routinely passed me at the mile mark and finished two minutes ahead. She wasn't alone. I watched scores of people fly by me and then recede into the distance ahead. It was discouraging.

Carol assured me that a slower start would make me faster overall. I resisted her advice. How could you go faster by going slower? She said I was a classic rabbit, full of enthusiasm without the staying power to keep up my frantic pace. Like most newbies, I ran out of steam.

Marty Ellowitz, a mad crazy runner older than I, advised me to save my best mile for my last. "It's better to pass people at the end than to be passed," he said. As I realize now, there are no prizes for winning the first mile.

Although I cannot be taught, I can be badgered. I finally caved in to friendly pressure and altered my approach to races. I resolved to begin nice and easy, gradually picking up my pace. On my first attempt, I got a personal record. In a month, I finished with Carol and sometimes ahead of her. I came close to beating Marty, too. It marked the beginning of my slow realization that I had a few things to learn about running, things that would make me faster.

About then, a natural runner, John Pajer, who won the first race he ever ran at forty-four years old, told me that each extra pound you carry costs you three seconds per mile. His formula proved itself during the period when I was losing weight. On weeks when

I dropped two pounds, my 5K would improve by nineteen seconds without noticeable effort. Unfortunately, once I reached my weight goal, the party was over. My times plateaued. Hard work drove them down slightly. Better and lighter shoes, synthetic shorts, low-top synthetic socks, and a sleeveless singlet helped too. I even clipped my nails, shaved my beard, and cut my hair wicked short. All to the good. Check it out. You'd be surprised how light some racing shoes are. They can make you feel like you are barely wearing shoes at all. In fact, some runners have started going barefoot not so much for speed as for healthier body mechanics. As crazy as I am to reduce weight, I haven't gone that far yet.

When cold weather sets in, I adopt the motto, "If I'm comfortable at the start, I'm wearing too much." I cannot tell you how many runners I have seen fall back because they are overdressed. I'd rather be cold at the outset and comfortable a mile in than miserable at the end. I wear a singlet eight months a year and shorts on all but the most windy and bitter cold days. I have gained a reputation for going light. People raised eyebrows when I showed up in my sleeveless Central Mass Striders shirt and shorts for Stu's 30K when the temperature was thirty-eight degrees, but I was vindicated on the hills where the bundled-up broke into an uncomfortable sweat. Ironically, my Spartan approach to cold weather racing doesn't carry over to any other part of my New England existence. On frosty days, my preference in the car and at home is to bask in temperatures that most nursing home residents would find a bit high. I suit up like Admiral Perry when I go to our weekly one-hour-long peace vigil. It's a mystery to me how I resist the cold while running, but I do.

In my second year of pounding the pavement, I suffered another injury. The miracle worker Dr. Wellen (she's actually a physical therapist, but I have made her a doctor because of her great skill) turned me over to Dr. Joanna Donato (another PT with gifts). She diagnosed a new pain in my foot as plantar fasciitis, a runner's nightmare.

"The plantar fascia," Joanna explained, "are a bundle of muscles that go from your forefoot to your heel. Plantar fasciitis is caused when they are irritated and inflamed."

She recommended rolling my arch on a frozen water bottle along with a break from running to give the muscles a chance to heal. She also added more exercises (strength prevents injuries) that I did and still do religiously.

Other runners gave additional advice. Some said it would take months to heal. My friend Tracy Flynn took a year off running when she got plantar. Her foot felt better after a couple of weeks' rest and started hurting immediately when she tried to run.

John Pajer told me about a thing called the Strassburg Sock that had worked wonders for him, so I bought one. It's a kind of torture device that combines a tight white compression sock with a Velcro band to keep your foot from stretching while you sleep, a joy the sadistic footwear is designed to prevent. I bought a plastic rocker to stand on to stretch my calf muscles. I stopped running altogether. Nothing made the slightest difference.

In response to my hysterical fear that I would regain weight, Joanna said that cross training on a bicycle would keep up my fitness without aggravating the plantar. What she didn't tell me was how dissatisfying biking would be. I used a white stationary bike my kids found abandoned on a curbside and my blue mountain bike. I had to work twice as hard to keep the pounds off. I biked to the pub and watched my friends run. It made me want to cry. Whenever I drove by strangers running, I pulled my car over to ask them wistfully, "How far are you going?"

After a month of faithful effort, I decided I would rather run with pain in my foot than not run with grief in my heart. I told Joanna that I would go eighty/twenty on her advice, keeping all the stretches and strengthening exercises while ditching the cross training. She said I was a problem patient. She was not the first to tell me that. Three blood donor centers have banned me because I make such a fuss it scares other donors away. I never sit down in a doctor's waiting room when pacing satisfies so much more. Agreeing to eighty percent of Joanna's advice constituted a historic compliment to her skill.

You might think that running while injured would be foolish. A life-long, talented runner named Frank Rucki called me "out of my mind." There was a consensus that he was right. If pushed too far, muscles tear, and then even surgery cannot guarantee that I'd ever run again. I was in a serious no-fly zone. And yet, a year and a half later, my old nemesis plantar just gave up trying to bother me. I outlasted him. Go figure.

In December of my first year running, talk at the pub started building about the Boston Marathon. Although the race isn't held until mid-April, the Central Mass Striders (CMS) receive twenty numbers to award to members just before Christmas. In 2011, those individuals had to pay three hundred dollars for a time-waived spot. Each year, the Boston Athletic Association (BAA) sets aside a certain amount of such entry bibs for people who raise funds for a charity or for members of a running club that volunteers at other BAA races. CMS is one of those clubs. The only other way to get a number for the Boston Marathon is to qualify in your age group. Benchmarks to do so have dropped significantly in recent years, making it very difficult for ordinary people to qualify. CMS awards its quota of numbers on the basis of how often members have volunteered over the year at various races.

As someone who did not race longer than 3.1 miles, I considered the Boston Marathon out of my league. Nonetheless, I got caught up in the general excitement. By the time April came around, I was so inspired by the marathoners that I signed up for the first Worcester Half Marathon. Before the race set out in June, I had to increase my weekly mileage and practice on the steep hills included in the course. It was challenging. 13.1 miles seemed an impossible distance. And yet, I finished the race. Unfortunately, I went out alongside Scott Stevens and foolishly ran too fast early on. Thirty-five people passed me in the final stretch. There was still too much rabbit in me.

Running the Worcester Half Marathon opened my mind to other distances. Claire and I went to a race in Oxford called The Dam Trail Race or unofficially The Damned Trail Race. It featured a five-mile and ten-mile course in woods near its namesake, a large earthen dam. Claire wisely ran the five, but I took on the longer challenge (can somebody get me a testosterone suppressor?) where I learned the hard way that genuine trail races are not for the faint of heart. The course wound up and down over hills and loose rocks and through dense and often thorny overgrowth. The "trail" had so many turns, I was hopelessly disoriented in minutes. We ran through a stream soaking our shoes and then through a sandpit coating them with dirt. Finally we climbed a steep hill. I stumbled to the finish loaded with scrapes all over my mud-splattered legs. Jack Goolsky, the CMS president, bleeding from a fall, came in after me. He wasn't the only victim. Apparently, getting injured in a trail race is considered standard fare. Runners actually seek out especially crazy courses. Before the race, we all received white cotton shirts each with a drawing that looked like it had been done by a nine-year-old. After the ordeal ended, we were offered oranges, bananas, and watermelon, but caviar would not have compensated for the suffering.

Claire finishing a Worcester Half Marathon

New challenges began to pour in, usually preceded by the phrase, "You're not a real runner until you've raced the . . . ." I think that the real-runner finish line gets pushed back every time I get near it. My brother twisted my arm to run The Cave Hill Classic in Leverett to benefit a community of Buddhists dedicated to world peace. I had been to many a peace demonstration with Buddhist monks and the Buddhist nun Clare Carter who lived at the Peace Pagoda in Leverett, so I agreed to participate. The five-mile race occurred in April when snow lingered on the ground. It began with a gentle downhill but ended with a relentless mile-and-a-half incline. On the last stretch, the road was so steep I felt like I could reach out and touch it like a ladder. The slowest zombie could easily have outpaced me. The friggin' race ended five hundred feet higher than it began. Finishers got an origami peace crane followed by a mile-long walk in the cold back to their cars.

But I was a sucker for the taunting that veterans heaped on me. Scott Stevens assured me that Worcester's Newton Hill Trail Race each Tuesday night in August would improve my 5K times. So, I did them all: up, down, around, in the woods, over roots, through brush, and on pine needles, leaves, stones, and through tall grass. The finish is down a terrifying slope studded with sharp rocks and broken glass. I feared I'd fall headfirst and be killed. Instead, I won my age group and a nifty commemorative pint glass. I have since acquired eighteen similar glasses, enough to set our table for Christmas and Thanksgiving dinner.

At one of the Newton Hill races, Mr. Stevens took a bad fall and limped to a bench at the finish. Jack Goolsky, Dave Wynja, and I examined his foot and assured him that it was just a boo-boo.

"If you can wiggle your toes, it can't be serious," I said.

Jack and Dave agreed. Scott's doctor, on the other hand, called it a compound fracture. It grounded Mr. Stevens for five months.

I wasn't the only one taking on bigger challenges. Claire caught the bug, too. She and I joined numerous friends from War Resister's League in running the second Worcester Half Marathon. I was determined to run it more intelligently than my first. My determination paid off. I started slow and finished fast at one hour and thirty-six minutes, not too shabby for a geezer. Claire also beat her goal. My college classmate and friend Tim McCaffrey, the only person I know who is more competitive than I, came in far behind me. I warned him not to measure his performance against mine, as such a high standard would only make him feel worse about himself. Tim blamed his poor finish on a pulled gluteus muscle. Is that even a real thing? Can you pull a muscle in your rear end? Was he setting me up for a later race? In fact, he beat me twice at the Washington, DC, Turkey Trot, or, then again, did I let him win? The jury is still out.

When my third December as an older runner loomed, talk escalated once again of the Boston Marathon. Qualifiers apply in September, but time-waived numbers are Christmas presents. John Pajer's wife, Karen, wanted in. Like me, she never saw herself doing a marathon, but, as she put it, "They suck you in." Although I wasn't sure if I had enough volunteer hours to get a CMS number, I submitted my name. The club chose twenty lucky runners. I led the waiting list until a woman ahead of me got injured, thanks be to the trickster god of competition. I was already three weeks into my training when the good news was confirmed. Two weeks later, I had the coveted invitation to the 116th Boston Marathon in hand. All I had to do was triple my mileage without ending up in an emergency room.

Training for the Boston Marathon sucks for New Englanders. You have to run longer and longer miles outside in the coldest weather for a race day that might not even be cold. Thankfully, that winter was mercifully snow-free and relatively warm. On the one day temps skated near zero, CMS vice president Bill Gonsorcik, Matt Grigas, Hicham Maalouf, and I ran thirteen miles. It was so cold that hoarfrost coated my eyebrows, and

photo by Claire Schaeffer-Duffy

marathoners Bill Gonsorcik, Karen Pajer, and Scott, from left, at the Celtic 5K

icicles dangled from my beard. When we stopped at a diner to use the bathroom and customers gawked at us, I said, "If we'd have had sled dogs, we'd have made the Pole."

Hicham, a native of Brazil and Lebanon, moaned at ten miles, "I can't feel or move my fingers." I sacrificed my mittens, which saved his digits for three future marathons.

As part of their marathon training, most area runners take on the Stu's 30K in early March, a brutal race through Clinton, Sterling, and Boylston around a reservoir and up three mountainous hills. Two weeks later, thousands do a rehearsal run from the Boston Marathon start line in Hopkinton to the top of Heartbreak Hill, twenty-one miles into the course. I ran both and felt pretty confident. I told John Conceison, who writes the running column for the *Worcester Telegram & Gazette*, that I hoped to finish under three hours and thirty minutes. After he read the article, Scott Stevens told me that predicting one's finishing time in the press is a sure jinx.

Unfortunately, Marathon Monday featured the second highest temperature in the race's history. It peaked in the mid nineties with high humidity. This premature April inferno came on all of a sudden and disappeared just as quickly. It would be many weeks later before the thermometer registered above eighty, never mind ninety. We were just unlucky, I guess.

In such hot weather, you would think the BAA would focus its attention on making sure every runner was properly hydrated. Instead, they sent out a terrifying warning of a potentially fatal condition called hyponatremia caused by drinking too much water. Not wanting to drown on the course, I drank more modestly than I should have, which caused my quads to seize up at mile ten. My race went down the toilet from there. I stopped in three medical tents to beg for help. I loaded up on water, Gatorade, and every other perk offered along the course. I was forced to walk long stretches. All too late. The pain was excruciating. At mile eighteen, a doctor told me that I was seriously dehydrated and that they'd take me to a hospital. I asked him for a bottle of water. While he was gone, I got off the stretcher and crawled back onto the course determined at least to get the finisher's medal. I was so slow that multiple costumed characters passed me, including a man dressed as a cheeseburger. Nevertheless, I finished at four hours and fifty-five minutes. Joanna Donato followed my race online and shared my humiliation. I was in so much pain I couldn't walk for three days.

What do you do after working so hard for five months only to see your marathon collapse before your eyes? I'll tell you what you do. You scan the horizon for another marathon and sign up right away. As luck would have it, the Worcester Marathon would take place seven weeks later. I didn't care that signing up to run Worcester didn't allow sufficient recovery and training time nor that the Worcester-into-Holden course posed more difficulty than Boston's. I was on a mission.

It turned out that Scott Stevens undertook the same pilgrimage. He had designed the course, which (surprise, surprise) went by his house in Holden. He told me that unless I could maintain a 7:50 pace per mile for the first sixteen miles, I had no chance of reaching my age group's Boston Marathon qualifying time of three hours and thirty minutes. That was pretty fast for me. I tried to set my sights lower, on beating my previous Boston time and not coming in on my hands and knees.

Race day weather with temperature around seventy and partly cloudy skies was paradise compared to the Boston Death March. The Worcester Half Marathon, which Claire and Vin Garofoli ran, started at the same time and followed the same course for almost five miles.

When the gun went off, I fell quite a bit behind Vin and Scott Stevens. I could barely see them at the two-mile mark when I began to settle into a faster pace. To my delight, I gradually closed the gap and, on Bancroft Tower Hill, I caught up with them. Was I ruining another marathon by going too fast early on? Time would tell. Vin veered off to the left on Salisbury Street while Mr. Stevens and I headed toward Holden on, you guessed it, Holden Street. For the better part of three miles, we slowly gained altitude while maintaining a 7:40 pace. We continued side by side into Holden center and onto roller coaster Bailey Road through woods. He stopped for water, and expecting him to catch up, I went on, but he did not. As a rule, I never look back (just another idiosyncrasy), so I had no idea where he was. I passed the eighteen-mile mark feeling strong. As we had arranged before the race, Bill Gonsorcik waited to hand me a packet of energy paste called GU. I squeezed the stuff into my mouth looking forward to a refreshing burst of lemon lime only to discover that Bill had given me peanut butter flavor. Have you ever taken a drink of milk only to discover your cup contained orange juice? He could have killed me, but remember. I was on a mission. I cruised to twenty-two miles, slowed quite a bit up the last big hill, and managed to finish at three hours thirty-two minutes: not too shabby.

I learned later on that Scott Stevens took a nasty fall not long after I left him. He finished almost forty minutes behind me. I found him in the medical tent on a gurney with an oxygen mask over his mouth. When he saw me, he removed the mask and asked, "Isn't there any security in here?"

Of course, I comforted him. Yes, siree. I sat my first-place-in-my-age-group trophy down on his bedside table and focused exclusively on him. There are times to be competitive and times to be solicitous.

I had not yet completed my pilgrimage. By two minutes, I still had not achieved the elusive Boston Marathon qualifying time, so, after a week and a half recovery, I hit the roads again to train for Lowell's Bay State Marathon in October. Suffice it to say, mission accomplished. I came in at three hours twenty-seven minutes, three minutes below my age group qualifying time for the Boston Marathon.

Aside from improving my health and gaining me more friends, running landed me a dream job. My son Aiden ran cross country at Worcester South High Community School for a very nice coach who teaches Spanish. Unfortunately, he also coaches the girls' volleyball team and recognized that he could not give both volleyball and cross country his full attention. He encouraged me to apply for the job, which I did: my first completely online application. The athletic department hired me despite my long criminal record as a civil disobedient. I took courses in CPR and concussion awareness as well as a general course required of all coaches. We watched a video of a bad coach berating his players, which reminded me of the coach who tormented my dying high school teammate. "Suck it up, sissy!" had fallen out of favor as an acceptable motivational phrase. It heralded a new dawn for coaching. Alleluia!

To say I enjoy the job would be an understatement. Coaching is challenging and exhilarating. I tell my runners at the outset, "There are three ways to win in cross country: to win outright (something very few people ever do), to get a personal record (something most of you will do), and to finish the season (something all of you can do)." I remind them that ours is a sport that nonrunners look upon with awe.

When considering our three-mile races, nonrunners say, "I could never run that far."

By running cross country, even if you are the slowest kid in the state as I was in high school, you accomplish something the public sees as impossible. I like to think that my obvious enthusiasm for the sport is infectious. Running delivers tangible rewards. When I'm coaching, I keep individual stats for each runner and compile them into a yearbook with color photos. I bring organic grapes and lemon water for them to practices. And, when I'm not timing them, I run with them.

I don't ask them to do things I wouldn't do. And they blossom. They go from kids who feel they have to walk up every hill to talented athletes. They each get faster and more confident. They even win races and, more importantly, gain a reputation with other teams for their excellent sportsmanship. What amazes me most is that the Worcester Public Schools Department pays me for the privilege of coaching.

Between 2010 and 2015, the South High cross country team grew from seven runners to thirty-seven. With fourteen girls, twenty-three boys, and no assistant coach, you might think my latest season would be a nightmare, but nothing could be farther from the truth. These remarkable young people— blacks, Asians, Latinos, whites, rich, poor, experienced and beginners—get along marvelously. When the slowest runners on the team come to the finish line, their teammates all gather to cheer them on. Their respect for one another is a tribute to them and to the positive atmosphere that the incredibly dedicated South High principal, Maureen Binienda, and her staff have engendered in an underfunded school which nonetheless boasts the highest number of students taking advanced placement courses in Worcester if not the state of Massachusetts.

At the end of each season, every runner gets a team jacket or sweatshirt with his or her name on it. I paid for them out of my salary my first year as a coach, but my runners

photo by Scott Schaeffer-Duffy

*Sovibol Keo, front, runs for the South High School, Worcester,
cross country team with Leo Orellana, left, and Joseph Appiah*

2015 South High School, Worcester, cross country runners include,
from left, front, Mary Vu; second row, Britnie Nguyen, Emma Younge, Peter Bacon, Sovibol Keo, Ramon
Perez, Annie Huynh, Evlyn Wah, Thaw Htoo, and Kevin Nguyen; back row, Lilly Wright

insisted thereafter on fundraising most of the costs. Last year, the team voted to feature a new motto on the gear: "We run better than the government."

Between coaching gigs, I regularly raced 5Ks and prepared for more marathons. Unfortunately, at the 118th Boston Marathon, my quadrupeds seized up at eighteen miles. Despite perfect weather conditions and plenty of hydration, several hamburgers passed me and I came in at four hours and nine minutes.

My son Aiden jumped in to help me complete the final two miles. We had just finished getting our picture taken on Boylston Street when we heard an explosion behind us. We turned, heard a second blast, and saw plumes of smoke. It was a terrible moment followed by hours of confusion and anxiety over the injured and runners who had been stopped on the course. When Claire and I walked across Boston Common the next morning to go to Mass at the Paulist Center on Park Street, we saw deserted Boylston Street surrounded by heavily armed police and military Humvees. It felt like a war zone.

That afternoon we gathered runners and supporters in Worcester for a vigil to pray for the bombing victims and to pledge our determination to continue running the Boston

Marathon. Claire promised herself that she'd run it in 2014 as a gesture of nonviolent resilience. Such determination became stronger when police killed the elder Tsarnaev, put five towns under a kind of martial law, and then fired hundreds of rounds before apprehending the unarmed younger Tsarnaev brother.

For my part, I began immediately to train for the Vermont City Marathon in Burlington, Vermont, one of the first marathons after the Boston bombings. Many runners wanted to run it to show they would not be cowed by violence. It is a beautiful race in a lovely city with terrific local support. Unfortunately, my friend Hicham

Aiden, left, and Scott near the Boston Marathon finish line just before the 2013 bombing

Marathon photo

Maalouf and I ran it in cold driving rain. He did well. I fell apart again in the second half. My final miles were as painful as Napoleon's retreat from Moscow. I was getting a reputation as a choke artist.

But then again, I've had little victories since then. Vin, my brother Michael, and I joined several hundred people in scenic Shelburne Falls in western Massachusetts for a formidable ten-mile race with a sweet name: "The Bridge of Flowers." Vin had talked up the monster hill that appears at the three or four mile mark and goes on for more than a mile. I approached the race with considerable trepidation, but, to my surprise, I won my age group and received a medal while standing on tiered boxes like an Olympic champion.

Claire and I started training for the 2014 Boston Marathon in mid-December 2013. With each successive week, mileage increased. Each Sunday's long run got longer and longer no matter the weather.

After her first twelve-mile run, Claire said, "What was I thinking?!" She later disparaged her pace saying, "I'm just a chuggaroo." What in the world is that? And yet, she never quit.

To nonrunners, why anyone would run so many miles is a mystery. An acquaintance asked me if I expected to win the Boston Marathon. I told her, "If I beat thirty-six thousand people, I will."

"Good," she replied. "There's no point doing it if you aren't planning to win."

Actually, there are probably as many unique goals as there are runners. In March, after Claire completed the twenty-one-mile Boston Marathon rehearsal run, she sent out the following letter explaining her motivation:

Dear Friends and Family,

I don't recommend proclaiming your intentions in an article published for a national newspaper. Words in print may come back to haunt you. But this is what I did last spring when I wrote an essay for the *National Catholic Reporter* reflecting on my family's experience of the Boston Marathon bombing. Many of us were there that day. In the final paragraph, I impetuously declared I would join Scott in running the 118th Boston Marathon on April 21, 2014.

That blasted paragraph launched me into a training routine which began in December. The old saying describing the fidelity of our postal carriers— "neither rain, nor sleet, nor snow"—applies to winter marathon training. Scott and I have been out there running in bitter cold and eyeball-stinging snows. After our weeks of long Sunday slogs up and down the hills of Worcester County, the big race is almost here.

The newspapers predict one million spectators. Thirty-six thousand runners have registered to run the course. Each one has his or her own reason, but the general spirit seems to be one of positive defiance. No one

Scott and Claire

wants the bombing to be the last word on a traditionally happy event that brought together so many people for so many years.

When Scott and I take off from the start line in Hopkinton, we will be wearing shirts inscribed with the word "PEACE" on the front and a quote from Dorothy Day on the back: "Love is the solution." It's a tiny act of peacemaking, a gesture really. Our intent is to affirm the solidity of love, the persistence of peace. The perpetrators and victims of last year's bombing were young. It was this detail of the tragedy I found hardest to bear. So, I am going out there as a mom and a new grandmom to remind all of us, especially the young, that no matter how breathtaking the violence, love will always be more durable.

Muttering decades of the rosary is how Scott and I have kept our sanity on those long, tedious slogs. Come race day, I'll continue the habit. I'll be praying for Dzokhar Tsarnaev (of all the souls affected by last year's devastation, he has the hardest path to walk), the family members of his victims, the victims of US bombings, and for all of my friends and loved ones, including you. Believe me, there will be enough miles on the journey to cover these topics and more.

I have felt shy about announcing this unusual project. Unlike Scott, I have never run a marathon. Despite months of training, I'm not certain I'll be able to run the distance. (There is the possibility this peacenik might crawl across the finish line!) But I don't want this to be an individual endeavor, so I am informing you . . . .

The Boston Athletic Association's race packet for this year's runners includes an African proverb: "If you want to go fast, go alone. If you want to go far, go together." What I want on Marathon Monday is for our collective love to outpace destruction and despair. Join me in rooting for compassion.

Claire

Our small gesture was not alone. A multitude of runners raced in shirts remembering Martin Richards, the eight-year-old boy killed by the bombers. Others proclaimed other worthy causes. The crowd was phenomenal. The old adage about the Boston Marathon rang especially true that day: "If you want to be loved, run the Boston Marathon." Enthusiasm, joy, generosity, and gratitude of the spectators warmed all of our hearts.

But then, as might be expected, my quads seized up at fifteen miles, a terribly frustrating experience after training so hard and long, but I told my brother Michael who always watches the race on Heartbreak Hill, "My quads are killing me, but I'm determined to beat last year's time."

"You'd better pick it up then," he warned me.

Michael was right. At thirty-five kilometers, I checked in at six minutes slower than the previous year. It's not easy to increase your pace when your muscles are screaming in pain and you feel like you might fall down. It's not even easy to walk, much less run.

But the crowd, that amazing crowd, reached out to me in the sea of runners. As I wince-walked by Boston University, a group of students hung over the barricade repeating, "You can do it, Peace," referring to my shirt. "Peace! Peace! Peace!" they chanted. Their earnestness was so strong, I dug down very deep and started to run again. You might have thought I'd have won the race the way they cheered. Their earnest support for a complete stranger invokes the very antithesis of the violence inflicted on strangers the year before. Thanks to their kindness and many of my own prayers in the final two miles, I finished strong and beat the previous year's time by twenty seconds.

Claire crossed the line not too long after me. We proudly wore our race shirts and medals to dinner in Boston's Italian North End, where the bus boy asked if he could have a picture taken with my finisher's medal. He told us he could never run 26.2 miles, but I assured him that it was possible. Only six years earlier, I couldn't run 26.2 yards. I had proven that potential often exceeds our imagination.

On the way to the restaurant, a passerby thanked us for running. It was gratifying to see how the race emboldened strangers to speak to one another. The sense of community was palpable.

Still, running is a "What-have-you-done-for-me-lately?" sport. So, after a few days off, I laced up again and set my eyes on winning the Holyoke Twelve-Week Points Series trophy. In the first week, I placed fourth in my age group behind Norm Fuller, Kevin Pfau, and Vin. I knew I had to work hard to get back into the medal round but decided to add a dimension that might give me an edge. After each race, I posted faux online news stories to heighten tension, and I gradually moved up in the standings. My August 14, 2014 release, titled, "Schaeffer-Duffy Defies the Odds" is typical:

Marathon photo

Claire Chuggaroo triumphant

> HOLYOKE—With both of the heroes of the Central Mass Striders beaten up by the arduous Newton Hill Trail Race (a race with a twenty-five percent fatality rate), many experts wondered whether Scott Schaeffer-Duffy and Vin Garofoli would even be able to race tonight, but these champions would not let their bruised bodies deter them . . .

Race Director Dick Arsenault said, "they are both such exceptional athletes. I hated to see only one of them win."

But win one of them did. Schaeffer-Duffy not only seized the laurel wreath in tonight's battle but also took over first place in the age group. With only four races remaining before the ultimate prize, there can be no doubt that the competition will be white hot. Garofoli attributed his loss tonight to the discovery of two rocks embedded in the underside of his shoes. A reporter from *Competitor* magazine asked him, "Was the sun in your eyes? Was there a flood? Did you encounter a swarm of locusts?"

Garofoli ignored the jabs and sought the help of Rich Larsen, Schaeffer-Duffy's former marathon coach. Larsen said, "Coaching Schaeffer-Duffy was like coaching someone without ears. It will be a pleasure to advise Vin."

For his part, Schaeffer-Duffy plans to continue his program of over-training and binge dieting. "If I could only find a fifth race to run this week and get my weight down to 130 pounds, I know I could go faster."

The Guiness Book of World Records is keeping an eye on Schaeffer-Duffy and Garofoli. It is unclear whether their records will be for speed, rivalry, or stupidity.

Thankfully, both Norm and Kevin (runners I could only rarely beat) missed some of the series, leaving the question of first and second to Vin and me. Our final finishes were all less than five seconds apart. A growing number of runners began reading my "blog."

On August 23rd, after a loss to Vin, I posted:

WORCESTER-In a stunning turnaround, Vin Garofoli came back from consecutive defeats to handily defeat Scott Schaeffer-Duffy at CMS's Worcester State University 5K. The fifty-nine-year-old beat his younger rival by a staggering forty-nine seconds. His finish of 20:18 was a personal record.

Schaeffer-Duffy said, after the race, "Vin is living proof that Geritol can help seniors retain their youthful ways." Former CMS president Jack Goolsky said, "Schaeffer-Duffy ran like he had a load in his pants." Jen Hogan, another CMS standout, said, "When I saw how slow his time was, I cried my eyes out."

Holyoke Race director, Dick Arsenault, said, "If Schaeffer-Duffy craps the bed on Thursday, we'll have to hide all the sharp objects."

But the gods of running took pity on me. I bounced back and went on to win the series. In the spirit of good sportsmanship, I posted a *"Sports Illustrated"* cover.

Oscar Wilde said it so well, "Nothing succeeds like excess."

Scott's **Sports Illustrated**
customized victory cover

Days after Hicham Maalouf sprained his ankle on a 10K race up and down Mount Wachusett, he ran another 5K while pushing his son in a stroller. When asked if running while injured was wise, he replied, "I'm Schaeffer-Duffying."

In an article entitled "Moderation? No Thanks," that appeared in the February, 2015, issue of *Competitor*, triathlete Susan Lacke said,

> Moderation is the guy who saves all his money for a rainy day only to die of a heart attack before he can spend it. It's the girl who wonders what would have happened if she had moved away from her hometown after high school. Moderation means stepping back from the precipice— sure, it's safe, but you miss the best views . . . . So go ahead: Turn your dial all the way to the right. Dive in headfirst. Absorb every last drop of what you love and ignore the people who try to ration your enthusiasm. Run until you discover what's waiting for you at the finish line. It's sure better than whatever's in the middle.

Challenges, rewards, camaraderie, and devilish fun of this arduous sport are nothing short of addictive. I don't know how long a run I will have, but I am determined to squeeze the most I can out of it.

I know some pretty fast racers in their sixties and even in their seventies, but should injury or circumstance cut my racing career short or even land me in that wheelchair the podiatrist warned me about, I will, nonetheless, remain eternally grateful that Claire inspired me to get off my expanding derrière and start running.

photo by Patrick Duffy

*Scott, left, and Vin,
still friends, still competing,
and each winning trophies at the
East Bay Half Marathon in
Providence, Rhode Island*

Jail

Two jail movies, *Brubaker* and *Stir Crazy*, came out in 1980. The first is a drama based on the true story of a new prison warden played by Robert Redford who goes undercover to experience jail conditions first-hand. He experiences shocking, capricious cruelty and ferocious brutality, primarily from the prison staff.

The second film, a comedy, has Gene Wilder and Richard Pryor mistakenly sent to jail. They are so afraid that they affect a tough-guy walk while repeating, "We bad." Unlike Redford, who exposes jail as a place where the innocent risk death, Wilder and Pryor come to realize that their time behind bars isn't that hard if they just be themselves. For example, after three days in solitary confinement, Wilder asks the warden, "Do I have to come out right now? I was just getting in touch with myself." Punished by being put into a cell with an angry brute, Pryor discovers that the man loves to play "Go Fish."

If I had to go by these movies alone, I wouldn't really know what to expect in jail.

Thankfully, I did not have to go in headfirst. My earliest time behind bars stemmed from a 1982 Good Friday protest at GTE's Westborough, Massachusetts, facility, home to the guidance system for the MX nuclear missile. Tom Doughton, Tom Lewis, Ray Demers, Celia Jessa-Ivy, Margie Farren, and I carried a large Paschal (Easter) candle, given us by the Trappist monks of Saint Joseph's Abbey in Spencer, Massachusetts, onto the GTE property. When blocked by GTE security, we knelt down. Symbolically bringing the light of Christ's Resurrection into the darkness of the arms race, we called our demonstration a prayer for disarmament. The Westborough police called it blocking the driveway. They arrested us and packed us into three police cars.

one of Scott's jail sketches

drawing by Scott Schaeffer-Duffy

On the way to the station, a cop warned me, "You're in for it now. You're about to spend the weekend in the crow-bar Hilton." Since it was too late in the day to take us to court for arraignment, we could either post bail or sit in lock-up. Tom Doughton paid the bail, but the rest of us refused. The police took us into the basement and placed us in cells. Mine had a seatless steel toilet, a mattress-less steel bunk, concrete floor, steel walls, low steel ceiling, and steel bars. The only light filtered in through the bars from a dim fluorescent in the adjoining hall. I could talk to my co-defendants in other cells, but couldn't see them. Graffiti, most notably "PIGS SUCK," covered the walls.

1982 Good Friday prayer for nuclear disarmament at
GTE in Westborough, Massachusetts

It was chilly and dirty, but I didn't have to face cruel inmates or guards. It struck me as novel. The time didn't drag. We enjoyed disembodied conversations. Ray wanted to become a monk. A trained artist, Tom participated in 1962 in his first demonstration— against a segregated carnival in Baltimore, Maryland. He later served three years in jail for burning draft records to protest the Vietnam War. Celia Jessa-Ivy was a very good-humored counselor. Margie worked in a nursing home and had volunteered at the Mustard Seed Catholic Worker house in Worcester. She wove liturgical vestments. I got to know each of them better and shared my own stories.

When conversation lagged, I sang Irish anti-war ballads and Gregorian Chant. On the back of leaflets from our demonstration, I drew sketches of my cell, wrote a poem, and made an Easter card for a friend. Guards brought us each a burger and cherry pie from McDonald's on Friday night followed by coffee and a doughnut in the morning. Tom said he felt spoiled to have breakfast served to him in bed. On Easter Sunday, Father Leo Barry, pastor of Saint Luke's Catholic Church in Westborough, persuaded police to allow him to bring us Communion and Bishop Bernard Flanagan's regards. Father Barry looked more pained at our circumstances than any of us actually felt. His obvious admiration for our "sacrifice," although overblown, encouraged us.

We appeared before Judge Francis Larkin on Monday morning in Westborough District Court. Tom told him that the MX missile

> represents too great a darkness to be ignored . . . . Its enormous cost is a
> theft from the needy members of our society . . . . As Bishop Flanagan said,

"There are times and situations when civil disobedience is not only morally justified but may actually be a duty." We did not break civil law. We were obeying divine law.

In a gesture of sympathy, Judge Larkin continued the cases without a finding and allowed our twenty-five-dollar court costs to be given to the poor.

Afterwards, Ray Demers told a reporter for *The Catholic Free Press*,

Being jailed for something you believe in gives you a real sense of freedom and clarity. All of a sudden, the fears that rendered you helpless before fall away, making the fear unfounded . . . . We prayed and prepared for our action for seven weeks, keeping ourselves constantly open to the Spirit so that our action might be a pure response to God's will. The issue is serious to us and, as such, we had to complete it, to go all the way with it. That meant jail, not bail.

Tom told the press, "In these times of nuclear madness, I can think of no better way to celebrate the Resurrection."

My next arrest, also at GTE, occurred on December 28, 1982, the Feast of the Holy Innocents recalling King Herod's massacre of the children of Bethlehem. This time Margie, Tom, and I acted with Jim Connolly, a Catholic priest; Theresa Guisti, a member of the Mustard Seed Catholic Worker, and Carol Markarian, a weaver for Saint Joseph's Abbey. We conducted a somber protest that included pouring our own blood on the concrete before GTE's main doors to make visible the human cost of their work in dramatic fashion.

Interestingly, in 2007, twenty-five years after that protest, Claire and I met a woman named Barbara Roberts who worked at GTE on the day of our protest. She saw us mark the plant's walkway with a large red cross and then kneel to pray. She told Claire and me that she and her coworkers had nuclear nightmares inspired by the nature of their work and our continual demonstrations. She had one dream in which she saw enormous black clouds rolling across the horizon. "I just knew it was the end of the world," she said.

During our many protests, Mrs. Roberts and her colleagues gathered at the plant's upper windows to watch and discuss the scenes below. The blood pouring particularly jarred them because the workers convinced themselves that nuclear technology they worked on would either not be built or would never be used.

"While you were working there, you didn't feel you were working on a missile system," she said. "You didn't see the missile. You didn't see the warhead. You were dealing with pencil and paper requirements." But you can't easily ignore blood on the walkway.

Who knows what effect we had, but I know one thing. Since at least 2010, Barbara has counted as one of Worcester's most passionate champions of peace and justice. She and her husband, Arthur, who worked for years in the Pentagon, regularly participate in a weekly peace vigil. They stand as powerful reminders always to have faith in people and possibilities.

Judge William Brewin presided at our trial for the blood pouring on January 28, 1984 in Westborough District Court. We were charged with disorderly conduct and criminal trespass. A World War II era Cold Warrior, Judge Brewin loved to say, "I will not have political statements in my court" immediately before giving a speech about the morality of the US nuclear arsenal. After a brief trial, he convicted us. Because of his long record for many acts of civil disobedience, Tom got thirty days in jail. Perhaps in deference to his occupation, Father Connolly received a suspended sentence. The judge sentenced the rest of us to thirty days in jail with twenty suspended and a year's probation. When we refused to sign the probationary agreement to obey the law, Judge Brewin was furious. He revised our sentence to thirty days and ordered that we return to court after ten days to see if we'd sign the probation at that time. "I think time in the House of Correction," he said, "will give you second thoughts."

Hours later, transported in handcuffs and shackles, Tom and I arrived at Worcester County Jail in West Boylston. A tall chain-link fence opened for us to enter the sally port. Along with other prisoners, we shuffled inside where corrections officers unchained us and told us to strip and shower. They bagged our clothing and property. They gave us a receipt, a pair of jeans, white T-shirt, long-sleeved denim shirt, gray blanket, and a set of old sheets. Some of the items were damp.

They then escorted Tom and me to a room with sixteen bunk beds, a former infirmary used as an overflow from maximum security. The room had a black-and-white TV, a desk for a guard, two phones that accepted only collect calls, and a side bathroom with two showers. It was pretty clean and bright. The other men were reasonably friendly. After they heard the reason for our sentences, they nicknamed us Proton and Neutron.

Card games broke up monotonous days as well as walks to the dining hall, where we ate in less than fifteen minutes at long stainless steel tables. The first time I had a visitor was jarring. Guards strip-searched me before escorting me into a room with a bank of telephones facing windows with phones on the other side. Why they strip-searched prisoners for a non-contact visit escapes me. Half of the phones did not work, so some visits went on in mute conversation. All were painfully short.

At ten days, they woke me early and transported me to the Westborough Courthouse. Theresa, Margie, and Carol were already there. When Judge Brewin asked if we were ready to promise to obey the law, Theresa replied, "With all due respect, your honor, unless you have something different to say, I'd like to be returned to jail now because if I don't go soon, I'll miss gym." As you may imagine, he sent us straight away to serve out the balance of our time behind bars.

Two events from that incarceration stick in my mind. The first came about when a guard apparently had to work unexpectedly on a Friday night. He took out his anger on us by shutting off the TV, turning out the lights, and ordering all of us to go immediately to bed. A short while later, I heard a prisoner mimic *The Three Stooges* by pretending to snore. Others took it up until the guard yelled, "Shut up!"

Then, in a tip of the hat to *National Lampoon's Animal House*, a chorus of inmates began softly humming "America the Beautiful." It was priceless.

The second event happened when an illiterate inmate asked if I would read him a letter from his wife. This fellow had been convicted of driving without a license. Dyslexic, he could not pass the written driving test but had driven for years on a farm. He was the only breadwinner for his wife and three small children. I saw them at one visit, and they looked like homeless Okies from John Steinbeck's *The Grapes of Wrath*. His arrest came after his boss asked him to make a delivery. In addition to jail time, the judge had assessed a large fine.

As I read the letter from his wife, I could tell that she and the children were in dire straits, a fact she bravely tried to keep from him. I could feel her love for her husband and his for all of them. I felt sick to my stomach that such a decent fellow was in jail. After he dictated an encouraging reply to her, I took a shower and wept.

I had never before run into a human need that I had absolutely no power to address. In frustration, I prayed,

> God, I cannot comprehend why this family has to suffer like this. Your thinking is beyond me. But, if there's some kind of quota for suffering that you feel you have to dispense, then take it away from them and give it to me.

I can't say if my prayer helped this man or his family, but I can say that my next few months counted among the most difficult of my life.

Carl Siciliano and I, both then members of Saint Benedict's Catholic Worker, joined a "Peace Pentecost" protest on November 2, 1982 against the MX missile organized by the Washington, DC Sojourners community. Along with three hundred others, we occupied the US Capitol Rotunda before police arrested us. After the court found us guilty of disorderly conduct, the district attorney recommended the judge sentence Carl and me to sixty days in jail.

Horrified, the judge chastised her. "Haven't you been listening to these people?" he asked. He then gave us three days in jail, insisting that the day of our sentencing be counted as a full day with instructions to release us as early as possible two mornings later. Our entire incarceration lasted forty-one hours, much of it spent waiting to get fitted for a white T-shirt stenciled with the word "JAIL" and a bright orange jump suit.

On the morning of the third day, Carl and I wore our jail shirts at our release into a courtyard encircled by a high wall. A thirty-foot-tall metal gate slid open for us to exit. Carl leapt and danced through shouting, "Free at last! Free at last!" A woman standing on the sidewalk with her husband, turned to him and said, "Wow. Those two must have been in there a long time."

On August 9, 1985, the thirtieth anniversary of the United States atomic bombing of Nagasaki, I joined Dan Ethier, Dan Sicken, Paul Giaimo, Connie Riley, Mary Jane Rosati, Deirdre Doran, Ann Sorensen, and Mark Johnson in another prayer vigil for disarmament on GTE's property. Mark Johnson was given a fine. The women received between seven and thirty days in jail, while the action landed the two Dans, Paul, and me in the slammer for thirty-nine days.

We spent the first week in the upper right tier of maximum security, much more like the movie versions of jail than my previous stay. At Worcester County, everyone goes to maxi, as they call it, until classification, which sent us to a minimum security building that once served as a dormitory for nurses.

Our accommodations in mini comprised an open dorm on the third floor with powder blue walls, polished wooden floor, and bunk beds. Once a day, guards took us outside either to a basketball court surrounded by tall fences topped with razor wire or to an open baseball field encircled by pine trees. Inmates called fence-less recreation time "going to the big yard."

On my first visit to the big yard, I took the opportunity to jog around the perimeter where a couple of bored guards stood watch. After my first lap, an inmate confided, "Rosario's taking off." On my second lap, another prisoner said "Rosario split." All the way back to the dorm, everyone whispered about the escape. We expected the alarm to sound once we lined up for the count, something that happens four times a day in mini. It surprised us when the guard on duty did his tabulation and picked up the phone without urgency to call in the results. His calm amazed us.

Four hours later, just before lights out, the same guard counted us again and asked, "Where is Rosario?" Apparently, he had not noticed Rosario's absence earlier. The guard's screw-up tickled the prisoners, who began peeking under their pillows and lifting up the toilet seats and saying, "He's not here." While Rosario could have been in New York State with such a head start, in reality, instead of getting far away, he did what most inmates do when they escape—he went to see a local girlfriend. A quick search through his property gave the guards plenty of letters with the girl's address in nearby Worcester. Before midnight, Rosario was back in jail where he did the rest of his sentence, plus extra time, in maximum security.

A day later, the youngest prisoners joked around with a friendly guard. When that corrections officer (CO) went off duty, his stony-faced replacement demanded to know the whereabouts of the logbook. Someone found the vinyl-covered book in a waterless toilet, a foolish prank undoubtedly perpetrated by one of the teen inmates.

The new CO picked up the phone, spoke into it quietly, hung up, and announced suspension of our recreation, phone access, visitation, and commissary until we turned someone in for the logbook incident. Jails allowed smoking back then, and inmates took the prospect of losing commissary very seriously. They quickly turned on the most timid fellow prisoner. "He must have done it," they said, even though everyone knew he hadn't.

Armed with a rulebook every inmate receives on arrival, I said, "Hold on. According to jail rules, the guards have to hold an investigation and prove someone is guilty of a violation. It's not up to us to rat on anyone."

I then asked the guard if we could talk with a deputy. He refused, so I suggested to the men that we start a hunger strike. They didn't like that idea, so I suggested a work stoppage until we could meet a deputy. This was well received. We wrote a statement of our grievance and determination to speak with a deputy, and everyone signed. The inmates elected Scott Palmeri, a fellow serving time for breaking and entering, and me as spokesmen.

We gave the petition to the CO who took it to a deputy.

Minutes later, Scott and I got a call downstairs. When we went to put on our denim shirts, protocol for a meeting with a deputy, the guard said not to bother.

Minutes later, I found myself shivering in a pitch dark room clad only in jeans and a white T-shirt. Guards guided me to a seat where a gooseneck lamp blinded me. A deputy named Larry Meerschman, a very nice man who had arranged for my previous release early enough in the morning so I could attend my Uncle Walter's funeral, asked me what had happened. I described the incident and said I thought the guard had made too much of it. Then Larry asked if I took responsibility for the written statement.

Almost before I could finish saying, "Yes," two guards chained and handcuffed me behind my back and dragged me to a place in maximum security called county lockup. Scott Palmeri had the same experience. The deputy informed the other inmates of our fate and asked if anyone else wanted to join us. My co-defendant Dan Ethier volunteered. Dan Sicken moved to follow suit, but Paul Giaimo, serving his first sentence, asked Dan to remain with him.

A collection of six cells facing each other, county lock-up was as Spartan as holding cells in Westborough, only twice as cold. No bedding was provided, and no access to visitors was allowed. Inmates considered it worse punishment than solitary confinement in cells called "the hole." Ironically, the jail also kept inmates who attempted suicide in county lock-up. Across from my cell was one such prisoner, whom an inmate worker watched twenty-four hours a day from a nearby stool. At least the guy who tried to kill himself had a mattress. For the rest of us, sleep on cold steel was intermittent at best.

On Sunday morning, a guard asked if anyone wanted to go to Mass. Dan and I jumped at the chance. Thanks be to the chaplain, Father Andy Remillard, who let me use his phone, I could inform my wife Claire of our predicament.

Each of us in turn faced a disciplinary board hearing. These are hasty affairs wherein officials accuse an inmate of an infraction, find him guilty, and give him a punishment. No evidence is produced or witnesses allowed. Unclear on the perfunctory nature of the process, I told the presiding CO that our rights had been violated. He pressed his face up against mine and screamed, "RIGHTS! You have NO rights! You're a prisoner! A ward of the state!" Veins bulged out of his forehead and spit flew from his mouth.

"Well, despite current appearances," I said when he finally backed off, "you and I are actually children of the same God with identical rights. So I'm going to pray and fast until this unjust punishment is lifted."

"You do that," he snarled and then sent me off to complete my sentence locked up in maximum security. Dan received the same punishment but on a different tier. From that point on, the prison authorities denied us visits, commissary, and the right to send mail or attend Mass.

Dan and I fasted for two and a half weeks as guards brought us meals and lied to us that the other had broken the fast. This was a pointless endeavor on their part since guards took Dan and me to the nurse's office each morning to have our vital signs checked. I could talk with Dan during the medical visits.

Eventually, after some media pressure compliments of Claire and a visit from Bishop Timothy Harrington, Worcester's auxiliary bishop, the jail released us from lock-up and had us transferred to medium security, a place identical to maxi save for housing inmates in medium security in single cells across a hallway from each other instead of two to a cell. As in maxi, cells were left open for several hours each day with inmates free to visit each other, hang out in the hall, or watch TV in the day room.

Upon arrival on the upper tier of medium, I went to the barred door at the end of the hall and called to guards below to get me some bedding. While I made the appeal, a young inmate came over and asked me, "What kind of ring is that you're wearing?"

"It's an Irish wedding ring," I replied without looking his way.

"Want to sell it?" he snapped back.

After so much fasting and aggravation, I turned to him and said, "Take a fucking wild guess."

Later on, when I got a blanket, sheets, and towel, I noticed the inmate locked in a cell opposite mine. I walked over to him and apologized, "I'm sorry I swore at you earlier. I've been pretty stressed out."

"You swore at me?" he asked. Then he shot his hands out, grabbed my head, and began banging it into the bars. It turns out the guy was the most tightly-wound person I've ever met. He said he regretted he wasn't old enough to have killed babies in Vietnam. Once he learned I was a peace activist, he grilled me about whether or not I'd shoot him under various circumstances.

He tried so hard to push my buttons that I finally said, "Look, I'm a pacifist. I will never kill you, but, if you don't stop yelling, one of the other inmates will."

Shifting gears, he started throwing paper, magazines, and clothing into the hall. Once he amassed a sizable pile, he tossed in an aerosol can followed by a lit match. Under pressure, those cans explode. Inmates on both sides of me put mattresses up against their bars to protect themselves from shrapnel. I followed suit just in time. After the explosion, guards doused the burning debris with water. Undaunted, the wild inmate stuffed a towel down his toilet and began flushing it over and over. In no time, the tier was flooded.

Instead of dealing with the situation themselves, the guards released two burly men jailed on the tier below to walk our hall. The flood poured down into their cells, ruining photos stuck on the walls. These dudes were pissed. As it happens, the building was not level, and my cell flooded more than most. When the enforcers came by, they misjudged me as the culprit and said, "Your number's punched, buddy."

My crazy neighbor laughed his head off. The guards charged Dan Ethier, in a cell five down from Mr. Psycho, with lighting the fire and inciting a riot. He faced another D-board, and I fully expected to be bundled on my way to breakfast. Bundling is a sweet sounding euphemism for covering someone with a blanket and then stabbing it until it turns red. Thankfully, before breakfast began, the jail released Dan and me.

You might think we'd try as hard as we could to forget our experience, but we did the exact opposite. Dan and I co-authored a fifteen-page report detailing human rights abuses we had witnessed at the jail. We presented the report to the Sheriff two days after our release.

"Since you aren't inmates any more," he scoffed, "how do you know any of these alleged 'violations' are still going on?"

He was a master of the Catch 22. Inmates who sign petitions get punished. Former inmates get ignored. We were not so easily put off. We took our findings to *Worcester Magazine*, which did a cover story on them. I like to think we contributed to the Sheriff's eventual election defeat.

Claire and I were arrested in 1984 with members of Boston's Haley House Catholic Worker for blocking the entrance to Draper Laboratories in Cambridge, a high-level weapons development facility once tied to MIT. Although fifteen of us were arrested together, everyone was tried and sentenced separately. I received three days that turned out eventful, unlike the time in DC.

I did my sentence in Middlesex County Jail in Billerica, Massachusetts, a Civil War era behemoth of brick and stone. At Billerica, I finally got my adolescent wish to be thrown into a dungeon. Upon arrival, guards took me down a dark stone stairwell into an even darker hall lined with cell doors opened with skeleton keys on a ring that the turnkeys had hooked to their belts.

It was incredibly dark. I later heard a story of how a guard slipped and fell on what he imagined was a puddle of water. Only later when he emerged into daylight did he realize that he had slipped on blood oozing out from under an inmate's cell door. Those steel-bound oak doors sported a small barred window at eye level. When my guard reached for my cell door, he needed both hands to swing it open.

The dank cell had crumbling, horsehair plaster walls. It was so small that, from the top bunk, I could easily reach out and touch both side walls. My cellmate, a beefy white guy named Jake, did not look up or reply when I said hello.

The next morning as I ate breakfast at a stainless steel table in the dining hall, I asked another inmate if he knew Paul Hood, an activist who had served thirty days in Billerica.

Jake slid into a seat next to me and asked, "You know Paul Hood?"

"Yeah," I replied. "He's a friend of mine."

"Well," Jake continued, "I guess I won't kill you after all."

Once back in our cell, Jake explained that, before I arrived, he had had a longtime cellmate named Bob caught with marijuana the day before his sentence would end. The guards told Bob that unless he revealed how the drug got into the jail, they'd delay his release, so Bob told them that Jake's wife smuggled it in. As a consequence, Jake lost visitation privileges. He was so angry that he told the guards, "Don't give me another cellmate. If you do, I'll smash his head against the wall." For two weeks, Jake enjoyed a single until they put me there.

As a side note, Jake told me in great detail how he planned to murder Bob after his release. At first I tried to persuade Jake that killing was ethically wrong, emotionally unsatisfying, and risky. Making no headway at all, I took a different tack:

> Jake, it's pretty clear that I'm not going to win you over to pacifism, so I'm going to go way out on a moral limb. Instead of killing Bob, which would be over so quickly and could land you in jail for the rest of your life, you should consider another approach.

photo by John Brassard for
Worcester Telegram&Gazette

Scott Scheffer-Duffy is currently jailed in the medium-security prison at Montville for his role in protesting the deployment of Trident nuclear submarines from the Electric Boat shipyard in Groton, Conn.

Scott behind bars with
Old Glory

"What do you have in mind?" he asked.

"Well, I'm just spit-balling here, Jake," I said, "but have you considered breaking one of Bob's kneecaps instead of killing him? It's my understanding that the pain is incredible and lasts for a very long time."

He said he'd give it some serious thought.

I sure hope I don't have to face Bob at the Pearly Gates.

I served two longer sentences, one in Connecticut and the other in Georgia. The first resulted from a 1989 Martin Luther King, Jr. Day protest against the Trident sub and the second from a 2002 protest at Fort Benning calling for closure of the US Army School of the Americas (SOA) where the army trained some of Latin America's worst human rights abusers.

In Connecticut, I was arrested with fifty-two other arrestees. No one had gone to jail for one of these large protests for so long that activists began calling Groton, Connecticut "the wading pool" of civil disobedience. We assumed there just wasn't room in jail for fifty-three peaceniks.

Unfortunately, Judge Paul Vasington decided the jails had plenty of room for one. He arbitrarily dismissed charges against the rest and, no doubt because of the luck of the Irish, threw the book at the sole victim, me. On January 9, 1990, he empaneled a jury stacked with Trident sub workers who convicted me in five minutes, record time for a jury in the state of Connecticut. Why'd they even bother leaving the courtroom?

And then Judge Vasington sentenced me to a year in jail. Not thirty days. Not even sixty days. But an entire year. Had I been wearing brown britches, I might have soiled myself.

Although I feared that I was already circling the drain, I made a plea for mercy. Judge Vasington smiled tightly and replied, "I'll take that as a motion to revise and revoke your sentence." He took my paperwork back from the clerk, crossed out the original sentence, and amended it to 364 days. I realized only later that inmates serving sentences of a year or longer qualified for very early release while others generally served their entire terms.

By reducing my sentence by twenty-four hours, Judge Vasington actually extended my time behind bars. I was screwed big time.

I didn't realize that I had a worse hurdle to overcome than simply doing time. It began with my assignment to work in the kitchen for a dollar a day as a dishwasher, a task that earned me "Outstanding Meritorious Good Time." Not to be confused with plain old-fashioned good times. After I foolishly revealed that I had worked in restaurants, they "promoted" me to head cook, a thankless task that lasted twelve hours a day with no days off for a whopping fifty-cent-a-day raise.

In no time at all, I was fantastically tired. A guard once came into my cell looking for extra mattresses. Seeing that I had two on my bunk, he tried to wake me up to remove one. I was so dead to the world that the CO finally just grabbed the bottom mattress by the side and lifted it up until I was pressed face first into the bars. He pulled out the bottom one and dropped me back onto the bunk with a thud. My amazed cellmates later told me I had never even opened an eye.

I couldn't quit working, though, because it was my only hope of early release, something I owed to my wife Claire and our children. You see, when a father or mother goes to jail, the punishment extends to the entire family. Claire remained at our very busy Catholic Worker house juggling the needs of our guests and those of our children. They came to visit once, but it was a frustrating and unpleasant experience talking through a wire mesh so thick that you could hardly see each other. I encouraged them not to put themselves out again.

I wrote an average of ten letters a day, at least one of them to Claire and the kids. I also wrote articles and letters to the editor. A local television station interviewed me once. The other inmates found that hysterical. The cameraman made me walk in and out of a barred gate six times before the shot satisfied him.

On my sixtieth day in jail, immediately after I had finished an article about forgiving my judge, a guard told me I was going back to court. Soon I stood before Judge Vasington once again. After calling me up to the bench, he gestured to a big pile of letters and said,

> You have a lot of friends. You also have gotten a lot of press. I didn't send you to jail to promote your cause. I'm not going to give you a fine because you won't pay it, and I won't put you on probation because you won't obey it. You are hereby released.

Free at last. Free at last.

Jail in Georgia was a different story. A campaign to close the SOA had gone on for years. Annual demonstrations at Fort Benning occurred in November around the anniversary of the murder of Salvadoran Archbishop Oscar Romero. Opponents of the SOA gathered for a weekend of events culminating in a march and an option to commit civil disobedience.

While legal consequences of civil disobedience are usually unpredictable, they were clear at Fort Benning. First-time offenders got a "ban and bar" letter from the base commander, second-time offenders got thirty days in jail suspended, and third-time offenders got six months in federal prison with a thousand-dollar fine. No exceptions. When I left Worcester on November 19, 2002, I had two prior arrests at the base. Claire gave me strict orders not to get arrested. Indeed, the vast majority of the five thousand protesters in Columbus that weekend had no intention of getting arrested. Only a few dozen souls would cross the line onto base property and incur the preordained consequences.

But, after a moving talk and Mass the night before the civil disobedience, I began guiltily to question my decision. Was it cowardly? Was I letting myself off lightly? I thought about Romero's assassination and the rape/murder of American nuns by SOA graduates. The following day would culminate in a procession with thousands of placards bearing the names and ages of Latin American victims. Was I doing enough to end that violence?

Finally, I decided to take a page out of Claire's spiritual playbook. When she can't decide what to do, she asks God to send her a sign. (Claire is a convert to Catholicism. They believe everything.) During the march to the main gate, organizers announced that those risking arrest should follow a blue banner. When I saw it emblazoned with the base's motto "Follow Me," I couldn't help but do so.

Hours later, stripped of my clothes and wrapped in an itchy jail blanket as I waited for my arraignment and release until trial, I made a collect call home to my angry spouse and crying daughter.

"You're going to miss my birthday," Grace wept.

"Did Thomas More ever feel this shitty?" I wondered.

But God will not give us burdens we can't lift. After my testimony at trial on January 27, 2003, US Magistrate G. Mallon Faircloth (who had replaced an equally severe magistrate named, I kid you not, William Slaughter) said "I like you" and cut my six-month sentence in half. He also waived my fine. On my release before Grace's birthday, I'm happy to say, a dear friend gifted our family with a trip to Ireland.

During my Georgia time in jail, I received wonderful letters from many people—especially interesting ones from Grace—but my letters, on the other hand, were pretty boring. Face it. Not that much happens in jail. Fires, riots, and fights don't happen often. You can't make much of a letter out of descriptions of your victories in cards or your commentary on *The Jerry Springer Show*.

So I decided to write a serialized book for my children entitled *The Treasure of the Lord*. I included each of them as characters and set it in the thirteenth century full of heroes, villains, pirates, saints, and knights. Each chapter ended in a cliff-hanger. Byron Jenkins, an older man appealing a death sentence for murder, found the book so intriguing that, at the end of each day he announced to the other men, "Turn off the TV." When they did, he pointed to me and said, "Read the chapter."

The guys gave me great feedback: "You've got a misplaced modifier there. . . That's an anachronism. . . That sentence is a hopeless run-on."

When I got home, I found the book bound with cover art by my son Aiden, a description of the book on the inside flap by Patrick, and a profile of me by Justin on the rear flap. It said,

> Scott Schaeffer-Duffy (1958-) is a father of four and a current advocate against the war in Iraq . . . . There have been no articles ever written about Mr. Schaeffer-Duffy, and he has never been to a war zone. He is also attempting to write a biography of his humble life.

The back cover was filled with reviews:

> A work of startling genius! Particular praise is merited for the character Lady Grace, an alluring and charismatic protagonist.
> —*The New York Times*

> Schaeffer-Duffy makes a stunning debut with the dramatic tour de force: *The Treasure of the Lord*. Filled with endearing characters such as the star, Lady Grace, it is a real page-turner.
> —*The Washington Post*

> Lady Grace is a paragon of feminine ideals! A character- clever and compelling.
> —*Ladies' Home Journal*

> Grace made it all worthwhile.
> —*Cosmopolitan.*

I wonder who wrote them?

Never before had I lived with people from the Deep South. As a native New Englander, I had negative stereotypes of Georgia and Alabama as places populated with trailer trash and rednecks, but it pleased me to find the least racism behind bars I have ever seen as well as quite a few individuals with brains to spare. It also surprised me that the warden responded to a protest I led against charging inmates twenty-five cents each for an envelope by dropping the price to a nickel. I liked the other prisoners so much that I almost let a guy named Shaggy give me a jail tattoo. My co-defendant, Eloy Garcia, and I, clad as we were in striped prison outfits still popular down south, nearly caused a riot at an evangelical Bible study when we challenged the angry minister's guilt-laden and hell-bent theology with one of mercy and freedom for prisoners. While I would not call my jail time fun, it was valuable and productive. I read more than a dozen books and reviewed several of them. I wrote hundreds of letters and had the rare opportunity to pray three times a day.

Jail is a cruel and inhumane institution, but it also provides a place where an activist can experience equality with the poor. At the Catholic Worker, I have some perks and lots of authority our guests don't have, but in jail, I am a prisoner like everyone else. It makes no difference how much money you have or what you have done, good or bad, in life. You are judged solely by how you treat those around you.

An ancillary, but invaluable part of civil disobedience is its openness to the prospect of being lumped together in jail with the poor. To voluntarily accept this risk is vital to protect civil disobedience from becoming a charade. The poor do not get special treatment. Quite the contrary.

Egalitarianism is part of the appeal of Christianity for me. I like the concept of a God who decided to live as one of the poor and oppressed in ancient Palestine. The way Jesus rolls is more attractive to me than the modus operandi of a god like Zeus who only came down from Olympus in his full power and might.

I should be clear, though. Jail is not "the new monastery," as I once foolishly called it. Graffiti I discovered on my cell wall in Middlesex County Jail says it well:

> The prison situation as presently arranged is guaranteed to generate severe enough pathological reaction in both guards and inmates as to debase their humanity, lower their feeling of self-worth, and make it difficult for them to be part of a society outside of their prison.

Jails are places of suffering where people are kept from their loved ones, places where local phone calls can cost thousands of dollars a month. Jails force human beings to overcome their surroundings. There's nothing constructive about them. They crush the humanity out of inmates and staff alike. And considering their sparse amenities, jails cost a shocking amount of money. I've heard that it costs far less to send someone to Harvard than the state penitentiary.

According to the Population Reference Bureau, the United States has the highest incarceration rate in the world. Ours is one of the few countries that sentences children as if they were adults. We spend more on jails than schools. As a civilized people, we can do better. New Zealand's restorative justice approach, for example, is far better for offenders and the victims of crime as well.

Despite my monastic disclaimer, my last jail tale involves a former Trappist monk, Dan Lawrence. He and I served a fifteen-day sentence in the Worcester County Jail. We shared a cell in maxi where we spent hours playing rummy.

Dan was a quiet and introspective sort. During our sentence, two men escaped from the jail, and even though they were promptly recaptured, the sheriff let guard dogs run loose between two perimeter fences as a measure of increased security. I woke up two days after this practice began to find Dan writing a letter. It reads:

Dear Sheriff Flynn,

For the past two nights there have been dogs outside maximum security making a terrible racket. This place is too loud already without their barking. Get rid of the fucking dogs.

Peace and Love,

Dan Lawrence

I looked up at him from my mattress on the cell floor and said, "You can't send this letter."

"Why not?" he asked.

"Dan," I said, "you can't swear at the sheriff."

Completely mystified, he told me, "Every other word out of the inmates and the guards is a swear. I think that's the normal way to communicate in here."

"Take my advice," I repeated. "Don't send your letter."

But Dan did, and in less than two hours, guards moved him to solitary confinement. I smuggled him a note asking if he wanted me to contact Amnesty International. The funny thing is, like Gene Wilder in *Stir Crazy*, Dan loved it in solitary. He got the peace and quiet he enjoyed in the monastery.

Husband and Father

Scott and Claire sitting in a tree
k-i-s-s-i-n-g.
First comes love,
then comes marriage,
then comes Scott pushing a baby carriage.
—my only formal sex education

In some times and cultures, the duties and roles of husbands and wives are well defined. Not so in the northeastern United States in 1985. Gone was the stereotype of the husband as breadwinner and wife as homemaker and mother. The feminist revolution had shaken things up. Men were no longer exempt from cooking, house cleaning, and, when it came time, child care. Women no longer contented themselves staying home while men pursued careers. The very term wife had fallen out of favor to be replaced by the more egalitarian label, partner.

Since Claire and I had been coworkers and friends before we were lovers, Saint Paul's expectation that wives should be obedient to their husbands wouldn't do. I hoped our marriage would rise above sexism. Claire's determination to assert herself as a person called by God to holiness bolstered my intentions. Had I made sexist suggestions, Claire would have squashed them dead on arrival. The only exceptions I can think of during our three decades of marriage have been in her dealings with auto mechanics and contractors. Then, Claire has sometimes played the damsel in distress to maximize benefits of whatever residual chivalry remains. Otherwise, she cuts a wide swath and tolerates no patronizing.

Unlike my folks, who had their parents near at hand for advice, many if not most newlyweds in the eighties did not live in their hometowns, home states, or even home countries. While Claire and I took up residence in Worcester, Massachusetts, her parents lived in Virginia and mine in northern New Hampshire. We had a copy of Doctor Benjamin Spock's book on parenting but no equivalent on marriage. Our only advice came from a retreat for engaged couples, which we attended months before our wedding. Two married couples, one young and one old, and a Catholic priest gave talks and took questions. The consensus among the presenters held that a good marriage required work and that the chief stumbling blocks were disputes over money, sex, and child care. They proved right on all counts.

Claire and I married on June 22, 1984 in Washington, DC. The steamy hot night began with Mass at Saint Patrick's Church and finished with great food, drink, music, and dancing in Saint Anthony's Church hall. We honeymooned on Massachusetts's Cape Ann, where the sun did not shine and the temperature never went over fifty-five degrees. Claire, a native of Tennessee who grew up in India, thought we had gone to the Arctic Circle. Without a cozy fireplace in the modest hotel where we lodged, the nights proved more bracing than romantic. Throughout our stay, Claire often exclaimed, "I can't believe I'm married."

Although it didn't have the quality of "What was I thinking?" her comment made me feel a bit like someone hired to play a husband on television rather than an actual one. As a couple that met in the hectic world of the Catholic Worker, Claire and I both were unaccustomed to the idea of taking of time off. We could do only so much walking on the beach, eating in restaurants, and sightseeing before getting antsy. So we curtailed our honeymoon by a day (Can you believe it?) and returned to our new 150-year-old basement apartment to begin actual married life.

Claire and Scott near the birth of their first child

To say we didn't really know what we were doing would be spot on. This was verified when we realized our plan to hyphenate our names should have happened when we got our marriage license when it would have cost nothing, but, because we didn't do it then, we had to pay for a legal name change. This was our first but not last screwup. Maybe we should have created an entirely new name like Schaeffy or Duffer. On second thought, it's just as well that we settled for Schaeffer-Duffy, although we did have a bit of a back and forth as to whose name would be listed first. Part of me thought Scott Duffy-Schaeffer preserved the original order of my name, but another part liked being the end punctuation of the new amalgam. In any event, the long name seemed pretty awkward and foreign to both of us until we met more people who knew us only with that name than those who knew the original ones.

I took two jobs, one at a group home for the mentally challenged and the other at a nursing home, while Claire cleaned houses and, later on, started an enterprise she called, "The Bread Not Bombs Bakery." We tried to keep flexible work schedules for the freedom to attend peace vigils, commit civil disobedience, and risk jail for nuclear disarmament. Claire decorated our apartment with thrift store acquisitions and gifts from her parents while I painted the floor bright yellow to lighten things up. She loved the community garden across the street, and we both loved the blues bar at the corner. Truth be told, she enjoys live music and adores dancing but has never been much of a drinker. I drank too much then and may have developed a problem were it not for our eventual decision to help found the alcohol-free Saints Francis & Thérèse Catholic Worker. But even without the constraints of a dry house, drinking loses its allure when you have to get up early for work or care for children.

When we got married, my Swedish grandmother told us, "If you are going to have children, have them in the spring. It's awful to be pregnant in the hot summer, and a baby born in the spring gets six months of decent weather before winter." She also told us to have our children three years apart to avoid have two at a time nursing or in diapers. She also said they will have less sibling rivalry. Her advice sounded wise and, since we were using natural family planning, we could pinpoint when we'd get pregnant. We had our first son, Justin, on May 30 and our daughter, Grace, three years later on June 13, the feast of Saint Anthony of Padua. For many years, we provided the only redheads in the annual procession of the statue of Saint Anthony through Boston's Italian North End.

Claire and I prepared for our first child by signing up at a prenatal clinic, attending birthing classes, and researching the kind of birth we wanted. We opted for a modified version of a cool thing called the Leboyer birth, a reaction to the traditional path of cutting the newborn's cord immediately under bright lights, dangling the child by a heel, smacking him or her to be sure the lungs are clear, putting erythromycin in the infant's eyes, inking the child's footprint, and then whisking the progeny away for swaddling.

Frederick Leboyer felt such an introduction into life outside the womb is too jarring. He favored turning down the lights, speaking in hushed tones, letting the cord stop pulsing naturally to give the child an opportunity to transition slowly from receiving oxygen that way to breathing it in, and then to give the baby to the father to place in a warm bath, a familiar environment. After immersion, the father places the baby on the mother's abdomen and so the child has a chance to nurse. Prodding, poking, and measuring would all have to wait.

When it came to actual labor, I learned that the father's role is worth about as much as ice cream in a blizzard. A friend put what he thought was a reassuring hand on his wife's shoulder during labor, and she snapped, "Don't you ever touch me again!" While I comprised half of the genetic make up, I performed absolutely zero of the labor. Offering ice chips and platitudes amounts to pretty paltry stuff, and after Claire made it clear she didn't want me to say a word, I had very little to do.

Claire's birthing coach had suggested it would help during transition, the most painful part of labor, for Claire to imagine herself as something powerful. When Claire hit transition, she began to roar. The doctor asked if she was okay, and she blurted out, "I'm a lion!" And so she was. Justin was born. He stared at me curiously with wide eyes when I placed him in the bath. He probably wondered what made Claire and me smile and cry at the same time.

After bringing home our firstborn in his stocking cap, we learned to support his neck so his head wouldn't flop and to beware of getting a shower when he made a fountain during a diaper change. My grandmother said it was good luck to get peed on by a baby, but I think she just made that one up. He looked so tiny that we started calling him our little peanut.

We were not home three days, though, when he exhibited violent convulsions. "What had we done wrong?" we wondered as we rushed him back to Saint Vincent

Hospital. The doctor took one look at Justin before calling in two other physicians who joined him in laughing, "Your son has hiccups." Years later, we would be equally embarrassed when we had to take our daughter Grace to the emergency room after she pushed a peanut up her nose. "Watch me make this peanut disappear!" she pronounced in a two-year old helium voice before sending the goober pea up her nostril. What in the world was she thinking?

The hiccup affair was insignificant compared to our biggest mistake. It came when Claire noticed that Justin still slept beyond the time expected for him to nurse. "Should I wake him?" she asked. Like an idiot, I said yes. That infant never slept for more than two hours straight again. And when he awoke, he screamed for an eternity. In short order, we both became exhausted and would remain that way. We took turns trying in vain to get him to go back to sleep. When I ran out of nursery rhymes, Irish ballads, and lullabies, I gave him history lessons of the American, French, or Russian revolutions. He had the stamina to stay awake at three in the morning all the way from the storming of the Bastille to the fall of Napoleon and the Bourbon restoration to the abdication of Czar Nicholas II. Claire slept soundly through my lectures on the Articles of Confederation and the liberation of the serfs. I only hope my accounts were as fair and balanced as we've all come to expect from the media.

Generally speaking, the only surefire way to get our angel to sleep involved putting him in a car seat and driving on the highway. On one particularly trying night, Claire and I headed east from Worcester and didn't stop until we reached Provincetown at the tip of Cape Cod. "Listen, kid," I told him, "This is as far as the continent goes." On the return journey, I detoured into the National Seashore, parked on a bluff by a lighthouse, and woke Claire to see a spectacular sunrise over the ocean. She took a quick glance, opened the door, and threw up. So much for that magic moment.

We braced ourselves for sleep deprivation in anticipation of the birth of our daughter Grace, but we learned to our pleasant surprise that some infants actually like to sleep. In fact, when I hovered over her crib and she opened her eyes, I was astonished to see her smile instead of hearing her scream. She was so jolly, I called her Chuckles and still do.

Each child is a unique delight. Grace sported curly red hair and seemed to hold onto the helium voice longer than most. She loved to sing and dance. Justin liked to read and put on magic shows. He was thoughtful. Asked at age seven if he would be Jesus in a skit, he thought for a minute and replied seriously with more than a bit of apprehension, "Will I have to be nailed to the cross?" Grace went through a period where she used various aliases including Baba Yaga, Manar Patanar, and Andre Kropoyen among others. Justin was a good eater. Grace let beans pass her lips only under protest. They both would have lived on macaroni and cheese if we had allowed it.

Unfortunately, cancer struck down my mother at only fifty-nine when Grace was two, denying our daughter any real memories of her grandmother. A month before her death, my mother told me that she once looked out the window when I was four and saw a boy chasing me with a meat-tenderizing hammer in his hand. Before he could fracture my skull, my mother took the heavy kitchen utensil away from him. In many ways, that was indicative of how she loved us without drawing attention to herself but by being there when we needed her the most. After her death, I found a box in which she preserved my birth notice, a lock of hair from my first haircut, photos, my report cards, newspaper clippings with me in them, every letter and card I ever sent home, and, at the very bottom of the box, the meat tenderizer.

My father had a more lasting impact on our children. He had always been eccentric and stuck to that script as a grandfather from whom you never knew what to expect. On one occasion, he appeared at our house without warning to give Justin an antique Victrola and dozens of old records, including one made at Coney Island of my grandfather Duffy telling humorous stories.

Claire's father and mother, although farther away, were effusive in their love for Justin and Grace. During our visits South and theirs to Massachusetts, they doted on their grandchildren. Long before the automated ease of e-cards, my mother-in-law, like my maternal great grandmother before her, never failed to mail actual birthday cards not only to the children but also to Claire and me along with beautiful Christmas ornaments and a quantity of gifts that she must have acquired over many weeks. We could not mail enough photos and made an annual Christmas video now quite precious to us all.

In one of those videos, Grace talks about her imaginary sisters. For many months, she referenced her faux siblings ad nauseam until, one evening at bath time, she announced, "My sisters are dead."

"Thank God!" Justin replied.

Nonplussed, Grace didn't miss a beat: "But they have thirty-two daughters."

I so loved my children's comments that I took to recording them on cassette tapes. In 1989 when Justin was four, I played him a Beatles song and, afterwards, he told me, "Dad, these guys are good. They are going to be popular."

"I think you are right," I replied.

Before she passed away, my mother told me that my grandfather took her and my father aside after the births of my older brother Michael and sister Kathy to say, "They don't make any other kinds."

But my parents were not to be dissuaded. They ultimately had seven children of whom I arrived fourth. At our Engaged Encounter premarital weekend retreat, Claire ruminated about whether or not she wanted children at all. When we told our friend Mary Laurel True that we planned our first baby to be born in the spring, she scoffed, "You'll have children when God is good and ready to give them to you!" So it goes. Claire became pregnant with our third, and we started to feel like real parents.

I went to every single prenatal checkup for Justin and Grace and missed only one for the third child. As fate would have it, the doctor could not find a heartbeat. I rushed to Claire's side and learned that we'd have to wait twenty-four hours for the results of a test on the baby's status. Distraught, we made the mistake of passing the time by going to see the movie *Ghost*, which featured the Righteous Brother's hit "Unchained Melody" in a particularly sad scene with Demi Moore. I still can't hear that song without recalling the dread we felt that night.

The next morning, we learned that the baby had died. When this happens, a mother usually miscarries, but, in the rare instances when she doesn't, doctors have to induce labor to deliver the dead child. Pretty rough. Claire ended up in the same room where she labored for our son Justin. We could hear other women giving birth. It was an ordeal. We appreciated that the hospital and Saint John's Cemetery allowed us to bury the remains of the child we called Patrice.

"Don't blame yourself for this situation," the doctor told us. "I'm sure you didn't do anything wrong. And don't feel the need to rush out and try to have a replacement child.

"Forget that!" Claire said. So we tossed out our spring birth plan and conceived as soon as we could. Claire gave birth to our son Patrick on November 26, 1991. A surprise pregnancy followed three years later producing our last child, Aiden.

"You wouldn't give five dollars for a new baby," my paternal grandfather said, "but once one is born you wouldn't take a million dollars to give that infant away."

Dorothy Day would say, "A baby is born with a loaf of bread under his arms."

I agree with both of them. Patrick and Aiden, our two children beyond the politically correct family size, proved to be absolute delights. Patrick was full of gumption and boundless energy while Aiden was a curly-haired cherub who inexplicably affected a Brooklyn accent until he was five.

One of our family's greatest joys besides Christmas has always been celebrating Halloween. In an effort to make the day more creative, we didn't buy costumes and often started making them as early as August. It began with Claire and me as Fred and Wilma Flintstone with Justin as their son Bam Bam and then Grace as a bumblebee. It took off from there.

Grace as the Mayflower II

photo by Scott Schaeffer-Duffy

As little boys, Patrick and Aiden portrayed The Blues Brothers one year. Another year, Aiden became Groucho Marx. Justin was Frankenstein's monster. One year, I dressed as Big Bird. Grace took us to the creative limit when she asked to be the Mayflower. I told her, "The *Mayflower* is a boat. You must mean you want to be a Pilgrim." But she insisted, so we went to Plymouth and saw the *Mayflower II*. I dutifully made her into the ship that carried my mother's great, great, great, great, great, great . . . grandfather to America.

To our delight, our children and their partners tackle Halloween with gusto. Grace makes fantastic decorations. Justin and our daughter-in-law, Patricia Kirkpatrick, made an adorable costume for our first granddaughter, the irresistible May Duffy. (After many years offering my first name to siblings and friends to use for their newborns to no avail, I decided on my own to call my granddaughter Scotti May. This, like many of my idiosyncrasies, is generally ignored.)

Over the years, Claire paid special attention to celebrating religious holidays with traditions that grew more and more dear

Scotti May and her "G'ampa"

as time went by to the point where Grace won't hear of it when anyone suggests that we celebrate Christmas Eve anywhere else but at our local parish's children's Mass where they all appeared at one time or another in the pageant.

I hide chocolate eggs on Easter morning. We make individual artworks each day to illustrate biblical readings during Advent and then place them on an Advent wheel on the wall. We always read a children's book about the Nativity called *Round the Back* and, in recent years, have read Truman Capote's "A Christmas Memory," which without fail elicits tears. I'm pleased to say Justin and Patricia hosted a group reading of Dickens's "A Christmas Carol." When I first tried to read it aloud, seven-year-old Grace burst into tears when Scrooge's fiancée broke up with him. "Is he going to get back together with her?" she wailed.

When I said, "No," she refused to hear another word.

One funny thing about being a parent is you can really be creative. As time went by, I understood better how my parents could suddenly decide to take us to the beach or a carnival. Parenthood should be fun. When Aiden was only four, inspired by an episode of *The Little Rascals*, I convinced Grace, Patrick, and Aiden to star in a play I called *MacBeth—the Short Form*. I did not re-write Shakespeare but did severely edit the Bard to distill his story of ambition down to fifteen minutes. Grace was wonderful as Lady MacBeth and Patrick played her doomed husband. Aiden played one of the witches and, in the finale as Duncan, he pointed a sword at his brother and yelled, "Turn hellhound, turn!" Cable access TV would have featured our troupe, but Patrick dug in his heels, as he often would, and refused to reprise the role.

While most children have tantrums, Patrick went so far over the top that we said, "He's having an octopus."

During such highly dramatic episodes, he would tell us, "Don't be a Gooser! Don't be a Darndy Dooder!" We have no idea what he was talking about but latched onto the first moniker as a good nickname for him.

Although universally sunny, Aiden didn't fare so well in the nickname department. While our family traveled in India, I found the deposits in his cloth diapers particularly pungent, so I called him Stinky. Amazingly, even well into adulthood, he has never objected to me calling him that malodorous name.

We used cloth diapers for all our children in an effort to be more environmentally considerate. It caused a bit of extra work at home but turned into a colossal task in India where I often had to boil water to hand wash clothes. In a mad gesture during the dark, early days of Claire's nursing with Justin, I promised her that I'd do all the laundry for our entire marriage since I was exempt from nursing. Here is one of those promises that sounded okay then but has grown less fun in her post-lactating decades.

No matter. As my hero Thomas More said, "When a man takes an oath, he's holding his own self in his own hands. Like water. And if he opens his fingers then—he needn't hope to find himself again." I took a similar approach in fifth grade when my friend Mike Seuss complained that he couldn't chew gum because he had braces and I promised to forgo gum in solidarity with him. His braces came off a few years later, but I've never had gum since.

Our children inherited Claire and my tendency to plant our feet and take stands. While we took it on the chin for peace and justice, they withstood the gale for the right to wear outlandish clothes, especially hats; to see more movies; in a time of utter parental defeat to get tattoos and piercings; and to join a screamo band.

"Where, oh where, did we go wrong?"

From the earliest age, I told my daughter, "There's nothing my Grace can't do." She twisted this motto into, "There are a few things Grace won't do." She won the battle of wills with Claire over music lessons. While the boys all made it through the musical boot camp to learn an instrument, Grace wore Claire down. And later, when Claire, who worried that Worcester's South High School wasn't challenging enough, insisted that Grace apply for admission to the highly-competitive Massachusetts Academy of Math and Sciences, Grace agreed. However, she turned down her acceptance (the only person ever to do so) when it arrived. She went on to graduate first in her class at South and get her BA at Columbia University and Masters at Clark University. She is not to be trifled with.

What with our peace work and hospitality to the homeless, we wanted to be sure that our children remained a priority, so we initiated a tradition that every Friday was Family Night. We served dinner to our guests separately and took turns planning an activity together. Although we heard a few moans and groans during their high school years, the tradition has endured into their adulthood. I like to tell them, "You can live anywhere in the world as long as you can come to dinner every Friday night." The corollary to that came about when Grace asked if she could use the family car to go on a date. Claire hesitated, but I said, "Of course you can take the car. We raised you with good values. I'll just sit in the back seat reading my book. You'll hardly notice me."

When Grace disputed this story's accuracy, Claire said, "Well, you know the original title of your father's creation was *The Book Of Lies.*"

"You cut me deep, Shrek," I thought and then recalled Matthew 6:4: "A prophet is not without honor except in his hometown and among his family."

One of our routine forms of recreation with our children nearly ended in calamity. Early on a crisp November Sunday afternoon in 2001, Claire took six-year-old Aiden hiking on the Appalachian Mountain Club trails bordering Worcester and Paxton. Claire and I had hiked various loops dozens of times. None of them were longer than a mile, but Claire and Aiden had not returned at three when I expected them. At four, shadows began to lengthen. I borrowed a car and drove up to the Appalachian Mountain Club parking lot where I found our van unlocked with the keys in it. I sped off down our usual trail calling out to no avail for my wife and son.

As darkness started to fall and panic to rise, I walked to the nearest house and used the phone to call friends and then the police, who asked me to go home and retrieve an article of clothing for Aiden and Claire. When I returned, the parking lot had filled with firefighters, police, EMTs, press, and spectators. Our van was surrounded by yellow tape marked "CRIME SCENE-DO NOT CROSS." As I approached, I heard several people whisper, "He's the husband," as if I was the chief suspect in Claire and Aiden's disappearance. To my enormous frustration, the police refused to begin searching the woods until a special dog could be brought up. By then, Claire and Aiden had been gone for six and a half hours. It was very dark and increasingly cold.

"Did they have warm clothes? Food? Water? Flashlights?" I was asked accusingly.

"Good grief," I thought. "This was an afternoon walk, not an overnight expedition."

Just as terrifying scenarios began to invade my mind, two super fit search and rescue professionals asked me to accompany them and a large German Shepherd into the forest. The dog sniffed the clothing and took off, straining at his leash. To my surprise, he led us down a path we never used. Every few minutes, the men blew a whistle and asked me to call for them. We then stood in silence listening before tearing off again. I could not believe how dark it was under the trees.

"Please, God, let them be okay," I prayed. And then we heard a scream. Like rockets, we rushed in that direction. I called their names and Claire replied. Minutes later, we found them sitting on the edge of the trail. Apparently, the scream was Aiden's from a fall that convinced them both to sit tight rather than blunder around in the dark. After many hugs, I learned that they had simply gotten turned around and lost their way, something the rescue people did as well. The dog was great for leading us to Claire and Aiden but had no idea how to get us back to civilization, so, after a radio call, a helicopter approached us, shined down a spotlight, and led us out the back side of the forest into Paxton where a police car picked us up.

The police said it was a good thing Claire and Aiden didn't wander off the trails because there are a number of abandoned colonial wells in the forest. Nonplussed, Claire told a reporter for the *Worcester Telegram*, "I was lost, but now I'm found."

Most of our other parental activities were less harrowing. We volunteered at school, coached youth soccer, read aloud daily, helped with homework, and tried to be always available should our children need us. One special pitfall I tried to avoid was the temptation to mold them into my own image. I once saw a photo of a child dressed in a Ku Klux Klan robe in the arms of his father in the same get-up. This disturbing image convinced me that Claire and my job as parents was to give our children good example and the tools to discover their own vocations and not to try and make them into our clones. To that end, we didn't dress them in peace T-shirts or drag them to demonstrations. While we served vegetarian food at home, we always told them that what they ate elsewhere was up to them. We did share with them our Catholic faith but tried to expose them to other traditions and make it clear that, as adults, they had to make their own choices, which we'd try to respect. Not always the easiest task. Just ask the father in *Fiddler on the Roof.*

Our attempt to give them room for self-discovery was aided by the fact that we gave them Schaeffer as a middle name and Duffy as the last, thus insulating them a bit from our notoriety/infamy. Ironically, now that they have each made significant marks in life, we increasingly meet people who identify us as their parents rather than them as our children. How quickly the sun sets on a generation.

With her father as a member of the US Foreign Service, Claire grew up in India, England, and Japan. Her experience convinced her that seeing the rest of the world was essential for child rearing. As good fortune would have it, a generous friend with a

photo by a passerby

Grace, Scott, Patrick, Justin, Claire, and Aiden visit Claire's childhood home in India (and take in the Taj Mahal)

sister who is a travel agent made it possible for us to go as a family to India in 1995 and to Ireland in 2003. We also managed to visit Vieques, Puerto Rico as well as Quebec and Nova Scotia. Justin and I got to see Niagara Falls and Toronto. We also went often to Washington, DC, northern Virginia, and the White Mountains region of New Hampshire. We tried to not let a year go by without going at least once to the ocean. We never took our children to Disney World, but we did show them the Taj Mahal, the Giant's Causeway, and the world's most beautiful bioluminescent bay in Vieques, Puerto Rico.

When ten-year-old Justin first saw the snow-capped Himalayas from the Indian village of Mussoorie he proclaimed dramatically, "I will come back here!" And so he did ten years later. We may have missed a lot of television, trips to the mall, and meals at McDonald's, but I don't think our children got shortchanged.

That's not to say our kids were always on board with some of the sacrifices of growing up in a Catholic Worker house of hospitality with homeless people and parents who sometimes went to war zones or to jail for civil disobedience. Sometimes, they craved the ordinary things that their peers enjoyed, like Grace when she pleaded with me to celebrate her birthday at Chuck E. Cheese. If you are unfamiliar with the chain, it combines a video arcade with a birthday party assembly line that can squeeze out as many as ten parties in a single day. I once went to a birthday party conducted at a long table with two other parties on either side. I felt like I was at one of those mass weddings you sometimes see in Korea.

Although I am not completely opposed to mainstream culture (I read the *Harry Potter* and *Lord of the Rings* books aloud to my kids and saw tons of movies with them), I just couldn't bear the tackiness of Chuck E. Cheese, so I told Grace we could do better. She was skeptical but came around when she discovered that I finagled the use of a nineteenth-century mansion replete with ornate fireplaces and multiple staircases for a night of live-action Clue. Claire and I along with Grace's siblings and friends dressed as Colonel Mustard, Professor Plum, Miss Scarlet, Mr. Green, etc. We then had a secret drawing to decide who would play the murderer. We left weapons visible throughout the house. Only the murderer could pick one up. Should he or she touch one of the others with the rope, lead pipe, wrench, dagger, or candlestick, the victim had to scream and fall "dead." A revolver, loaded with caps, could fell one of us from ten feet or less. Anyone who thought they knew the culprit's identity could call everyone to the ballroom by blowing a whistle and then make an accusation: "I accuse Miss Peacock of murder in the library with the candlestick." If the charge was correct, the murderer was handcuffed, and a mug shot taken. Then a new round ensued.

After several rounds, we upped the ante by playing without lights. Since it was a stormy night, (How could it not be?) the illumination came from distant streetlights. At one point, I heard screaming far away and assumed that Mr. Green, who was right behind me, was innocent. As we crept up a curled staircase, we found Miss Scarlett sprawled on the stairs.

"She's dead," I said.

Lightning flashed. I turned in horror to see Green raise the dagger and say, "I know. I killed her!"

I'm lucky I didn't have a heart attack. I still get goose bumps recalling the moment.

As anyone knows, despite parents' claims to the contrary, children are not always perfect. They scream and yell in public to try and wear you down into giving them whatever they want. They make poor choices and act irresponsibly. They can be deliberately difficult. During my sophomore year at college, I left my ten- and eleven-year-old brothers, Chip and Tom, alone with my studious and shy roommate for a half an hour, warning them before I left to behave themselves. When I returned, I was shocked to see Tom laughing while my roommate held Chipper by his ankles out our second floor window and shouted, "I'll drop you! I swear to God I will!" No one ever revealed what they did to drive him so crazy.

Of course, parents don't always get it right. The last thing my son Aiden wanted to see at his prom was me spying from the hallway. What children don't often appreciate is how big a responsibility being a parent is. The consequences of confusing a viral infection with a bacterial one, of sending them to the wrong school, of letting them be on their own prematurely, or of not playing the heavy sometimes can be serious. Unlike many activities in life, you can't just zone out in parenting. There are no leaves of absence or vacations. Even if you do find someone to watch your children, the buck still stops with you for their entire lives.

photo by Claire Schaeffer-Duffy

not all parental ideas are equally popular: Scott as Santa with Aiden

While parental responsibility can be daunting, it is offset in so many ways. The joy of watching your children go from taking their first steps to their college graduations and wedding days is a priceless treasure. I cannot tell you how elated Claire and I were to see Justin play the lead in *The Importance of Being Earnest* and Grace play the cowardly lion in *The Wizard of Oz* and then Patrick row for Harvard in the Head of the Charles and Aiden, in full zombie make-up, win Worcester's Monster Dash 5K. Children have failures for which parents inevitably blame themselves, but they also have spectacular triumphs that redound on them and them alone.

Parenting does cut into time for romance, though. With a child or two tugging at your or your partner's shirt and a haggard look on both of your faces, it can be very difficult to be amorous. With a good sense of humor, you can still connect in times when the kids are struck down by the flu, diarrhea, vomiting, sunburn, or, the mother of all nightmares, a splinter that can be removed only with a needle. More often, tempers get frayed, and the parent who is in the deeper end of the parenting pool may take it out on the wader. I learned early on that, when I returned from a peace mission overseas, I had to wait at least an hour hearing about how things went for Claire before I talked about my trip. Forgetting to acknowledge your partner's trials can be more perilous than failing to speedily answer the question, "Do I look fat in this dress?"

Aiden, Justin, and Patrick, from left, in Claire's comfy chair

I did have one romantic triumph when, in response to Claire's complaint that she had no comfortable chair to sit in while nursing, I rustled up a recliner. To surprise her, I snuck the chair into the house in the morning while she was out. As fate would have it, Claire was on her own secret errand to ease the tired bones she knew I experienced from long hours at work. By the end of the day, we had not one but two comfy chairs.

Sometimes, Claire or I suffered from poor-me syndrome. We'd look at the tidy houses and outfits of childless friends, hear about their blooming careers, or, worse yet, romantic getaways and fear that we might melt with envy. On occasion, we'd take it out on each other and argue over ridiculous things. Claire usually won, and then I'd mope around afterwards trying to win back her favor by doing extra household chores.

Often when I tried to play the martyr with Claire, the children would sing in chorus, "Dad the sacrificer. Dad the giver-upper!" The candor of children can burst a crabby balloon. Grace wrote me a Father's Day poem when she was ten. The last stanza read:

My dad is the best!
He beats all the rest!
We think you're especially great!
You're the top of the toast,
a lot better than most!
We overlook farting, belching, and weight.

In a marvelous way, children help us keep our feet on the ground. But when our youngest set off for college, during that short space before our oldest started leaving our granddaughter here with regularity (a joy we would never relinquish), Claire and I experienced a genuine empty nest in spite of the continuous presence of up to six previously homeless guests. We re-learned the art of talking to each other without

outgoing Patrick, perhaps thanks to growing up in a house of hospitality

photo by Scott Schaeffer-Duffy

interruption. We also continued to pursue life goals that gave us something, other than our children, to talk about. Claire is especially good at this. She's taking an online poetry class as I type this chapter. She's the chairperson of the Center For Nonviolent Solutions. She's an award-winning freelance writer who has reported from war zones, inner cities, and even death row. She has never lost her desire to learn new things or visit new places.

Although, I don't share all her interests or dislikes (she could care less for mystery novels or practical jokes), I am really proud of her joie de vivre.

And so in this time of low marriage versus high divorce rates, how have we stayed together since 1985? We know plenty of couples as loving if not more so than we whose unions did not endure. We do have the good fortune of parents who never divorced, although mine came perilously close. I agree with Claire, though, when she said, "As I grow older I feel the effect of their commitment. It wasn't a storybook, but when I look at couples who didn't have that commitment, I appreciate my parents' example."

Also, Claire and I have been enormously blessed in our siblings Michael, Kathy, Chris, Judy, Chip, Tom, Eric, Susan, and Michele with their spouses Charlotte, Ernie, Sam, Maggie, Lauren, and John; in our nieces and nephews Angela, Jenny, Joanne, Barbara, Jack, Elizabeth, Emma, Laura, Thomas, Charlie, India, Byron, Jesse, Max, Hannah, and Miles; in our children's spouses Patricia and Anthony, and of course in our granddaughter Scotti May. And happily, we all enjoy spending time together.

Nonetheless, given how little day-to-day guidance Claire and I had on marriage and parenting, it'd be outrageous not to say that we've been very, very lucky. We had no experience. I can't think of any task that I took up for the first time that I didn't bungle in one way or another. We probably avoided some disasters by seeking advice from friends and by working decisions out between us. I'm grateful, for example, that Claire prevailed in her insistence that all the children take music lessons, and she's no longer furious that I prevailed in the choice to send our children to public schools instead of home-schooling. Some arguments last a lifetime, by the way.

For the most part though, I think we just have to bow to the hidden God of parenthood who nudged us this way and that. Left on our own, Patrick would still be limping from a break in his leg that we thought was nothing. His guardian angel prompted us to take him to the hospital after a week, just before setting his broken leg might have been impossible. Angels also watched over Aiden as a toddler when Claire and I each assumed the other was watching him and he followed me across a busy street.

Our marriage and our parenting were far from perfect but much better than we could expect from our own efforts by themselves. Maybe that's part of the mystery of a Catholic wedding. Matrimony is the only Catholic sacrament that is not administered by a priest. The couple actually administers the sacrament while the priest and congregation are witnesses. In our case, the prayers of those witnesses, beloved family and friends, must have reached some heavenly ears. What can I say save, "Thanks be to God!"

photo by Scott Schaeffer-Duffy

Patrick, Grace, Justin, and Aiden, from left
"Children are a heritage from the Lord, the fruit of the womb, a reward."

—Psalm 127

Peacemaking and War

Along with five other unarmed peace activists, I was boxed in by two armored personnel carriers with mounted machine guns and an M1-A1 tank. The formidable weapons stood less than twenty feet from us. Their operators were "buttoned up" inside, so we had no idea of their intent. We stood frozen in place as the turret of the huge tank began to turn slowly until we stared down the barrel of its long gun.

Just how did I end up facing down a tank in a war zone? It's a twisty road that begins with wounded pride. In response to President Jimmy Carter's plan to introduce registration for military service, I sat at an information table in 1977 in the lobby of Holy Cross College's Hogan Center. US Marine Corps Major Townsend, a Reserve Officer Training Corps (ROTC) instructor, approached me. Major Townsend and I had exchanged numerous letters to the editor in the campus paper on the ethics of war.

Despite Major Townsend's martial stance and my pacifism, we fell easily into a friendly debate. As our conversation deepened, students gathered round to listen. After two hours with the lobby packed, we both had exhausted our arguments. Consensus emerged that on religious topics, I had the upper hand while whenever we focused on personal experience, the major held all the cards. I scored a few points with references to historical peacemakers, but I could not compete with his familiarity with combat. While it always galls me to lose an argument, it especially rankled to lose this one since lives were at stake. One out of ten of my classmates were heading to the military via ROTC while the US and Soviet Union were never more than three minutes away from global nuclear annihilation.

"No," I thought. "This debate is far from over."

In 1982, my coworkers at the Catholic Worker, Claire Schaeffer, Carl Siciliano, and I attended a talk by the theologian Henri Nouwen at Washington, DC's Catholic University. Nouwen said that his presence in Nicaragua had acted as a deterrent to attacks by US-sponsored opponents of the left-wing Sandinistas. When the talk ended, Claire plowed through the crowd and cornered the speaker to ask, "Do you think the fighting stopped because of your celebrity, or is this something that any American could do?"

Nouwen's reply that the presence of any internationals could have the same impact set us on a course to go to war-torn Nicaragua where I hoped to put flesh on my theoretical pacifism. Carl had just received a small inheritance, and he gladly used it to finance the expedition. Our friend Theresa Grady from Ithaca, New York, agreed to join us. Save Nouwen, everyone we approached stateside for advice called our proposed venture suicidal. Even after arriving in the Nicaraguan capital, local activists, humanitarians, and government workers warned against the dangerous, potentially insane journey toward the northern border.

Luckily, on our third day in the country, we met two Maryknoll nuns in the capital to pick up a jeep. The sisters readily agreed to take us with them to their mission in Ocotal, where counterrevolutionaries (Contras) had already attacked several times.

Once we arrived, Sister Joan Uhlan asked us to use the convent's indoor toilet only at night and the outhouse during the day to save water. On my first journey to the wooden privy, I discovered a black-and-orange-striped spider on the toilet seat. A profound arachnophobe, I achieved the not small accomplishment of finding a long stick and prodding the monster twenty yards away before I sat on the john. In the middle of my business, I happened to look up and saw, to my everlasting horror, three more spiders just inches above my face. I never went to the bathroom during the day again in Nicaragua.

Later that night, I asked Sister Joan if she had ever had spiders in the house. She said she saw one the previous week. When I asked her what she did with it, she replied, "I shot it." The thought of a spider large enough to kill with a gun has probably done more to keep me from returning to Central America than any fear of being killed by soldiers. (On the other hand, when I took my two-year-old granddaughter, Scotti May, to a pet store, we saw a tarantula climbing the glass in its cage. Scotti May approached the arachnid and began to sing, "The itsy bitsy spider went up the waterspout.")

While in Ocotal, we learned a great deal about the brutality of the counter-revolutionaries, known as Contras, from family members who had suffered deaths and injuries. We visited a poor woman who lived in a single room hut with a dirt floor, who offered us two eggs for lunch. She told us that three of her four sons had been killed after the government drafted them.

"Which government?" I asked her. "The current or previous?"

"All the governments are the same," she shrugged. "They take and kill my sons."

I later learned that the Sandinistas subjected males between sixteen and forty to a military draft with no provision for conscientious objection.

That night, the nuns presented us to a church full of locals who wanted to meet us. When they learned that we sheltered the homeless in Washington, DC, the Nicaraguans immediately asked, "What can we do to help?" It blew me away that these very poor people, victimized by American geopolitics, would want to help street people in our nation's capital.

After a few days, I came to realize that our presence in Ocotal might deter the Contras but had no effect on the Sandinistas, who still patrolled the mountains beyond us. I told Claire and Carl that a real pacifist would situate himself between the warring parties and not behind the lines of either side. The idea appalled them, and they persuaded me to save it for another day. We ended up leaving the country with greater awareness of war's impact, but only a partially effective pacifist technique.

I learned in 1988 that the Arab-American Anti-Discrimination Committee (ADC) was recruiting human rights observers to live for a month with Palestinian families in the Israeli-occupied Gaza Strip and West Bank. I applied, and ADC accepted me. ADC trained my fellow observers and me in what constitutes human rights abuse under international law, how to collect affidavits, and how to document findings with photographs. The team included a Protestant minister from the Midwest, a housewife from Florida, a nursery school teacher from Rhode Island, a Muslim immigration lawyer from Boston, a Jewish college professor from Brooklyn, several others, and me. ADC planned for each of us to spend fifteen days in a location of our choice with one family and then fifteen more days in a different place. At the end, our group of eleven would author a report based on observations and data collected in twenty-two different locations.

After flying into Amman, Jordan, we drove by bus over the Jordan River and then by taxi on to Jerusalem. The following morning, I settled in on the second floor of a prefab concrete home in the Palestinian refugee camp in Rafah on the Egyptian border of the Israeli-occupied Gaza Strip. My host family consisted of a father, mother, and nine children. The second son, Mohammed, shared his room with me. His older brother was a medical doctor. His father held a PhD in linguistics. Half the family spoke impeccable English, and I added a word at a time to my very limited repertoire of Arabic. They served dinner on a low, round table, around which the male members of the family reclined on pillows. Women ate separately. I learned the hard way that, in a Palestinian home, unless you leave an uneaten portion on your plate, it will be refilled over and over. Four helpings later, I went to bed looking forward to conducting my first interview the next day.

The sound of gunfire woke me. I quickly joined Mohammed at a window where we saw Israeli helicopters dropping tear gas canisters and showering glass balls the Palestinians called marbles onto the rooftops and streets where they shattered. I saw teenagers hurriedly piling rocks and debris into the road to form low barricades. Mohammed told me that the gunfire came from the souk, a large open market four blocks away, but the shots appeared to be moving closer. Family members quickly dropped venetian blinds on all the windows. Through cracks in the blinds, I saw an armored Israeli jeep with a mounted machine gun crash through the barricades as soldiers aboard fired steel-coated rubber bullets and tear gas canisters in all directions.

After a second jeep passed, we heard terrible screams from the shuttered house next door. The Israelis had fired a tear gas canister into the home, and the disoriented family inside could not escape. Mohammed's older brother rushed to our roof and jumped across the alley. Like Batman, he grabbed the upper beam of a second-floor window and smashed open the shutters with his feet. Not long afterwards, he returned to the courtyard of our house carrying two unconscious children.

He rescued the remainder of the family and went out one last time to retrieve the gas canister. He placed the still-hot metal tube in my hands saying, "This is yours."

On its side, I read, "FOR OUTDOOR USE ONLY • INDOOR USE MAY CAUSE INJURY OR DEATH • Federal Laboratories, Saltsburg, Pennsylvania."

Later that day, I called Joel Brinkley, *The New York Times* bureau chief in Jerusalem, to tell him that I had seen a six-month-old Palestinian girl shot by an Israeli soldier.

"How long have you been here?" he asked.

"Two days," I answered.

"Let me tell you something," he replied. "What you saw is not news. It happens every day. I'll tell you what is news. When Palestinians were bulldozed to death a couple of weeks ago, that was news because it's different."

"Mr. Brinkley," I offered, "I realize I'm a newcomer here and you're an experienced journalist, but let me ask you, if that injured child I saw had been Jewish, would the shooting then be news?"

He didn't answer.

The conversation reminded me of one Claire, Carl, and I had in Ocotal with a *Washington Post* correspondent, Christopher Dickey, then researching a book on the Contras. We asked him why we didn't see stories in the *Post* describing the Sandinistas accurately as democratic socialists rather than the Communists President Reagan said they were.

"You have to realize that if the President says the sky is green, we have to report it," Dickey said. "If he says it every day, we'd be going out on a limb to say otherwise."

When we looked surprised, he said, "I could write the plain truth for the alternative media, but then I'd only reach a handful of people."

"So how do you preserve your integrity?" we asked.

He told us with a hint of pride that he made sure that each article he filed was "nuanced toward the truth."

After my call to Mr. Brinkley, the Israelis declared a curfew. I assumed it meant that people could not go outside after a certain hour at night, but the Israeli definition was more stringent. During a curfew, Palestinians could be shot if they so much as looked out their windows. Indeed, Susan Atkins, another member of my team, photographed a three-year-old girl after an Israeli soldier shattered her jaw with the butt of his rifle when the girl peeked over her windowsill. Years later in the West Bank city of Ramallah, I saw the corpse of a Palestinian mother killed by an Israeli sniper as the mother stood in her living room four feet away from an open window.

On the third day of the curfew, while I copied notes upstairs, a soldier burst into the room, brandished his gun, and shouted in Hebrew. After I said I didn't understand him, he demanded, "What are you doing here?" Afraid of repercussions to my host family and of losing my notes and film, I gestured toward my roommate and said, "Mohammed went to the University of Texas," which was true.

The soldier assumed we studied together and withdrew. He and other members of his squad compelled the father and other sons at gunpoint to clear debris from the road. I knew intuitively that lying to the soldier was risky but figured that letting him draw a bogus conclusion was okay.

Unlike my time in Nicaragua, in Gaza and the West Bank I not only heard reports of violence but actually witnessed it. Ultimately, our team documented hundreds of human rights abuses. We found it impossible to be anywhere in Israeli-occupied territories for more than twenty-four hours without seeing a shooting, unlawful arrest, beating, home demolition, land seizure, or denial of food, water, or medical care. It was a relentless onslaught against a defenseless population. We did see Palestinian teens throwing stones at soldiers, something we did not condone, but we also saw many nonviolent forms of resistance including boycotts of Israeli products, tax resistance, and nonviolent marches.

The expedition deepened my awareness of and aversion to violence but failed to provide an effective antidote. Publicizing human rights violations, while an important step towards more just policies, does not address the immediate need to save lives. I believed that a pacifist needs to offer something more.

And then, in 1993, I heard a National Public Radio report about a peace demonstration in the besieged Bosnian capital, Sarajevo. Not long afterwards, I learned that one of the participants in that daring march, Kathy Kelly of Chicago, was recruiting Americans to join a larger effort to stop the Bosnian bloodshed. Called Mir Sada ("Peace Now" in Serbo-Croatian), the idea involved gathering thousands of international activists who would pass through the battle lines and establish a peace camp in no man's land, prompting a ceasefire and negotiations to end to the war. I yearned to pursue precisely such a grand ambition. Along with Chris Allen-Douçot of the Hartford Catholic Worker, I joined a team of about thirty Americans who journeyed to Split, Croatia, on the Adriatic Sea. There we met six thousand other peacemakers from nineteen countries led by Italians from an organization called Beati i Costruttori di Pace, Blessed are the Peacemakers.

We left Croatia for Bosnia on August 4, 1993 in a caravan of buses that stretched over a mile. After inching through many military checkpoints, we reached a small town called Prozor where we camped by a lake. The sound of Croatian artillery firing towards the nearby town, Gornji Vakuf, awakened us the next morning. To their credit, the Americans rolled up their sleeping bags and gathered their packs to proceed, but a sizable portion of participants felt it too dangerous to go on. After three days of contentious meetings conducted in five languages in the hot sun, a frustrated contingent of Communists commandeered two vans to press on towards Sarajevo. Appalled at their break with consensus, a group of American Quakers lay down on the ground to block them. Unfortunately a reporter from the BBC arrived at that moment just in time to see the peace movement demonstrating against itself.

Not long afterwards, a French humanitarian organization, Equilbre, pulled out taking most of the water with them. Before joining Mir Sada, the Americans had recognized that, given the ferocious nature of the Bosnian war, it was more likely than not that some of us would be injured or killed. Many Americans had written their wills. We didn't want to throw away our lives, but we had come because we knew that bloodshed couldn't be stopped at a safe distance. Leaders of Equilbre, on the other hand, had anticipated a general ceasefire upon their arrival, as was common in other places where they had delivered aid. Before he withdrew, the leader of Equilbre, Alain Michel, said, "Going further takes on the logic of the martyr. The need to continue is pretentious and futile."

The next morning, members of Beati announced that they had made an exploratory trip to Gornji Vakuf the night before and been fired on. They concluded it was indeed too dangerous to go forward and proposed instead that the group retreat ten kilometers to a United Nations base to demand action. I was heartbroken. I didn't need to come to Bosnia to appeal to the UN, and I had no illusions that soldiers in blue helmets were apostles of nonviolence.

Hot and exhausted, I opened my pack and looked at a clown costume inside I had brought along to amuse orphans in Sarajevo. I put the costume on and let Kerri Berineck, a friend from Chicago, make up my face as a tearful clown. I took out a small banner with the religious symbols of the Muslim, Catholic, and Orthodox belligerents in Bosnia and the word Peace in Serbo-Croatian. Then I started walking out of the back of the camp toward Sarajevo.

A Spanish Franciscan asked what I was doing, and I earnestly replied, "I don't want to judge anyone else, but I can't go home with a sunburn as the greatest sacrifice I've made to stop the Bosnian War."

To my surprise, seven others followed me. They were Kathy Kelly, Chris, Reverend Michael Morrill, Father Steve Kelly, SJ, along with a Dutch priest, Keyes Koenig, and a Greek couple whose names we never learned. Before we had gone far on the curvy mountain road to Sarajevo, Don Albino Bizzotto, the practical and spiritual leader of Beati, and his translator Lisa Pelletti Clark caught up with us in a Range Rover. In front of a small group of Bosnian civilians who had come out of their houses, Albino pleaded with us for the sake of our families not to throw away our lives foolishly.

I gestured toward a two-year-old girl and said, "Why should my daughter Grace's life be more precious than this child's?" The Italians begged us with tears in their eyes. We embraced and continued up the road toward the Bosnian capital, thirty or so miles away.

When we had gained quite a bit of altitude, a group of Croatian soldiers pulled up behind us. Through a translator, the incredulous officer asked, "What are you doing?"

"We are marching to Sarajevo," we replied.

After a shell burst close enough to make the soldiers crouch, he stated the obvious. "There's a war."

"If you continue," he warned, "you men will get shot and you women will be raped." He gestured for us to go back.

I stepped forward and said, "You and your men are soldiers, willing to lay down your lives to defend the people you love. We are pacifists who love people on all sides of this war. We need to be willing to sacrifice our lives as well."

Despite the fact that I was dressed as a clown and he in military attire, he gazed at me with great seriousness and finally said in a softer voice, "Please go back."

We declined, and he reluctantly left us.

An hour later, at a crossroads littered with shell casings marked in English, Arabic, or Cyrillic script, we sat down to take stock of our food and water supplies. While we did so, the Croatian soldiers reappeared with Don Albino who said, "Your actions have inspired the whole group. We are now planning to try to reach Sarajevo through Mostar, a Bosnian city whose suffering perhaps exceeded Sarajevo's. Please rejoin us."

Acknowledging that we had always wanted to act with the entire group if possible, we agreed. The soldiers cheered and offered us brandy to celebrate.

We went to Croatian-controlled West Mostar but could not cross the Neretva River to the besieged Bosnian side. As I boarded the ferry in Split along with my comrades, I felt dejected that we had accomplished so little.

The media treated Mir Sada harshly. A writer for the *National Catholic Reporter*, who accompanied us to Prozor, wrote an article with the headline: "Peace crumbles on the way to Sarajevo." My local paper, the *Worcester Telegram & Gazette*, lampooned my clown march as a symbol of the peace movement's lack of seriousness. Only *The Catholic Free Press* and New York *Newsday* described the gesture as meaningful.

Regardless, I was sure that the peace movement could do better. As soon as I returned home, I immediately put out feelers in published articles, public talks, private meetings, phone calls, and letters for people interested in another project. Working without a computer, email, or fax machine, I was amazed that a group managed to come together in just four months. I couldn't have managed it without the strong support of Christine Schweitzer from War Resisters League in Cologne, Germany and others in Vienna, Amsterdam, Antwerp, London, Florence, and Chicago.

Sjeme Mira

We called the project Sjeme Mira or Seeds of Peace. In size it was much more modest than Mir Sada: instead of six thousand, we had nineteen participants from nine countries. We wanted to reach the Croatian, Bosnian, and Serbian sides of Mostar to offer a nonviolent witness against war, to promote reconciliation, and to be in physical solidarity with victims of war. Oral historian Studs Terkel, former US Attorney General Ramsey Clark, and activist singer Joan Baez as well as Nobel Peace Laureates Mairead Maguire, Betty Williams, the Dalai Lama, and Elie Wiesel endorsed our effort.

Sjeme Mira was a diverse group comprised of Ron Renkowski, a soft-spoken Midwesterner; Jack Winn, a

logo by Rita Corbin

Boston businessman; Keyes Koenig, a Dutch priest with tireless enthusiasm for walking due to his conviction that fossil fuels are destroying the future; Hans Uwland, also from Holland, a conscientious person not willing to let us sugarcoat any situation; Bradford Lyttle, of Chicago, a longtime Quaker peace activist; Marlou MacIver, a Pennsylvanian who does not let Parkinson's disease hold her back; Gary Shapiro, the grandson of concentration camp survivors, who, in order to gain his mother's blessing, promised her that he would not be killed; Sister Anne Montgomery, a petite and powerful opponent of nuclear weapons who had served years in jail for civil disobedience; Jürg Rohweder and Kurt Südmersen, Germans who kept up our spirits with humor and song; Jesuit priest and peacemaker Steve Kelly, Jim Reale who started each day with yoga; an Austrian named Christian Demmer and an Irishman named Marc Chapman who did much of the driving on mountain roads with hairpin turns, not to mention the danger of snipers and mines; Yves Struyven, one of the kindest people I have ever met; two American Vietnam veterans, Claude Thomas and Bill Ledger, invaluable when we confronted soldiers at checkpoints; Christine Schweitzer, and me. Everyone proved vital at one point or another.

We introduced Sjeme Mira in a leaflet:

WHO ARE WE? WHY ARE WE HERE?

We are private citizens from many countries. We are not official representatives of any government, combination of governments or the United Nations. We are here because we could not stay in the relative peacefulness of our homes watching while yours are being destroyed. We are believers in peace who are deeply disturbed by the war that is going on in the former Yugoslavia. It grieves us to see your people being displaced, injured and killed, and your beautiful towns and cities destroyed.

We represent several religions and philosophies. The majority of us believe in God, but several do not. All of us believe that truth and love are supreme values, and that nonviolent resistance, rather than military force, is the best way to pursue justice and peace. We are inspired by peacemakers like Mohandas Gandhi, who said, "For a nonviolent person, the whole world is one family." In this sense, you are our brothers and sisters, children and parents. How could we not come to your aid?

We come hoping to speak to people on all sides of the conflict here, and to help relieve the suffering. We do not take sides, in the sense of believing that someone is completely right and someone else is completely wrong. We believe that, over the centuries, injustices have been perpetrated by all sides in the former Yugoslavia (and in our own countries for that matter). We believe that these injustices have occurred largely because all sides have tried to gain their way by military force. In killing and otherwise hurting people, and destroying valued property, war always violates truth, perpetrates injustice, and generates hatred. We believe it is impossible to build lasting peace on a foundation of war.

We ask all the people of the former Yugoslavia to abandon military force as the means by which you struggle for freedom and justice. We ask you to adopt nonviolent resistance as your means of struggle. We know that nonviolent action, like military force, involves sacrifice, and the risk of suffering and even death. But it does not do irreversible harm and generate hatred, and it will win the approval and support of most of the people of the world. It can end the cycle of violence, vengeance, and destruction in former Yugoslavia. It can enable the children of this land to grow up free of hatred, with their parents alive, not casualties of war, and able to see their dreams for a better life realized. It can make this land a place that people throughout the world would like to visit and enjoy.

We try to come without a sense of self-righteousness. In our own countries there is injustice and violence. We are painfully aware that we have been unable to overcome these evils. We welcome suggestions that you may have to improve our own societies.

We are not armed. We will not retaliate against anyone who may attack us. We do not seek the armed protection of any nation or combination of nations. We come with the conviction that, in a world of increasingly destructive weapons, if the human species is to exist much longer, people must give up military violence, and use nonviolent means in their quest for freedom and justice.

We produced the leaflet in Serbo-Croatian with Latin characters on one side for Croats and Muslims and Cyrillic characters on the other for Serbs. We distributed the leaflets everywhere we went. We also offered a daily interfaith prayer for peace and delivered medical supplies to civilians on all sides.

It took us almost a week to get through checkpoints into the Croatian part of Mostar, where, over three days, we witnessed how the war had affected people. The kindhearted family with whom we stayed had a blanket blocking the doorway to a portion of their house that had been obliterated by a Serbian shell. The head of an elementary school told us that Bosnian snipers shot one child a day. We saw damage to buildings, including a mosque Croats had burned to the ground, and we also saw semi-normal daily life.

Bill, Jack, and I went out early one morning to take photos near the front line dividing the city when we were stopped by a Croatian soldier who insisted we come inside his

Bosnian Croat Fascist

unit's social club. Apparently, he and his comrades had been fighting all night and wanted us to drink with them. The scene seemed innocent enough until we noticed Nazi regalia adorning the walls. Our host posed for photos giving the Hitler salute in front of a picture of Croatia's World War II pro-Nazi ruler, Ante Pavelić. As the drunken soldier smiled and waved his .45-caliber pistol around, we made as quick an exit as we gracefully could. Lashed to the door was a doll of a child with a bullet hole through the forehead. These guys were proud of their brutality. To say the least, we felt a mixture of compassion and revulsion for West Mostar's people.

At a fairly modern hospital, we interviewed a wounded Croatian soldier who said,

> Maybe after ten years I would live with Muslims in peace and brotherhood but not now. They captured me. They tortured me. They forced me to work, but I must also say they saved my arm. The Muslim doctors treated me like a human being. But they are mostly monsters on that side, savages, primitive people.

Notwithstanding his anger, the man concluded, "I would not talk to my children about the war. I would never make stories about the war and my taking part in it. I would raise them like war didn't exist. War is stupid. Physical force is an argument of stupid people."

"In an ethnically cleansed neighborhood," a sixteen-year-old Croatian girl told us, "Muslims, Serbs, and Croats could live together again in peace. All this war is in the hands of a few men. If we stop them, the war will stop and the people will live together. Most people want peace."

Getting into the besieged Bosnian side of the city proved much more difficult. After days of unsuccessful efforts to convince the Croats to let us pass their lines, we approached Jerry Hulme for help. A retired British general and representative of the United Nations High Commission for Refugees in Medjugorje, Bosnia, Hulme told us that passage through no man's land presented extreme danger. Still, he felt it vitally important for outsiders to experience conditions in East Mostar. He offered to try to bring us along in a UNHCR vehicle, almost certainly a violation of UN rules. We told him that we wouldn't travel with an armed escort or wear helmets and body armor. He said he liked our spunk and agreed to take us a few at a time.

Brad and Gary went first and returned to tell of appalling conditions and unspeakable devastation.

The next day, Bill, Claude, and I made the harrowing five-mile trip up the Neretva River Valley, with Jerry dodging craters and anti-tank mines while swerving to deter snipers until we reached the portion of Mostar that had been surrounded on one side by Croats and on the other by Serbs for more than a year. Devastation here exceeded many times what we had seen in West Mostar. Each cross street, open to the river and the West, was marked with the sign "PAZI SNAJPER'" (RUN, SNIPERS!). Virtually every building was damaged, many completely destroyed.

We walked through piles of worthless Yugoslavian currency on the floor of a shattered and roofless bank. We met people huddled in dark basements where former college professors burned library books in an attempt to stay warm. We offered our leaflet to an exhausted doctor in a hospital that had sporadic electricity, few supplies, virtually no anesthesia, and no running water or other utilities. We saw several amputees in the streets.

We also met the head of the Bosnian War Presidency, Alija Alikardic, who told us, "They are all Nazis over there. We will all be slaughtered if we lay down our weapons."

When I told him that we saw evidence that his troops were also sniping at children, he waved our leaflet and replied, "How can you pacifists possibly understand the reality of war?"

Bill put his palms down on the front of the man's desk and said,

> For a year in Vietnam, it was my job to scoop body parts out of a river from a PT boat and put them in plastic bags for later identification. When I see the destruction of this city, what has been done to your people, I feel like taking a gun again to stop those who are doing this, but I know now after Vietnam that this is wrong and will not save you.

At a ruined radio station, our host Selma, a woman whose boyfriend was imprisoned by the other side, said, "I don't understand what's happened, but it's hell. I'm so sorry because I have no private life. I've lost my identity. It's very terrible and dangerous."

Selma pleaded with us to bring her candles, matches, batteries, sardines, cheese, flour, and oil. We told her that we couldn't be sure to survive the trip out, much less promise to return, but, if we did, we would. As it turned out, Claude gave her much of what she

Scott, the Sjeme Mira banner, and Bosnian graffiti

wanted two days later. The following summer, on the way back from a successful trip to Sarajevo with Beati, I managed to visit Selma during a ceasefire in Mostar. She told me that her spirits had been so low before our visit in December that she had contemplated suicide, but that after Claude returned, she decided to hang on.

"In a way," she said, "you people saved my life."

As gratifying as Selma's comment was, when I returned from Bosnia, my four-year-old son Patrick heard a radio report of genocide in Rwanda and asked, "What are you going to do about that?" He reminded me that violence is relentless and the need to oppose it goes on. We cannot sit in smug satisfaction over past efforts while new outrages are being committed.

But then again, while our ambition is always to end conflict outright, it is important not to dwell dejectedly on what we have not accomplished. Perhaps dispensing a bit of hope was Sjeme Mira's best contribution toward ending the Bosnian War. As if reinforcing the thought, six months after Sjeme Mira disbanded, I received a letter from a man in northern Bosnia giving me positive feedback on our leaflet. His home stood hundreds of miles from anywhere we had visited. When the press asked Claude before we left if he expected Sjeme Mira to stop the war he replied, "No. I'm not that naive. But we can be like that stone you throw in the pond. When it hits the water, the ripples spread out. We could start ripples for peace."

There it is. I would later either lead or participate in peace efforts in Iraq, Afghanistan, Darfur, and Egypt as well as six more trips to Israel/Palestine. We never walked on water. In fact, we often screwed up and even bickered among ourselves, but doors that everyone told us were shut tight always seemed to open for us, sometimes through the auspices of unlikely people.

When a Catholic Worker Peace Team I led tried to reach the Palestinian refugee camp in Jenin after Israelis had devastated it with tanks and helicopter gunships, a large contingent of soldiers stopped us. We had walked miles and been through many adventures, including being detained and threatened with deportation, but only a mile outside the camp an Israeli general told us that he had orders not to allow anyone to get closer.

"What would you do," I asked, "if, knowing you cannot give us permission, we walked on anyway?"

"I'd have my men gently bring you back," he replied.

He then left us under the guard of an officer and several privates. Kathy Kelly began arguing with the officer as to why we should be allowed to proceed.

After a bit, the officer gestured to Kathy and Grace Ritter and Audrey Stewart of the Ithaca, New York, Catholic Worker, and said to me, "How can you let these girls go into a war zone?"

"Those girls," I replied, "have been to war-torn Iraq, Bosnia, Haiti, and elsewhere."

Taken aback he said, "You people have a lot of faith."

"Faith?" I returned. "It was your people who fled the largest army in history to the banks of the Red Sea when they didn't have a single boat."

He paused and then gestured toward the cornfield between us and Jenin and said, "Go."

And so we did.

In that situation, an Israeli officer threw a stone in the pond. I do not know if he suffered any repercussions, but I do know that an Italian named Gabriele Moreno Locatelli, inspired by my clown march, carried a rainbow peace banner into the no man's land surrounding Sarajevo where he was shot to death on October 3, 1993.

And then on March 16, 2003, twenty-three-year-old Rachel Corrie from Olympia, Washington, was killed in the Gaza strip when she tried to stop an Israeli military bulldozer from demolishing a Palestinian doctor's home. Peacemakers in war zones have paid the ultimate price.

Nonetheless, nonviolent responses to war have grown exponentially in the past thirty years. Groups like Peace Brigades International, the International Solidarity Movement, Christian Peacemaker Teams, The International Peace Force, and many other individuals including human rights activists and journalists continue to explore the possibilities of

Gabriele Moreno Locatelli and Rachel Corrie

nonviolence in places of intractable harm. No one is naive that such work is without risk. Gabriele and Rachel are just two of many activists and journalists who have died without a gun or bomb in their hands.

The realization that death is a very real possibility has sometimes paralyzed me with fear. During a curfew in Bethlehem when even the UN considered it too dangerous to distribute food, I joined a small group of internationals delivering what we could carry to homes in the Old City. As we moved toward the Church of the Nativity, the scene of a fierce Israeli attack at that time, I saw journalists in helmets and heavy body armor far behind us peeking around buildings to sneak pictures of us. I realized that they were much more aware than I was of the likelihood of being shot. Their extreme caution tempted me to seek cover, but, when I looked ahead, I saw a Swedish peace activist clad as I was in a white medical shirt and blue pants striding forward intent on feeding the hungry. I knew her parents were from Argentina, where they had been tortured during the Dirty War. I knew she was not naive. I knew she focused on what must be done to be fully human.

I hurried to her side and resumed distributing food even as Israeli soldiers charged up to us and cocked their guns. Perhaps it was her courage. I don't know, but the soldiers did not shoot. Far from it. After some discussion, they actually allowed a Red Cross/Red Crescent ambulance to deliver more food than we could carry.

Jon Krakauer, a member of the ill-fated 1996 climb of Mount Everest when eight people died, says when the stakes are life or death there is no margin for error when calculating risk. In the 2015 documentary *Meru*, Krakauer describes how in 2008 Conrad Anker turned his team around only a hundred meters from the summit of the most daunting peak of the Himalayas. But after his climbing partner, Renan Ozturk, suffered a fractured skull and severed artery to the brain in an avalanche, Anker still included him in a second assault on Meru and even allowed Ozturk to summit after he appeared to endure a small stroke.

Dramatic inconsistency in risk taking like that described by Krakauer reminds me of how carefully the Sjeme Mira team plotted how much risk to take. At a three-hour meeting, Brad Lyttle from Chicago insisted we should proceed into the no man's land only if we met six stringent conditions. However, when the moment of truth arrived with none of his benchmarks visible, everyone turned to Brad who said, "What the heck. Let's go." Reason is important, but loyalty to and faith in friends as well as the grandeur of the venture can outweigh reason. It may seem wildly irresponsible, especially for those with children, but as Conrad Anker says, "By walking our highest paths, we can show our children how to be strong and complete."

More often than one might expect, my compatriots and I have plunged into danger. The ability to do so increases with one's awareness of how very much greater and long lasting are the risks indigenous people face in war zones. After touring a pediatric hospital in Basra, Iraq with only a one percent survival rate and a camp of thirty thousand displaced women and children in Darfur, Sudan, and seeing an Afghan man whose eyes were burned out of their sockets by NATO bombing, my grief-stricken friends and I felt almost grateful to take a risk on their behalf.

And while war zones are places of unspeakable violence, they are surprisingly often places of hope. During an Israeli assault on Ramallah in the West Bank, I happened upon Raja Shehadeh, the Palestinian author, lawyer, and founder of the human rights organization, Al-Haq. Despite incessant gunfire from Israeli soldiers, he was outside his home digging a hole to plant a tree. When I asked why he was not under cover, he smiled and told me, "In the midst of death, one has to continue to affirm life." When Raytheon Corporation tried to open an arms factory in Derry, Northern Ireland, Catholic and Protestant residents of the blue-collar city with a long history of strife, came together to oppose it. A man whose brother was one of fourteen unarmed Irish Catholic civil rights marchers shot and killed by British soldiers in 1972, told me, "We don't want our prosperity to be based on the export of more bloody Sundays to other countries." In a Bosnian refugee camp that had been attacked multiple times by Croatian fascists, I encountered a multi ethnic group of teens who, in their words "had to do something to keep hope alive" and formed themselves into a circus troop. Despite their red noses, juggling, and festive antics, they powerfully demonstrated that the real clowns were the politicians and generals telling Bosnians to slaughter each other. And then, in Kabul, Afghanistan, a place that has seen almost continuous warfare for thirty-five years, I met another group of courageous young people who call themselves The Afghan Youth Peace Volunteers. A sixteen-year-old member named Abdulai told me:

> My father was killed by the Taliban in 2000. We had to run away in the snow. My older brother had to carry me. Today, people are suffering at

the hands of three groups: insurgents, the US, and NATO. If the US has not brought security in ten years, why should we hope it would do so in twenty? We are so tired of war. I don't want the Taliban to come to power, but blood cannot wash away blood. I want reconciliation.

Scott, left, and Abdulai

The courage of indigenous peacemakers is at once humbling and inspiring.

It all brings me back to the time in the Israeli-occupied West Bank when two armored personnel carriers and a tank pinned a group of activists and me against a wall. Moments before that Israeli tank swiveled its gun turret towards us, we had heard the continuous firing of its .70-caliber machine gun at the Dheisheh Refugee camp around the bend. We knew bullets that large go right through parked cars and concrete walls to obliterate any human beings in their path.

When that tank stopped shooting at Dheisheh and rushed around the corner to confront us, we felt more concern with keeping it away from defenseless families in the camp than with fear that we would be wounded or killed.

As I have so often seen, our presence sufficiently confused the tank commander that, after questioning us, he did not fire but merely escorted us back to the center of Bethlehem. We didn't disarm him, but our presence stopped the shooting for an hour. While that's only a moment in a maelstrom, I am grateful to hold back senseless death for every second that I can. That brief interval could have provided space for civilians to reach safety or the tank commander to rethink his orders.

My British friend David Polden recently informed me that on March 8, 2014, sixty Israeli Jewish students refused compulsory military service. Who knows what ripple in the pond inspired them?

One thing is certain: we know not the day nor hour of our death. All we can do is live without fear of anything save the failure to try to make the world a more peaceful place. Such a life, short or long, cannot fail to be a richly satisfying one.

A Problem Patient

When my grandfather brought my father to the dentist as a young boy, he avoided the appointment by jumping out the office window and running home. While I have never taken his approach, I admire the clarity and simplicity of it. In the face of impending pain, he did the rational thing. He fled.

My own relationship with the medical profession has been more social but no less dramatic. It began deceptively when, as a nine-year-old, I was struck by a car and taken to Woonsocket (Rhode Island) General Hospital. They tell me I ran between parked cars onto Rathbun Street in Blackstone, Massachusetts, to get a ball. The car hit me in the forehead and threw me twenty feet.

I take their word for it, because I had and still have no memory of the event. I was so unresponsive on the pavement that my friend Henry Valati called my mother to tell her I was dead. Actually, I was deep in a coma from which I tried to arise two days later. I saw my mother and father waving at me, but, before I could reply, darkness encircled them.

On my fourth day in the hospital, I awoke fully to the sound of the theme song of *The Three Stooges* and the sight of the backside of a television facing the conscious children on my ward. Although I had a scab and still have a small scar on my forehead, I didn't feel a whit of pain. On the right side of my bed were heaps of presents and cards. It was like winning the lottery without buying a ticket.

Seven years later, when I was a junior at Pelham (New Hampshire) High School, a friend named Jimmy scribbled on my shirt with a fat black magic marker, so, naturally, I retaliated on his sleeve. He responded by dislocating my pinky finger, so I stabbed him in the wrist with my Number 2 pencil.

Scott's still dislocated pinky finger:
"Live long and prosper, Jimmy!"

selfie by Scott Schaeffer-Duffy

When we went to the nurse's office and asked her to remove the lead from Jimmy and snap my finger back in place, she replied, "Do I look like a magician? Get outta' here!"

Twenty years later, Jim's doctor charged him two hundred dollars to have the lead removed. I took the lower road: my pinky still sticks out at an angle.

"I'll never play the piano again," I moan to anyone who'll listen.

Despite these incidents, I really had no association with

205

the medical profession and my archenemy, physical pain. That changed in 1973 when I cut my finger on a meat slicer at the Anchor Restaurant where I was illegally employed doing tasks a fifteen-year-old is forbidden to do. My boss rushed me to a modern hospital in Lowell, Massachusetts, where a very sleepy intern looked at my wound and announced, "This is going to hurt you more than me."

He then did a kind of torture underestimated as a mere muscle pinch. It felt like the doctor tried to cut my finger off with a pair of dull kindergarten scissors. Before I could even catch my breath from the screaming, he said cheerfully," Okey doke, now I've got to do the other side."

The sadist promised that I'd not be left with a scar. This was the first of many medical lies I would be told. He didn't tell me that when my nerves got over the pinching, I'd feel like my finger was being dipped in molten lead. It throbbed so hard that I swear I could hear it. I was schooled by adults in my life to choke down the pain, to man up, to tough it out, to not be a baby, and other repressive responses, but I had other plans. I couldn't pull off the macho thing and didn't want to go gently into the dark night, so I chose hysteria.

If this sounds like an overreaction, that's because it is. If I complained proportionally to the actual pain, people might feel sympathy, but that would do nothing, really, to distract me. In fact, their platitudes would just remind me of my plight. But hysterical ravings have an entirely different effect. People don't sympathize. They laugh. Sometimes I do too. It takes the focus off a lamentable current situation and transforms it into improvisational theatrics. It's a creative challenge and fun.

Unfortunately, I would not get another chance to practice the histrionic method until I started donating blood. Here is a noble pursuit absolutely necessary for saving lives in medical emergencies. It also amounts to an experience of escalating pain beginning with the application of a blood pressure cuff attached tighter than the tightest tourniquet followed by piercing of the index finger, squeezing out of a drop of blood, and impaling of the forearm with a needle wider than the Keystone XL pipeline. Cookies or crackers are offered as a sop to the exsanguinated victims in post-op, but nothing can erase the memories. Where are the support groups for blood donor PTSD? There are none. You are on your own to cope as best as you can.

When I went to my first donor center, I started making a fuss before anyone initiated any of the aforementioned torments. According to one nurse, she had never had a more difficult patient. "Why, oh why do you give blood?" she asked.

"Irish Catholic guilt," I answered.

I routinely sought painless medical conditions that would exempt me from giving blood, but despite my emotional stress, my body refused to cooperate. I was never anemic. My blood pressure was spot on even after I ran up and down the clinic stairs to try and elevate it. I never fainted after donating blood as more Spartan donors often did. My blood gushed out so freely that The Red Cross appealed to me every six weeks to give again.

In time, though, I found myself banned from various donor centers ostensibly because I frightened the other donors, but who knows the real reason? In any event, I resolved to try to donate in silence.

I went to a blood drive in Holy Cross College's Hogan Center ballroom. I made it midway through the pumping without a peep. I had my eyes closed and imagined myself floating away on a bed of clouds when a disc jockey from a local radio station thrust a microphone into my face and asked, "So what would you like to say to our listeners about giving blood?"

I snapped open my eyes and the dam burst. I grabbed the mic and shouted, "It kills! It hurts! They are trying to kill me! The needle is as big as a basketball pump needle! I can feel shards of metal shooting up my veins! Oh God! Oh God! Help me!!!"

The broadcast went out live. The deejay froze until I collapsed onto the gurney sobbing. Suffice it to say, I was not chosen as a poster child for giving blood.

Eventually, two hospitals and as many donor centers banned me, but blood drives are like funerals. No matter where you go, they host them. Thanks be to God, they finally gave me a two-gallon pin and assurance that my exposure to tropical diseases in Latin America made me ineligible to give blood again. It may have been a lie, but if it was, it's one I'm not going to challenge.

Since most of my personal heroes wore glasses (Gandhi's are even preserved in a museum), I have always wanted them. During college, I wore a pair of wire-rimmed glasses with clear lenses for a few months to verify my desire. For many years, I went to Doctor Thamel, a friendly optometrist who examined me for free, but he always disappointed me by saying that I had spectacular vision.

But then in my forties, it started to slip, so, at long last, I could legitimately become a four-eyed person. Most medical aids—walkers, crutches, wheelchairs, and the like—have downsides, but glasses opened my horizons. They transformed me instantly into a person who looks much wiser than I actually am. I don't even make too much of a fuss in the optometrist's office save complaining about the "acid" they put in my eyes before the annual exam.

Other than getting the coveted glasses, my middle years were free of medical intervention. Save colds, a bit of hay fever, and occasional sunburn, I felt like I would live forever. Handy, since I had no medical insurance.

For what few concerns I did encounter, I called Anne Marie Kaune, a nurse practitioner at Worcester's Homeless Outreach. From my father-in-law, I inherited a bright red copy of *The Merck Manual of Medical Information*, an indispensable book for a hypochondriac. You can look up the smallest ache or pain and endow it with an impressive name. I routinely called Anne Marie announcing I had serious maladies. She sometimes saw me but more often told me that I was imagining things and that I should get a primary care doctor.

One day after wolfing down a spicy lunch, I experienced chest pains and called the Homeless Outreach and left the message, "Help me! I'm having a heart attack!"

A different nurse heard my message and was frantic to find me, but, when Anne Marie arrived, she recognized my voice and told her colleague, "Trust me. It's nothing."

As my hero, Rodney Dangerfield liked to say, "I don't get any respect."

But then Governor Mitt Romney turned my life upside down. He made healthcare widely available to the poor in Massachusetts. I jumped onto MassHealth without any of the glitches associated later on with its cousin, ObamaCare. By then, I was middle-aged, getting a bit portly, and starting to hear about peers with serious health issues. A couple of them had even died.

Nonetheless, most people continued to associate me with Woody Allen in the film *Hannah and Her Sisters* when he reminded a skeptical friend that his health concerns were not imaginary: "Don't you remember when I had that black spot on my back?"

"It was on your shirt," his friend derided.

Despite my many complaints, no one ever diagnosed me with anything consequential.

And so, on a dark and stormy night, when I complained to my wife, Claire, of severe abdominal pain, she ignored me for hours until she got fed up and dumped me at the emergency room.

"Call me when they tell you it's nothing," she said as she drove off.

I was in so much pain that I crawled to the admission desk and reached up my hand to wave to the receptionist, who either didn't see it or didn't care. I lay on the floor for quite a while before someone helped me to a curtained off bed. A nurse and later a doctor looked me over and concluded that I might have appendicitis but that my contradictory symptoms necessitated more tests.

For my part, I moaned loudly and sang sad Irish songs about the inevitability of death. They wouldn't give me painkillers because they might interfere with a diagnosis. Hours into my ordeal, they concluded that I must have my appendix removed. Then, finally, they gave me some morphine by IV.

They must have given me only a couple of drops, because I didn't notice any reduction in my pain, so I complained, "What is this? Spit-back morphine? Will somebody open the spigot?" But that was not to be. They put me on a gurney and whisked me away to the operating room. En route, I told the orderlies, "You should probably stand back because I think an alien is going to burst out of my abdomen any minute now."

A much-chastened Claire stood at my side in pre-op as I spoke nonsense and drifted into drug-induced sleep. I awoke to the harsh voice of a burly nurse saying, "If you don't pee into this cup in the next ten minutes, I'm going to catheterize you."

"Ma'am," I replied. "I am an Irish Catholic. *I* don't even look at my genitals. There's no way *you* are going to see them."

Surrounded by medical students, a doctor approached. He looked at my chart and said, "Your appendix had a micro burst. That must have really hurt. We barely saved your life."

Finally, I stood vindicated for years of health vigilance.

Now I had a real scar, unfortunately located below the Speedo level, but nonetheless a real scar. I could say ad nauseam, "I nearly died. Don't you remember."

But then calamity struck again. I noticed a black spot on my nose. My friend the red book told me it was cancer. Not a pimple. Not a blood blister. Cancer! The ultimate killer. The big C. My doctor took one look at the evil spot and ordered a biopsy. When technicians at the biopsy asked my level of pain, I told them that their little smiley face/ frowny face chart didn't begin to capture it. I told them I had the lowest threshold to pain imaginable and that, when I had a splinter removed as a child, a neighbor called the police thinking I was being murdered. I said, "I cry when I get my hair cut."

I refuse to sit down in waiting rooms, preferring to pace in circles, muttering about pain. When nurses call my name, I shriek. They might as well announce, "Dead man walking."

Despite my prognostications of trouble, the doctor scheduled me for day surgery to have the offending spot removed. As time dragged by toward my ordeal under the knife, I distracted myself by putting my affairs in order and reading Sylvia Plath poetry. Claire accompanied me to the hospital. Nurses escorted me to a waiting room where I saw several radioactive warning signs and biohazard labels.

I asked a nurse if I was being prepped as a medical school cadaver.

For basal cell skin cancer, the mutilation, aka surgery, proceeds in stages, supposedly to make sure they don't remove more than is necessary. Actually, the fiends revel in stretching out the nightmare. Are they paid by the hour or what?

When I emerged from the lowest depths of hell, I looked like they had taken an ax to my nose. The nurse told me to call if I had any concerns. I called her eight times that afternoon. She finally asked, "Do you have this number on speed dial?" Claire shopped at a mall the next day, and an orderly who had been working two floors above my operating room asked her, "Is he okay?"

I'll say one thing, though. These guys told the truth when they promised me that the disfigurement would disappear. Unfortunately, the threat of a recurrence lingers. The doctor asked me to go to a dermatologist twice a year for three years and then yearly for five more so she could check for additional hated spots. I routinely offer the dermatologist twenty bucks to let me go home without an examination, but she has principles.

When I sit in the waiting room, I worry about catching leprosy, psoriasis, or more exotic skin maladies. The other patients come fully dressed, so I have no idea what misfortune afflicts them. For all I know, the waiting room is a virtual incubator for pathogens.

Despite the near explosion of my appendix and loss of a section of my handsome nose, my body seemed to hang together. I began running on February 11, 2009. Since then, my blood pressure, cholesterol, and weight have been terrific. Things looked pretty good. I even started wondering if I might live forever.

But then, after a victorious 5K race, I went to the bathroom and saw blood in my urine. That I did not faint testifies to my composure. I saw a doctor the next day who did multiple tests, all painful, of course.

"It could be a urinary tract infection, kidney stones, kidney failure, an enlarged prostate, or colon cancer," he then informed me

"Don't sugarcoat it, Doc," I said. "How long do I have?"

He couldn't have been more confused but refused to give a prognosis without a sure diagnosis. I wasn't encouraged by the fact that all his choices were dreadful. Why don't they always toss in "Or it could be nothing"? I didn't like Doors One, Two, Three, or Four.

And then like Stonewall Jackson at Bull Run, the doctor not only defeated me but chased me after I had surrendered.

"Did you know that you have a first-degree atrioventricular blockage?" he asked.

This appointment was surely going from bad to worse.

He discovered the condition quite by accident while taking my vitals and advised me to have annual EKGs to make sure it doesn't become a second- or third-degree blockage. When I asked what the difference is, he explained that there are no symptoms for a first-degree blockage. However, the second-degree requires medication and dietary changes while the third-degree demands vascular surgery. Visions of bypass surgery, pacemakers, and stents assaulted my imagination.

He then took x-rays of my abdomen. Just what a potential cancer patient needs: more radiation. He also scheduled me for a colonoscopy and promised to get back to me. This was surely turning into a very bad day.

Consulting the red book did not help. None of the choices appealed to me. A friend told me that he passed a kidney stone so large that he fainted. He also warned me that kidney stones travel in packs. Great.

Other friends informed me that the worst part of the colonoscopy is a noxious drink you have to consume to clean out your system prior to the procedure. They were not kidding. It tastes bad and leaves you chained to the toilet for hours and hours. You wouldn't think the human body could possibly contain so much poop. Happily, everyone also said the actual exam was painless. They put you into a gentle slumber, and you wake up with no ill effects whatsoever save the trauma of a possible cancer diagnosis. In my case, though, I woke up mid-exam screaming, a one-in-a-half-million occurrence, they later told me. Apparently, my colon is the twisty kind, and they couldn't get their probe around the corners. I'd have to have a different procedure called a fluoroscopy instead.

Oh, and by the way, the doctor said, "You have diverticulosis." What the flip?

"You've got little pockets in your colon that could trap seeds and lead to diverticulitis which is very painful and must be treated immediately."

Before sending me home, the doctor said I should never eat cucumbers, strawberries, or popcorn. It just kept getting better and better.

When I went for the fluoroscopy, the receptionist asked me to sign a waiver that disclaimed the provider's responsibility for possible side effects. The list of what could go wrong was longer than those on the television commercials for drugs, but, in fine print, near the bottom of the page, it included "possible fatality." Now this jumped out at me.

"This test could kill me?" I asked the woman at the desk.

"Don't worry about that," she assured. "We have to include it even if it's the remotest possibility."

"I don't care how remote it is. It makes no difference to me if there is one bullet in six cylinders or one in a thousand. I'm still being asked to play Russian roulette here."

When she had no response, I asked, "How long have you worked here? Has anyone been killed by this test since you were hired?"

She seemed happy to tell me that there had been no deaths but less eager to admit that she'd only worked there for a few months. But they needed my signature to proceed, so I sacrificed reasonable prudence and gave it to them.

They made me put on a johnny (I was starting to feel like that's all I got to wear) and escorted me into an operating room where they strapped me to an examination table and then gave me a radioactive beverage to drink. What's with all the treating of fire with fire these days?

"They tell me this is a painless procedure," I said to the doctor.

He chuckled and said, "Well, they tell you wrong."

An hour and a half later, I emerged in complete agreement with him. I think I would have rather been waterboarded. I won't even share the ugly details, but I will say that I learned to avoid all medical procedures that end in "oscopy." The good news is that my torturer concluded that my colon is cancer-free. One of five potential evil doors was now locked up tight.

My original doctor got back to me and ruled out a urinary tract infection, thereby sealing up another portal to hell. He scheduled me for a CT scan to explore the other cruel options.

The CT scan was kind of fun. Here was the first test I'd encountered that didn't hurt. I was so enthralled by the high-tech aspects of the set-up that I hummed or whistled the original *Star Trek* theme throughout. The only negative involved the television in the waiting room that broadcast shows and commercials referencing cancer. When I stopped my pacing to complain to the receptionist, she directed me to a pile of magazines. As chance would have it, the top one featured a story about a cancer victim.

"Is this some kind of conspiracy to make me panic?" I asked as I dropped the offending journal on the counter.

She glanced at it and said, "I don't think you have to worry. This person had ovarian cancer."

Oh, how the healthy love to sneer.

Unfortunately, the CT scan revealed a mysterious spot on the base of my spine. My prognosis seemed to get worse and worse the deeper they probed. So I was scheduled for an MRI.

Like a CT scan, an MRI doesn't hurt per se, but it remains fairly terrifying. The technicians clothed me in a johnny, had me lie on a gurney, and then wheeled me to the maw of a gaping tube. They told me that the test is very noisy, so I would be given head phones with music as a compensation. It was essential that I not move during the hour-long process or it would have to be done all over again.

"Some patients get a bit claustrophobic during this test," the techie said as she placed a device between my clasped hands on my chest. "Push this button if you are starting to panic."

So I pushed it.

"Not now," she said. "Only push it if the test makes you really agitated."

So I pushed it again.

"Maybe the button isn't a good option for you," she said as she pried it from my hands.

Before I could protest, she slid me into the circular coffin and noise began in earnest. It really was quite loud and discordant, like a fan belt was loose somewhere inside the apparatus. I wondered if it was a rebuilt MRI machine or a knock-off from Asia. The "music" was just a step above what is played in most elevators, but, thankfully, its lyrics never dealt with cancer or other morbid topics. I was so determined to make this test a one-time experience that I lay as rigid as I could, doing my best to keep my chest from rising too much when necessity forced me to breathe.

Thankfully, I survived, and, even more happily, the lawn-mower tube's results were negative for cancer. My regular doctor pronounced me healthy once again. After all was said and done, she concluded that the blood in my urine came from passing a single kidney stone.

"Since so much time has passed without a recurrence," she said, "I think there's a very good chance you'll never pass another stone."

Although you might think my antics would annoy medical personnel, I am pleased to say they mostly find my behavior amusing or at the very worst an interesting break from the forced stoicism of other patients. I like seeing the wide-eyed look in their eyes and hearing them chuckle when I ask bizarre questions. Ironically, my extreme self-indulgence distracts me from actual anxiety. I feel more like I'm in a skit about going to the doctor rather than actually going there. I am teleported back to eighth grade when I did quite a bit of improvisational comedy on stage. I free-associate and am amazed by what pops into my head and slips out of my mouth.

The spot-on-the-spine suggestion was an exception. It scared me. My mother died from bone cancer at fifty-nine, only two years older than I am now. As cancers go, this one is particularly merciless. It stole my mother's life over six nightmarish weeks. She endured the torment without complaint. She refused treatments that offered only the chance of prolonging her life and the certainty of higher medical bills. She was very brave. Could I be so other-centered if I were in as much pain as she was? I don't know if I could.

Like Scarlett O'Hara in *Gone with the Wind*, I mostly choose not to think about death. When I do, I tend to pin my hopes on a great improbability. You see, Catholics believe that the prophet Elijah and the Virgin Mary were assumed bodily into Heaven without having to die. Now that's only two people in all of history, but I figure there's still a chance for me, perhaps a better one than the odds of winning the lottery.

When I cannot help but think of death, though, I tend to fear the worst—not the nightmarishly painful deaths like my mother's but the ones that end up in curiosity columns, like one I read about a woman who was run over by a street sweeper, a vehicle that cannot go faster than ten miles an hour. I can just see myself slipping on a banana peel, falling headfirst into a toilet, and drowning. I suspect that God dreams up real doozies for prideful folks like me, so rather than mope around like Scotty Rain Cloud, I'd rather bank on being assumed bodily into heaven.

Despite all my denials, however, they tell me that death is inevitable. By accident, disease, or the intention of others, I will die. It is inescapable and almost certainly painful. Like everyone else, I cannot escape it. The awareness of my mortality initially prompted me to make certain I was not leaving a mess for others to clean up. Details like making sure Claire knew that I hid the house checkbook inside a hollowed-out copy of a Danielle Steel novel preoccupied me at first, but I also began to think about my dying itself. Claire's best friend, Judy Brown, died less than a week after a routine visit to the doctor. Before she lost her strength, Judy smiled and waved her arms to Bruce Springsteen's "Everybody Has a Hungry Heart."

I also take solace from the example of Claire's and my chosen patron saint, Thomas More who was beheaded for his refusal to recognize the authority of Henry the Eighth over the Church in England. When they took him from the Tower of London and led him to the block with his hands bound behind his back, More asked the executioner to move More's long beard off his neck because, "At least it hasn't offended the king."

In the same vein, there's the story of Saint Lawrence, the martyr roasted to death on a grill. Reputedly, his last words were, "Turn me over, please. I think I'm done on this side."

I also admire Oscar Wilde's last words. He looked at the ugly wallpaper on the wall beside his deathbed and said, "One of us has to go."

As an advocate for the terminally ill, my friend Jo Massarelli has seen many people die. When she kept vigil at the bedside of a cantankerous Irishman who had a longtime feud with his neighbor over the location of their property line, the curmudgeon beckoned Jo to come closer and whispered, "I want you to take my catheter hose and drape it over my neighbor's hedge."

Although I'm only a quarter Irish, I must admit to a partiality for gallows humor. When I told my pure-blooded, Irish friend Elizabeth Mullaney that I found myself reading the obituary pages more often, she said, "Well, after all, it is the Irish sports page." You'd be surprised how funny some obits are, often unintentionally, like the one which described a man as having "married his pre-deceased wife in 1943."

When I was a Capuchin-Franciscan novice, we ended every day with a prayer for a happy death. My Uncle Bob had such a death. He went to the doctor and learned his body was riddled with inoperable cancer. Typical of the way he spent his entire life, Bob spent his last days joking, praying, and reassuring others. When my cousin turned him in bed, he faced the blank wall and said, "Goodbye cruel world." He posed for photos and led family members in a rendition of "You Are My Sunshine."

A poet, photographer, crooner, mountain climber, biker, kayaker, and horror novel enthusiast who was also a faithful Catholic, husband (for sixty years), father, grandfather, uncle, and friend, Bob was an amazing person. Before he died, he insisted with a grin that I add "fighter of evil" to the list of his passions. I owe him a debt of gratitude for many things, but especially for taking me and my friends on numerous expeditions climbing New Hampshire's Mount Washington. When someone asked Bob why he climbed Mount Washington over and over, he said, "Because it's the highest, of course." Bob was one of those special people whose death left those who knew him feeling like their world had diminished. It's hard to imagine a wedding without him singing, "Sunrise, Sunset" or a family gathering without his mischievous smile. He was eighty-four but forever young. He taught me so much about how to live and how to die.

Many years ago, I wrote a poem that may bear recollection in my final hours.

> You be the one who does what is right.
> Find it and do it. You must dare.
> Filtering down through the darkness is light
> which will show you the where.
>
> Be of good cheer, stay clear of lies,
> let peace reign inside you, the dove.
> Conquer the pressure, utter few sighs,
> and never neglect, friend, to love.

And so, I hope and pray that, when my final moments come, I won't waste them moaning, screaming, or worrying but that I'll have the grace to bring joy to those within earshot. That to me is a really happy death. Given how difficult most deaths are, that may be a tall order, but, then again, as good Saint Luke assured us, and I have seen time and time again, "Nothing is impossible."

Everything Is Possible

Stephen King discusses the phenomenology of time in a short story called *My Pretty Pony*. He reflects on how fast time seems to slip during a vacation and how slow it moves at the dentist's office. From the standpoint of how it felt, the time I had to wait as a child from Halloween until Christmas was very much longer than the last ten years of my life that have flown by at breakneck speed. But King also points to a singular moment he had on a carousel when time seemed to stop. He calls it "pretty pony time."

Kurt Vonnegut's hero in the novel *Slaughterhouse-Five* is "unstuck in time." At one moment, Billy Pilgrim practices optometry in upstate New York, and in the next he rides in a cattle car on his way to a prisoner-of-war camp. He has no control over the phenomenon. He blinks, and he is suddenly a child. Blinks again and just as suddenly faces death. Unlike King, though, Vonnegut peppers his novels with humor despite the fact that they often deal with grim subject matter like the allied firebombing of Dresden, which Vonnegut actually experienced as a prisoner of war.

I believe that the simultaneous ability for the mind to make time stop and to catapult it backward or forward allows a person to savor his or her deepest experiences and to recall them whenever they may be needed.

I have witnessed an incredible amount of avoidable human suffering and have had joy beyond my wildest expectations. Like a person who treasures water after time in the desert, my heart is at once broken and then filled by the nearness of conflicting experience in my consciousness. Like a Quaker hymn written during a time of persecution, I echo the chorus, "How can I keep from singing?"

To me, time is an illusion. Everything is at once being born and dying and vice versa. This isn't some kind of New Age nonsense, either. It is literally true. Obituaries and birth notices appear virtually side by side in newspapers. I received a letter today from a friend in New Zealand who is getting ready to plant her garden as we are harvesting ours.

At a huge anti-nuclear rally in New York's Central Park, Tom Lewis said to me, "Today, half a million. Tomorrow, you and me."

I wish I had replied, "And the next day, a half a million again."

In Plato's "Allegory of the Cave," he asserts that most human beings live like slaves facing a wall and mistake shadows for reality, while lovers of wisdom break free into the light of day where risks and rewards are immeasurably greater.

I believe that when we follow our dreams and ideals, we open ourselves to intensified life full of paradoxes. On one hand, Jesus tells his followers to take up the cross, but on the other hand he tells them that the burden he recommends is light.

Was Jesus unstuck in time?

Saint Thomas Aquinas, who argued that God exists both inside and outside time, might have said so. Perhaps Jesus on the cross found the strength to forgive his executioners because of a pretty pony awareness of his impending resurrection.

And yet, I am no Pollyanna. It would be hard to sugarcoat life after having had dying infants thrust into my arms in Iraq. Sin and suffering are undeniable. I am frank with new runners, activists, and Catholic Workers that victories do not come cheap. But, at the same time, I assure neophytes that, if they persist, rewards dwarf the sacrifices. I go so far as to tell them that if they give their heart and soul to any worthy venture, they too will experience miracles.

In fact, if any individual gives her or himself fully to a worthy venture, I am confident that they will experience a miracle.

Can a book like this one ever end? Probably not. As long as one stays open to possibilities, the impossible recurs.

On Tuesday, August 7, 2015, Claire posted the following on Facebook:

> Life is a gift, and I am most grateful to be savoring it. This afternoon, when dark clouds banked in the sky, I rushed out to roll up the car windows. A ferocious wind was blowing down the street, an ominous wind. Seeing it, I knew I had to move our car out of range of our ancient, treacherous maple that I still love dearly. I put the key in the ignition, pressed the power button, and put the car in reverse. Flustered by the wind, I turned the car off and began to restart it again when an enormous branch, a branch as big as a tree trunk, crashed on the car. It forked right where it struck the vehicle, one branch falling on the hood of the car, the other landing on the far side of the roof, my head between the two. After less than a minute of shouting for Scott to help me get out of the vehicle, I was able to exit unscathed.
>
> So what saved me? My stupid habit of mindlessly turning the car off right after I turn it on? Had I been in motion, I might have been more in harm's way. The street lamp that deflected the fall of the tree?
>
> My neighbors had their own interpretation.
>
> "Angels are watching out for you," Lula hollered minutes after I emerged from the car.
>
> And this became the refrain of the afternoon as neighbors and passersby said, "Thank God, you are alive." The burly tattooed man in a beat-up car, the curly-headed youth strolling down the street, the women who stopped to take photos with their cell phones, even the men who came to clear away the street marveled my life had been spared and pointed to the heavens, "Someone is watching out for you," one said. Very quickly a scene of catastrophe became a monument to gratitude. What a miracle it is to be alive. I mean that literally tonight. Thank you, God, for the gift of life.

While relieved and grateful that Claire escaped without a scratch, I was nonetheless sad to see our 2007 Prius in ruins. A newspaper photographer asked me, "How do you feel?"

I looked wistfully at the crushed hybrid and said, "It was such a good car."

photo by Tanya Connor for *The Catholic Free Press*

Claire and Scott's neighbor Sadie hugs Claire after
Claire's close call with a falling tree

"But your wife was almost killed," he replied.

"Only seventy thousand miles," I moaned.

"But your wife," he persisted.

"Forty-five miles to the gallon," I said.

Claire overheard me and shook her head. When Claire told her mother what I had said, she laughed heartily.

Nevertheless, our car was a total loss. We had no money to replace it. But our wonderful daughter, Grace, started an online fundraising campaign that raised ninety-four hundred dollars in only five days, almost enough to buy a 2009 Prius with six thousand fewer miles than the dead car. So, on the seventh day, Claire and I went out and bought the car but had to put fifteen hundred dollars on a credit card. The next morning, while running six miles, I prayed that someone might send us a check in the mail to help cover the remaining cost.

When I got home, I found two more bills and a nasty card in the mailbox. "So much for prayer," I grumbled. But minutes later a woman came to our door, said she heard of Claire's accident, and wanted to help. She wouldn't give her name and then left an envelope containing fifteen hundred dollars in cash.

This book goes on and on. I hope all of you will join the adventure.

About the Author

Scott Schaeffer-Duffy was born in 1958, the fourth of seven children. He paid his own way through the College of the Holy Cross by working in restaurants. He has been a peace activist since 1978, a Catholic Worker since 1982, and a long distance runner since 2009. He has been married to Claire Schaeffer-Duffy since 1984. They are the parents of four children.

The author welcomes reader questions and comments and is available for talks, readings, and signings.

Readers can contact him as follows:

Scott Schaeffer-Duffy
Saints Francis and Thérèse Catholic Worker
52 Mason Street
Worcester, MA 01610 USA
theresecw2@gmail.com

Acknowledgments

I want to thank David O'Brien, Rosalie Riegle, Art Wortman, and Brayton Shanley for their early encouragement and confidence that this book would be published. I am also grateful to Brenna Cussen and Jo Massarelli who spent hours reading and responding to early drafts. Their suggestions made this a better book.

Appreciation also goes out to The Worcester Art Museum, *Worcester Magazine, The Catholic Free Press, Inside Worcester, The Telegram & Gazette,* and many individual photographers for their gracious premission to reprint their images.

I am especially grateful to my publisher, Marcia Gagliardi of Haley's, whose deep appreciation for good writing and layout, along with a charming personality, made every step of this process a pleasure. Special thanks also to Elsie Uffleman whose copy editing is marvelous.

I want to thank my dear wife, Claire, and our children for their consistent support and sense of humor that played a vital role in bringing this book to life.

But most of all, I want to thank the hundreds of remarkable individuals whose actions have enriched my life and this book.

Colophon

Text and titles for *Nothing Is Impossible* are set in Baskerville, an eighteenth-century font designed by John Baskerville of Birmingham, England, and cut by John Handy. Because Baskerville is a somewhat precise design that emphasizes contrast between thick and thin strokes, different digitizations provide a variety of interpretations of what Baskerville intended and of how the digitization should compensate for ink spread on paper. Designers may therefore prefer different designs for different text sizes, papers, and printing methods, since a design intended for large text sizes could look too spindly for body text. Therefore, with *Nothing Is Impossible*, design has not exceeded eighteen points while taking advantage of regular, italic, semibold and bold iterations.

Among recent digitizations, František Štorm's extremely complete range of versions features three optical sizes, the text version having thicker strokes to increase legibility as metal type does. Meanwhile, the common URW digitization of Baskerville Old Face features dramatic contrasts between thin and thick strokes. This makes it most suited to headings, especially since it does not have an italic.

Dieter Hofrichter, who assisted Günter Gerhard Lange in designing a Baskerville revival for Berthold around 1980, commented:

> We went to Birmingham where we saw original prints by Baskerville. I was quite astounded by how sharp the printing of his specimens is. They are razor-sharp: it almost hurt your eyes to see them. So elegant and high-contrast! He showed in this way what he could achieve. That was Baskerville's ideal—but not necessarily right for today.

Many companies have provided digital releases (some of older Baskerville revivals), including Adobe, Linotype, URW++, and Bitstream as well as many others. These may have varying features, for example some lacking small caps. Monotype Baskerville is installed on Macs as part of OS X, while many Windows computers receive Moore's adaptation under the name of Baskerville Old Face in the URW digitization (that described above) without an italic or bold weight.

CPSIA information can be obtained
at www.ICGtesting.com
Printed in the USA
BVOW11s0728150416

444169BV00002B/2/P